SO-BZZ-819

Contents

PREFACE	xi
ACKNOWLEDGMENTS	xiii
INTRODUCTION	xv
HOW TO USE THIS BOOK	xix
WALT DISNEY WORLD MAP	xx–xxi

1. GETTING TO MICKEY   3
Saving Money on Travel / 5

**2. WHEN YOU SHOULD GO AND WHERE YOU
      SHOULD STAY**   11
Timing Is Everything / 11
*Recommended Accommodations for the
      Cheapskate* / 13

3. WHAT'S IT ALL ABOUT, MICKEY?   49
*Background Information on Walt Disney
World* / 49
Tickets, Get Your Tickets! / 50

4. THE MAGIC KINGDOM   59
Main Street / 61
Adventureland / 67
Frontierland / 72
Liberty Square / 76
Fantasyland / 80
Mickey's Toontown Fair / 85
Tomorrowland / 87

E-Ticket Ride Nights / 92
Free at the Magic Kingdom / 93

5. **EPCOT**   **95**
FutureWorld / 98
World Showcase / 110
Free at EPCOT / 126

6. **DISNEY-MGM STUDIOS**   **127**
Hollywood Boulevard / 127
Sunset Boulevard / 130
Hollywood Hills / 132
Animation Courtyard / 135
Mickey Avenue / 136
New York Street / 138
Commissary Lane/Echo Lake / 140
Free at Disney-MGM Studios / 144

7. **ANIMAL KINGDOM**   **149**
Entrance Plaza and The Oasis / 151
Discovery Island / 152
Camp Minnie-Mickey / 155
Africa / 156
Rafiki's Planet Watch / 159
Asia / 161
DinoLand, U.S.A. / 163
Free at Animal Kingdom / 166

8. **THE "LESSER" ATTRACTIONS**   **168**
Downtown Disney / 168
Downtown Disney Westside / 169
Downtown Disney Pleasure Island / 173
Free at Downtown Disney Pleasure Island / 178
Downtown Disney Marketplace / 179
The Water Parks / 183
Blizzard Beach / 185
Typhoon Lagoon / 189
River Country / 192

9. OTHER ON-SITE ATTRACTIONS, DISTRACTIONS,
    AND DIVERSIONS   195
    BoardWalk Resort / 195
    Miniature Golf / 198
    Wide World of Sports / 200
    Where to Meet the Characters / 201

10. EXCLUSIVE CHEAPSKATE ITINERARIES   208
    The Ambitious Cheapskate's Itinerary / 215
    The Cheapskate's Family Itinerary / 227

11. SOURCES OF ADDITIONAL SAVINGS   242

12. THE FUTURE OF WALT DISNEY WORLD   245

    THE CHEAPSKATE'S DISNEY DIRECTORY   248
    KEEP IN TOUCH   253
    ATTENTION CHEAPSKATES   254
    INDEX   255

Preface

Okay, we admit it. We're both big Disney fans. Between the two of us, we've visited Disney World more than thirty times . . . and counting! So, while we strive to be objective in our criticism and analysis, we gotta level with you—we love this place!

In our search over the years for the perfect Disney travel guide, we've discovered that there's really no book for the cheapskate—that seasoned traveler who knows what he or she likes to do on vacation, but doesn't have the money of a Rockefeller with which to do it. In this book, we reach out to that guy (or gal) and his (or her) family. We offer herein time- and money-saving techniques, most of which we've tried ourselves, for enjoying the Walt Disney World resort. There's really no reason why a traveler on a budget can't have a great Disney vacation.

A word of warning: This will be more of a doing, active vacation, with just a little time for relaxation. But if you follow our advice, and luck is with you, you can *gain* some time for relaxation.

So join us on this trip to the world's favorite travel destination. You will have to loosen those purse strings somewhat, but probably not as much as you thought!

Acknowledgments

The authors gratefully acknowledge those family members, friends, and loyal readers who provided their support, advice, and travel tips and put up with seemingly endless Disney discussions. We especially thank Janet and Lee Pfeiffer for their input and encouragement, and Sue Pisaturo, Disney travel agent par excellence and friend to the cheapskate! (See her ad in the back of this book.)

We also want to thank the good folks at Citadel; and kudos to our friend Steve Brower for his help.

Introduction

THE WALT DISNEY WORLD CHEAPSKATE DEFINED; AVOIDING THE HERD MENTALITY; AND THE BENEFITS OF PLANNING

If you're reading these words, then chances are you're a cheapskate. Hey, that's nothing to be ashamed of. No matter who you are, whatever the size of your bank account, if you're someone who likes to get the most vacation for your dollar, then you're a cheapskate.

If you plan on taking a Disney vacation, you probably already know that there are many other books to help you get ready for your trip. Some of these (dare we say it?) might even be more thorough than ours (we've purposely left out some things that are simply out of the reach of the cheapskate). There's even an "official" guide out there—one that says that everything is perfect in the World. Our goal in *The Cheapskate's Guide to Walt Disney World* is to share money-saving and time-saving techniques acquired over many vacations enjoyed by us and our knowledgeable friends. By traveling smarter, you'll enjoy your trip more.

This book is anything but official. By making it unauthorized, we don't have to toe the Disney party line and tell you that everything in Walt Disney World is just ducky (sorry, Donald!). Rather, with your vacation enjoyment always in mind, we tell it like it is. Our frankness probably won't make us many friends in the Disney organization, but they probably won't buy this book anyway. (Get the lawyers on the phone, just in case!) While there's a lot we like about Walt Disney World, when we don't like something, you'll know it. Our allegiance is to you, our fellow Disney fan, not to some stodgy board of directors who take themselves too seriously.

Walt Disney World is the world's most popular vacation destination. More people vacation there than at any other place on the planet. And for good reason—it's clean, it's safe, it's fun, and, for the most part, the people who work there are friendly and helpful, and all the details have been well thought-out. It's so nice that you barely notice—or don't mind—that everything at Disney World is designed to separate you from your money. (You think it's a coincidence that when you exit most attractions you wind up in a gift shop?!)

On its busiest day, more than 80,000 people converge on the nine theme parks that make up Disney World. Most wander aimlessly about, virtually clueless. This is because human beings tend to hang out with their own kind. This herding mentality forces people to follow the crowds, lining up like cows waiting to be milked. To you, dear reader, we say, "MOO! No more!" Avoid the herd mentality. In Disney World, at least, do things against the grain whenever possible (read on, and you'll see what we mean). Follow our advice and, more often than not, you'll avoid the maddening crowd.

With everyone trying to see the same attractions at the same time, it's not easy to avoid long waits on lines—but it is *possible!* You should not have to wait more than ten or fifteen minutes, even for the World's most popular attractions. How is it possible? The trick is in knowing *what* to see *when*.

Most first-time guests flounder around with no idea of what they want to see and, in doing so, spend more time standing on lines than seeing the attractions. There's nothing more frustrating, especially if you have impatient small children in tow! Let's say you are able to see eight major attractions a day. If you wait thirty minutes at each attraction (a length of time that is not unheard of, even on average days), that's four hours wasted! We've heard so many horror stories from people who came back from their vacations having missed the best parts of the World because they didn't know what to see, or simply did not have the time to wait on all the lines they encountered.

(And we're sure they must have had lots of fun telling the kids they had to abandon a line they had been waiting on!)

It is the absolute truth that the more time you spend planning your vacation to Disney World, the more enjoyable that vacation will be. It doesn't take a lot of effort to become knowledgeable in the ways of the park, and the benefits can be extremely rewarding. Planning ahead virtually guarantees that you will see everything you want to see (sometimes more than once if you want to), in less time, and without unexpected hassles.

So, if you get nothing else out of this book, at least learn this: The trick to a great trip is to pre-plan and get organized. Get all the information you can (see the Disney Directory at the back of this book for helpful addresses and phone numbers). Decide in advance what you would most like to see on each day. Read this *Cheapskate's Guide* from cover to cover before you go, then bring it along with you to skim through each day of your trip. We've designed it to be vacationer-friendly!

We know the Disney parks backward and forward, and *we* still plan out each and every day we spend there. We start doing research a few weeks before leaving home. We have to— the Disney parks are in a constant state of change.

So many changes have taken place at Disney World since its inception that it's hard to believe it's the same theme park. In the early seventies, you didn't have to worry about long lines at Space Mountain, Big Thunder Mountain Railroad, or Splash Mountain—those rides simply didn't exist. The Magic Kingdom was all alone; EPCOT and the Studios were only twinkles in the eyes of the Disney brass! And the only form of admission to the park was a general admission ticket that cost about $5. Each ride then charged a separate admission (the old A, B, C, D, or E ticket program). Aside from the apparent money-exchanging hassles, the ticket media concept was great, because when people ran out of tickets they all went home. By late night, the park was deserted and you could literally walk right onto any attraction! If you were lucky, you could also collect tickets from people who came home with unused, undated extras, thus insuring that next time around you only had to pay for your general admission.

But those heady days are over. A one-day, formerly $5-admission today costs more than $40, and includes unlimited use of all the attractions. These days you have no other choice but to do a cost analysis in advance of your vacation to see which type of multi-day/multi-park admission ticket makes the most sense for your plans. For example, the difference in cost between buying a four-day passport and paying extra to visit a water park or Pleasure Island, or purchasing a vacation package that includes all admissions, can be astronomical.

So take some time, think about what it is you really want from your vacation. You've made your first right move by buying this book, but our information is just the tip of the iceberg in the process of planning the perfect trip. You *can* make your kids happy with a trip to Disney World, and also enjoy it yourself, without spending large sums of money. All it takes is the *right* information and a little advance preparation on your part.

So take *The Cheapskate's Guide* with you into the parks. Show the world you're proud to be a cheapskate (and give us a little free advertising! We'd sure appreciate it!). On the pages that follow, the emphasis is on having fun on a budget. Once your vacation is over, the memories about the fun will stick with you longer than the memories about what the fun cost.

Note: Since *cheapskate* might be considered a relative term, whenever possible, we've recommended food and lodging that vary in price, but always with an eye toward the lower end of the budget scale. You *can* have fun on a budget; you'll just have to do a little more research, soul searching, planning, and discussing to put together the vacation that's perfect for you.

How to Use This Book

After reading just about every Disney Book and article out there, visiting many Internet Web sites, and discussing this book with families, friends, and anonymous vacationers, we think we've set this book up in a user-friendly format, one that we ourselves would benefit from if we were the readers, rather than the writers.

We begin with background information on timing your visit and discuss the best places to stay. We recommend you do some of your own fact-finding well in advance of your trip. Allow at least four weeks for delivery of the brochures and information you seek.

Then we present each Disney park, discussing each individual "neighborhood's" attractions, food, and shopping. That way you don't have to flip around the book trying to gather the advice you need and can spend more time enjoying the park rather than riffling through pages. With that knowledge under your belt, you can move on to our itineraries—designed to enable you to see the most in as little time as possible.

We encourage you to read the entire book while you're planning your trip, *before* you leave for Florida. Discuss with your family which rides you consider must-sees and which you can pass on. Then bring the book with you to the parks each day and take advantage of our valuable tips.

The prices quoted and information provided in this *Cheapskate's Guide* were current and accurate at the time of writing. Every effort has been made to insure that the information presented is current and accurate, but as with everything in life, things change. And the way things have been going at Disney World the last five years, things *will* change . . . a *lot!*

Not to blow our own horn, but it's not easy to write a book

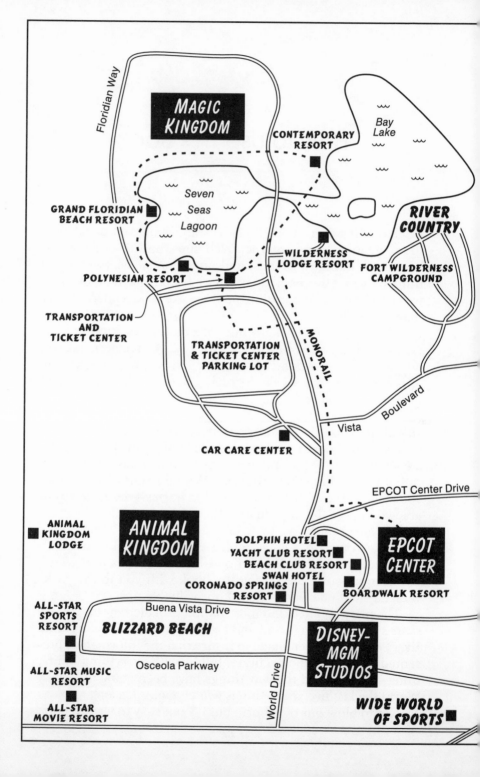

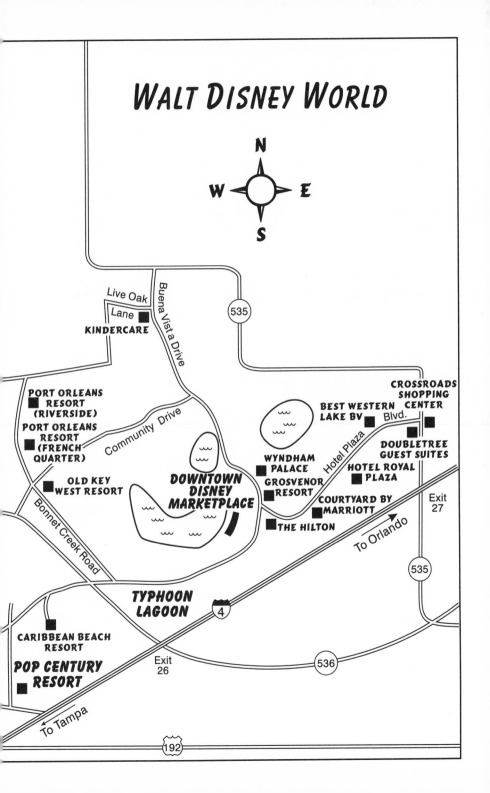

like this. No matter what you do, no matter how much information you include, there's always going to be something you've left out. There's always a danger that, whenever you quote prices, you leave yourself open for dispute. But our intentions are noble—we want you to have as much fun at Disney World as we've had.

We recommend you call well in advance for more information and the latest pricing for whatever accommodations or package deals even remotely interest you. We'd hate for you to have a rude awakening upon check-in. And in your own research, if you discover new information that could benefit future travelers, please write to us.

The Cheapskate's Guide to
WALT DISNEY WORLD

1

Getting to Mickey

By Bus

Greyhound and other major bus carriers offer direct service to Kissimmee and Orlando. Direct taxi service to Walt Disney World is available from the bus station.

By Car

If you're arriving by car, Disney World is conveniently located on I-4, which runs from the east coast of Florida to the west coast. Getting to I-4 is easy—you can approach it from I-95 if you're coming from the east, or I-75 if you're coming from the west. If you're traveling north on the Florida Turnpike, take the Osceola Parkway west (exit 249) to the Walt Disney Resort.

Disney's main gate is located on Route 192, which can be reached from an exit off of I-4. However, newer exits on I-4 and other, less-crowded roadways lead directly to EPCOT and the Disney on-site hotels (read on!).

By Plane

Walt Disney World is located in the little hamlet of Lake Buena Vista, Florida, about 20 miles from Orlando International Airport. This is one of the country's fastest-growing airports (undoubtedly due to the growth in popularity of Disney World) and is serviced by all the major airlines. And it's no coincidence that this airport was designed by Disney!

For those guests arriving by plane through Orlando and taking a rental car to the resort, a new road that many people don't know about (at least until they read this!) has opened that takes you directly onto Disney property.

After picking up the rental, follow large red signs for the south exit from the airport to Kissimmee. Take Florida 417 South (the Central Florida Greeneway). If you're staying at one of the EPCOT area resorts (i.e., BoardWalk, Caribbean Beach, Old Key West, Port Orleans, Yacht and Beach Clubs, Swan, or Dolphin), take exit 6 and follow the signs to your destination. If you're traveling to the Magic Kingdom or Animal Kingdom hotels (Magic: Contemporary, Fort Wilderness Campground, Grand Floridian, Polynesian, or Wilderness Lodge; Animal: the three All-Star Resorts, Animal Kingdom Lodge, Coronado Springs, and Pop Century Resort), take exit 3 to the Osceola Parkway. This takes you directly onto Disney property where you can follow the signs to your destination. Florida 417 is a toll road, and a one-way trip will cost about $2. However, it is a direct route and will save you time, while also avoiding heavy congestion on the more popular I-4. The trip should take no more than thirty minutes from wing to room.

For guests who arrive by air and stay on-site at a Disney hotel, a rental car might not be necessary, especially if Disney World is your only destination. Taxi service is available at the Orlando Airport, but reliable bus transportation is also available and will be more economical.

Mears Motor Shuttle operates from Orlando Airport to the Disney resorts, and the trip takes approximately forty-five minutes. You get the shuttle on the airport's second level, outside of the baggage claim area. The cost is currently $14 for a one-way adult ticket, and $25 for round-trip. Children age four to eleven are charged $10 for one-way and $17 for round-trip. Reservations can be made by calling 407-423-5566 or through their Web site at http://www.mears-net.com. (Mears transfers are often included as part of a larger tour package. Check with your travel agent.)

If you're a large family or group, you might want to try Quick Transportation. You arrange ahead of time to be picked up (call 888-784-2522, or visit their web page www.quicktrans portation.com), and a driver will be waiting in the airport (holding a card with your name on it!) whose sole purpose that day is to get your group from the airport to the hotel. For $110 roundtrip for up to seven people (tip not included), they'll take just your group and make just one stop—not a van load of people staying in six different hotels.

While You're at Orlando International Airport

Look for Disney's information booth in the main terminal—it's a great place to gather brochures and information that will build excitement on the ride to your hotel!

By Train

Amtrak serves Orlando with daily trains from the East Coast or the New Orleans-Miami route. After arriving at the train station, take a taxi or a motor shuttle to the resort. The Auto Train provides service from Lorton, Virginia to Sanford, Florida, which is twenty-five miles northeast of Orlando.

SAVING MONEY ON TRAVEL

Try a package deal through a travel agency, tour operator, or one of the airlines (read on). Through such a package, you may be able to get into a hotel that is otherwise sold out. (Read on for more information.)

Discount Tour Operators

There are hundreds, maybe thousands, of companies offering discount package deals to Disney World. Ask your local travel agent, or call them directly. Here are a few to get you started gathering information:

Adventure Vacations	800-638-9040
Globetrotters	800-999-9696
GoGo Tours	800-899-3999
Kingdom Vacations	800-626-8747
(www.kingdomvacations.com)	
Leisure Group Sales	800-327-2989
Travel Impressions	800-284-0044

Online Discount Travel

The Internet and the World Wide Web are empowering consumers to get the best for less, and the travel industry online is no exception. You can now avoid the middleman/woman and often get a better deal through an online travel service than you can from your hometown travel coordinator. And with the advent of E-Tickets, you can book a flight just hours before it hits the sky. Surf the Internet and you're sure to find bargains. Here are several places we've found:

Go here first—these sites offer links to hotel, resort, airline, and information travel websites:

- www.travelsites.com
- www.airlines.com

These sites offer complete travel services (e.g. air, hotel, rental car reservations). Many even offer an e-mail fare watcher service—

- www.aatoztravel.com
- www.Activatravel.com
- www.bestfares.com
- www.cheaptickets.com
- www.expedia.com
- Internet Travel Network: www.itn.net
- www.lowestfare.com
- www.onlinevacationmall.com
- www.site59.com
- www.smarterliving.com

- www.travelocity.com
- www.travelscape.com

These sites are of the "name your price" variety. If you don't mind not having complete control of when you fly or how many stops you'll have to make, check 'em out—

- www.priceline.com
- www.hotwire.com

These sites search the web to find the best deals, making your comparison shopping easier. They come with their own set of challenges (e.g. you often have to download their software program) but the savings may be worth the hassle:

- www.airlineguides.com
- www.farechase.com
- www.qixo.com
- www.sidestep.com

Simple Yet Effective Way to Save Money

Sometimes in order to get the best rate, you just have to ask for it. Often, when you call for a rate (on rooms, airfare, whatever) the operator will give you a rate that is not the best one available. If you ask for a better rate, sometimes you'll get one. Hey, it doesn't hurt to ask!

The Internet is growing daily, in users and in Web sites. Do your research and planning early and you're sure to find money savings.

Disney Information Online

As you'd expect, being the world's most popular vacation destination virtually guarantees that Walt Disney World will be one of the most popular topics on the Net. Type the words "Walt Disney World" into a search engine and you could spend days and still not have seen all the sites. We'll save you the trouble—here are some of the ones we use:

- www.disneyworld.com: Here's Disney's official site. Not quite as frank and opinionated as we are, but this site should be your first stop as you begin planning your trip and you should bookmark it for your return research visits.

- www.go2orlando.com: A helpful site for anyone planning a trip to the Orlando area (and that means you!)

- www.wdwig.com: Arguably the best unofficial Disney site. It even has restaurant menus!

- www.themeparks.com/wdw/default.htm: Operating schedules, resort information, and more.

- www.mousesavers.com: This site WILL save you money. It includes moneysaving tips and little-known, published codes that will get you the best rates. Here's how it works: do some research on the site, then call Disney's central reservations directly, using the specific code you found for the specific Disney resort you want, and you save hundreds of dollars on your trip. Some restrictions and specific dates apply. No-nonsense—nothing glitzy or glamorous—but still a must visit. Tell them we sent you!

As you search the web, be aware that it's constantly changing and don't be frustrated if one of these sites disappears from your monitor. And, by the same token, if you discover an especially helpful—and money saving—site, let us know so we can share it with our fellow cheapskates.

Tips on Saving Money on Airfare

This topic could be a book unto itself. But here are some quick tips:

- If you know when you want to go, book your flight up to 11 months in advance. The lowest available fares are usually the first ones the airlines release.

- Be flexible. There's usually less demand for midday and very-late-in-the-day flights. Sometimes even the *day* you fly can make a difference—ask when you call about flights.

- Go during the off-season when rates are lower.

- Be flexible on the route—changing planes or putting up with a layover will reduce rates.

- Book deep-discounted fares far in advance. They are usually nonrefundable, but if you have to cancel, you can apply the ticket to other flights during the year.

- Wait for the last moment—accept a bargain price on a leftover seat and hotel cancellation. This is not always a wise move if you've got kids—how will you explain to them that you couldn't get plane tickets?!

- Piggyback with a convention. Find out if there are any conventions coming up in the Orlando area, claim you're with them, and take advantage of their cheap airfare.

- Fly standby. Travelers with valid tickets can stand by for flights other than the ones for which they have reservations. If there are empty seats on the flight you really want, standby ticketholders can board. The trick is to book the cheapest seat on any flight, then show up at the counter just before the flight you really want to take, not the flight for which you have a ticket. You usually won't have a problem, unless you travel during an incredibly busy time. Call the airline the day before your flight and see how fully booked the flight is you'd like to stand by for. Check with the airline to see their standby policy—it sometimes involves your paying a $25 or $50 surcharge per ticket, but the savings could be worth it.

- Check directly with the airlines for unadvertised specials and package deals. Sometimes dramatically discounted airfares are offered exclusively to those who use the Internet. This allows the airlines not only to save money on travel agency fees, ticket printing, advertising, etc.—and pass those savings on to you—but also gives them the ability to fill seats at the eleventh hour that would otherwise fly away empty. Best of all, if you provide the airline with your e-mail address, you will be placed on their subscriber list and be kept up to date on their latest cyberdeals.

Here are the toll-free numbers and web addresses for some of the major airlines:

- Air Canada: 800-776-3000
  http://www.aircanada.ca

- AirTran: 800-247-8726
  http://www.airtran.com

- American: 800-433-7300
  http://www.aa.com

- American Trans Air: 800-225-
  2995; http://www.ata.com

- America West: 800-235-9292
  http://www.americawest.com

- Continental: 800-525-0280
  http://www.flycontinental.com

- Delta: 800-221-1212
  http://www.delta.com

- Frontier: 800-432-1359
  http://www.frontier.com

- Jet Blue: 800-538-2583
  http://www.jetblue.com

- Midway: 800-446-4392
  http://www.midwayair.com

- Midwest Express: 800-452-2022
  http://www.midwestexpress.com

- Northwest: 800-225-2525
  http://www.nwa.com

- Southwest: 800-435-9792
  http://www.southwest.com

- Spirit Airlines: 800-772-7117
  http://www.spiritair.com

- TWA: 800-893-5436
  http://www.twa.com

- United: 800-241-6522
  http://www.ual.com

- US Airways: 800-428-4322
  http://www.usairways.com

- Virgin Atlantic: 800-862-8621
  http://www.virgin-atlantic.com

If you'd like to find the Web page of an airline not listed here—perhaps because a Web page didn't exist when we were writing this—use one of the search engines, like AltaVista, Yahoo, or Webcrawler, and type in the airline name, then scroll through the search results until you find the airline's official Web page.

Many airlines now offer an e-mail service for discounted, last-minute fares. Go to their Web site and leave your e-mail address. They will notify you electronically when there is a rate change.

2

When You Should Go and Where You Should Stay

TIMING IS EVERYTHING

As you may have guessed if you've read this far, the best time to go to Disney World is when most other people aren't there. But there's one catch to this approach: If you go when the parks are the least crowded, the hours of operation tend to be shorter and some rides might be shut down for renovations or maintenance. There are also fewer nighttime parades.

So the time of year you choose is crucial. Choose off-season (which varies from hotel to hotel—check with your travel agent) and you'll face fewer crowds but somewhat less time in the parks. No matter when you go, you won't have difficulty finding a place to sleep—there must be nearly one million rooms in the Orlando/Kissimmee/Lake Buena Vista area—but if you prefer a specific accommodation, we recommend booking early.

Your greatest problem during your Disney World vacation will be dealing with the crowds in the parks. Use the following guidelines when planning your vacation:

Least Crowded Times   You've just about got the place to yourself (on average, about 25,000 visitors per day).

- The second week of January through the end of the month
- September through mid-November
- The first through third weeks of December

Moderate Crowds Expect up to 35,000 visitors per day

- The first ten days in February
- The entire months of March and May
- The first and last weeks of April

Heavy Crowds You'll have the displeasure of sharing your trip with up to 60,000 visitors per day

- New Year's Day
- President's week holiday
- The second and third weeks of April (due to Easter recess and Spring Break)
- June to August
- Thanksgiving

Too Crowded for Real Enjoyment Up to 80,000 visitors per day (we wouldn't even bother going)

- Christmas holiday

Weather in the World

The weather conditions in central Florida should also be considered when planning your trip. While most would consider the climate nice throughout the year, the heat can be unbearable during the summer months, and in the winter, while it's pleasant during the day, it can get downright nippy when the sun goes down.

Consider the temperature and rainfall statistics listed below, which were provided by the National Weather Service, before you go.

Month	Average High	Average Low	Mean Temperature	Rainfall (Inches)
January	70	50	60	2.28
February	72	51	62	2.95
March	76	56	66	3.46
April	81	61	71	2.72
May	87	66	76	2.94
June	89	71	80	7.11
July	90	73	81	8.29
August	90	73	81	6.73
September	88	72	80	7.20
October	82	66	74	4.07
November	76	57	67	1.56
December	71	51	61	1.90

Our Recommendations

We think the ideal time for a visit to Walt Disney World is from late April until Memorial Day; or any time in September after school starts. The weather's not unbearably hot, and most parks are open to a decent hour. Call ahead (407-824-4321) and check the operating hours for the dates you've got in mind. You may have to take the kids out of school, but remember: The dates when *all* kids are out of school are the days you *don't* want to be in Walt Disney World!

RECOMMENDED ACCOMMODATIONS FOR THE CHEAPSKATE

So, you want to go to Disney and you've decided when you want to go. Now you've got to pick a hotel. You can stay either on-site or off-site. Choose wisely, grasshopper, because whatever you decide can make the difference between an okay trip and a great one. Read this whole section, including our somewhat biased recommendations, before you choose.

Least Expensive On-Site Accommodations

Disney's Fort Wilderness Resort and Campground This is the least expensive spot for the cheapskate, but read on. . . .

Pitch a tent, park your camper, or rent a luxury Wilderness Home, or one-bedroom Wilderness Cabin. We'll give you one guess which is the cheapest alternative. All of the nearly 800 campsites on this secluded 784-acre site include electrical and water hookups and a charcoal grill, and most have sanitary hookups. Comfort stations, a trading post, and shower and laundry facilities are near every site.

While it can cost as little as $35 a night for a tent campsite during off-season, even a cheapskate needs some luxury. (Try sleeping in a sleeping bag in the summer and you'll see what we mean. And when you've been walkin' the Disney beat—take it from us—you need the comfort of a real bed!) Of course, you can pull up your RV to one of the well-equipped campsites, but then your per night room rate is hovering right around the price to stay at the All-Star or Pop Century Resorts described below. We strongly suggest you spend a few more bucks and choose the air-conditioned comfort of the All-Star or Pop Century Resorts. And for the price of renting a Wilderness trailer or cabin for a night (in the neighborhood of $200), you could stay at one of Disney's more fashionable/pricey hotels.

But, if you really like being out in the open, the direct phone for the Fort Wilderness Resort and Campground is 407-824-2900.

Disney's All-Star Music, All-Star Sports, and All-Star Movies Resorts   Not coincidentally, these budget-priced Disney hotels are located on a nearly 300-acre complex near their budget-priced off-site competitors on Route 192 in Kissimmee. As their name implies, they are themed around sports, music, and movies. All-Star Sports has 1,920 rooms in five buildings, each dedicated to a different sport: baseball (Home Run Hotel), basketball (Hoops Hotel), football (Touchdown Hotel), surfing (Surf's Up), and tennis (Center Court); while the All-Star Music Resort's buildings are centered around your favorite music: Broadway tunes, calypso, country and western, jazz, and rock and roll. The All-Star Movies Resort was inspired by five of Disney's most popular releases: *101 Dalmations, Fantasia, The Love Bug, Toy Story,* and *The Mighty Ducks.*

The three hotel complexes are located close to Animal Kingdom and Blizzard Beach, but since free transportation is included in your stay, getting to any of the other Disney theme parks is only a bus ride away. Each resort surrounds a main building, which includes a food court (called End Zone at Sports, Intermission at Music, and World Premiere Court at Movies), guest services desk, and an arcade. That means you can grab a quick early breakfast, buy admission tickets without waiting in the parks' general admission lines, and be in the parks as they open. And when you're beat, but the kids are still full of energy, you can grab a nap while they entertain themselves in the arcade.

The themes of each hotel are carried forward throughout your whole lodging experience—for example, the country and western building in the All-Star Music Resort is garnished with huge cowboy boots (we're talking twenty feet tall, folks), while a pool in the shape of a baseball diamond (complete with Goofy "pitching" water from a pitcher's mound, and more) flanks the Baseball building in the sports resort. The All-Star Sports Resort also includes a pool resembling the ocean (even the grass surrounding the pool is sculpted to look like waves), while the main pool of the All-Star Music Resort looks like a giant guitar. Each resort also has a kiddie pool for the littlest travelers.

As to the End Zone (sports), Intermission (music), and World Premiere (movies) food courts—these are large, often crowded, noisy places, but the lines move fast and you can grab everything from a late-afternoon snack to a decent full-blown meal. And there's something for everyone's taste.

Although adults might consider the appearance of these hotels tacky, kids enjoy them tremendously. The rooms are on the small side, but are adequate for a family of four. Besides, how much time do you really spend in your room, anyway? Most rooms are equipped with two double beds and a small bathroom (toilet and bathtub/shower). There is a countertop across the back of the room with a single sink and a closet bar with shelf. An armoire houses the TV and has three drawers for clothes, and a small table with two chairs rounds out the room.

For around $80–90 per night, the All-Star resorts offer a lot of theme for the buck. Look for package deals that combine your lodging with theme park passes, character breakfasts, and more. But bear in mind that if you want to stay in one of these, Disney's least expensive hotels, you must book your trip early to guarantee yourself the cheapest room for the time-frame you have in mind, and expect crowds at virtually every time of the year. If your kids have a favorite sport, type of music, or movie that they enjoy, try to book a room in that specific building. Disney won't guarantee that you'll get the preferred room on check-in, but it's worth trying.

And remember, when you place your on-site reservation, request a refrigerator. The $5-a-day rental fee will more than pay for itself. You can go off-site to stock up on groceries and soda rather than pay on-site food prices.

The All-Star Movies Resort is located at 1991 West Buena Vista Drive, Lake Buena Vista, FL 32830-1000; the direct phone is 407-939-7000. The All-Star Music Resort is located at 1801 West Buena Vista Drive, Lake Buena Vista, FL 32830-1000; the direct phone is 407-939-6000. The All-Star Sports Resort is located at 1701 West Buena Vista Drive, Lake Buena Vista, FL 32830-1000; the direct phone is 407-939-5000.

Disney's Pop Century Resort   This is Disney's newest value hotel. In fact, it's so new that it was still under construction while we were writing this edition. So, we'll give you as much information as we can about this sister hotel to the All-Star resorts, which was scheduled to open its first phase, The 1950's, in December 2001. By the time the hotel is completely finished in 2003, there will be twenty building, six swimming pools, and over 5,000 guest rooms.

The Pop Century Resort is similar in size and structure to the very popular All-Star resorts. The only difference is the hotel's themes. Rather than sports, movies, or music, this resort's theme traces the recent history of the American pop culture. Each building is represented by larger-than-life icons of different decades of the second half of the 1900's. The 50's building will have a huge jukebox and large bowling pins for the outdoor stairways. The 60's will star Baloo and Mowgli from the Disney movie Jungle Book feature (released in 1967), along with Duncan yo-yo's. The 70's will feature that wonderful plastic tricycle, the Big Wheel, and staircases made to look like giant 8-track tapes. The themes will also carry into the design of the pools, with the 50's resembling a large bowling pin, the 60's in the shape of a flower (flower power), and the 90's—what else—a computer!

The size of the room is expected to be the same as the All-Stars, with either two double beds or one king-sized. There will be a small table with chairs and a TV stand/armoire with a few drawers for your clothing. The bathroom is small (just a bathtub/shower and toilet), with the sink in the main room. That helps to save time when you have a family all trying to get ready at the same time to hit the parks first thing in the morning.

It's also expected that the hotel will have a food court instead of a restaurant. This also saves time in the morning since the first person up can get breakfast and bring it back to the room for the rest of the family. (One thing we discovered about the food courts at the value hotels is that they improved as they were built. In other words, the Music resort's is better than the Sports', which was built first, and the Movies resort's is much better than the Music. So, we're hoping that this trend continues at the Pop Century.)

The room rate is expected to be the same as the rates at the All-Stars. So, our theory is, if you're going to pay the same price for the room, you might as well pick the newer hotel and make your reservation at the Pop Century Resort.

The Pop Century Resort is located on 235 acres of land between the Caribbean Beach Resort and Wide World of Sports, at 1050 Century Drive, Lake Buena Vista, FL 32830-1000. At this point in time, the direct phone number for the hotel is not known, but reservations may be made by calling 407-W-DISNEY.

Moderate Priced On-site Accommodations

Okay, you're cheap, but you're not *that* cheap. If the All-Star and Pop Century resorts just aren't what you have in mind, or if they're booked solid for the days you want, don't give up hope! For a few dollars a day more, Disney offers four moderate priced hotels that are really very nice for the money—the two Port Orleans resorts, Coronado Springs, and the Caribbean Beach resorts.

Each hotel has basically the same design: There are a number of smaller buildings clustered around a main resort area. The main area houses the registration and guest services desk, gift shop, and restaurants. Outside is a large themed pool and marina (each hotel is on a small river or lake). Each cluster of rooms sometimes has a smaller pool. The only real difference between hotels is the theme of the buildings. All four also feature good-value-for-the-money restaurants.

The rooms are adequate in size and actually quite efficient for a family of two adults and two children. Each has two double beds, a small table with two chairs, an armoire that also houses a TV, and a double sink. The closet consists of a clothing rod on the wall next to the sink; not terribly pretty but very practical. The bathroom is small—just a bathtub with a shower and a toilet. The rooms range in price from a low of $129 a night to a high of $209. The difference in price is due to the view from the room, or the time of year. All rooms are exactly the same, except that a few have one king-size bed instead of two doubles.

Port Orleans Riverside (formerly known as Dixie Landings)   The biggest of Disney's moderate priced resorts boasts more than 2,000 rooms. The resort is in the style of the Old South, with plantation-type mansions and more rustic bayou-style country cottages. Close your eyes and you'll think you're Tom Sawyer!

The main recreational area, Ol' Man Island, covers over three-and-a-half acres and offers an ol' fashioned swimmin' hole (heated pool with water slide). The resort also has a stocked fishing hole where you can try your hand at landing the "big one" for a nominal charge (the charge is for the rental of a bamboo fishing pole and bait). But if you land one, be a good Mouseketeer and throw it back!

Port Orleans Riverside restaurants include:

- **Boatwright's Dining Hall**   Full-service, sit-down restaurant offering American and Cajun cuisine for breakfast and dinner. Entrees under $16.95.

- *Colonel's Cotton Mill* Food court serving breakfast, lunch, and dinner from 6:00 A.M. until midnight. Five different shops offer a variety of options: pasta and pizza, barbecue, Mexican food, hamburgers and hot dogs, spit-roasted and fried chicken, sandwiches and salads, and bakery items. Kids are fascinated by the thirty-two-foot-tall water wheel that powers a working cotton press in the middle of the court. Many entrees under $10.

- *Cotton Co-op Lounge* A casual cocktail bar featuring live entertainment Thursday through Monday evenings. Open until 12:30 A.M., serving light hors d'oeuvres.

- *Muddy Rivers* Grab a quick snack as you hang poolside at the Ol' Man Island swimmin' hole. Serving hot dogs, chips, popcorn, and specialty drinks, with most items $5–10.

- *Sassagoula Pizza Express* Have those hot pizzas delivered directly to your room (from 4:00 P.M. until midnight). Sure is nice to rest your feet after a day in the Disney parks!

Bike and watercraft rentals are available. There are also a playground and a video arcade game room for kids. Miles of walking paths ring the park. Why not take a walk to neighboring Port Orleans French Quarter Resort? Better yet, hop a boat to Downtown Disney.

Port Orleans Riverside is located at 1251 Dixie Drive, Lake Buena Vista, FL 32830-1000. The direct phone is 407-934-6000.

Port Orleans French Quarter Resort This 1,000-room resort is modeled after—what else—the French Quarter of New Orleans, made authentic by the ever-present sound of jazz music and the faint smell of freshly made beignets in the air. Each cluster of buildings is connected by narrow streets that intersect, creating beautifully landscaped courtyards.

Doubloon Lagoon, the main pool area, has a goofy-looking sea serpent for its water slide and alligator fountains adding to the festive atmosphere of Mardi Gras.

Port Orleans French Quarter restaurants include:

- *Sassagoula Floatworks and Food Factory*   Food court serving breakfast, lunch, and dinner from 6:00 A.M. until midnight. Offers many options including pasta and pizza, barbecue, hamburgers and hot dogs, spit-roasted and fried chicken, sandwiches and salads, and bakery items (don't miss the beignets and café au lait). The seating area is in a warehouse setting and surrounds you with Mardi Gras parade props. Many entrees under $10.

- *Scat Cat's Lounge*   Lounge offering live entertainment Thursday through Monday evenings. Open until 12:30 A.M., serving light hors d'oeuvres.

- *Sassagoula Pizza Express*   Pizza delivery direct to your room from 4:00 P.M. until midnight.

Bike and watercraft rentals are available, and there's croquet and a video arcade for kids. Miles of walking paths ring the park. Take a walk to the neighboring Dixie Landings Resort. Or, if money's burning a hole in your pocket, hop a skiff (that's boatsmen talk for . . . boat) to Downtown Disney.

Port Orleans French Quarter is located at 2201 Orleans Drive, Lake Buena Vista, FL 32830-1000. The direct phone is 407-934-5000.

> "Hey, what happened to Dixie Landings?" We can hear you ask the question. Disney, in their boundless wisdom, has decided to consider Port Orleans and Dixie Landings as one resort, under the umbrella name of Port Orleans (with Port Orleans Riverside now the name of Dixie Landings, and Port Orleans French Quarter the name of what was formerly called just Port Orleans). Confused yet? Remember when Sugar Pops cereal suddenly became known as Corn Pops? All that changed was the name.

Caribbean Beach Resort   Take a trip to the islands without leaving the U.S. of A! Disney's Caribbean Beach Resort offers five brightly colored "villages," each named and styled after a Caribbean island. The resort has over 2,000 rooms, plus a forty-five-acre lake with white sandy beaches.

The main recreation area features the Old Port Royale Pool. The pool is styled after a Caribbean fort with turrets and cannons. Kids love this pool the best! Caribbean Beach restaurants include:

- *Captain's Tavern*   Full-service, sit-down restaurant offering typical American cuisine for dinner.

- *Old Port Royale*   Colorful Caribbean food court serving breakfast, lunch, and dinner from 6:00 A.M until midnight. Six different shops serve a variety of food: pizza, broiled chicken, home-style meals, bakery items, and ice cream. Many entrees under $10.00.

- *Banana Cabana*   Snacks and drinks served at the pool.

- *Bluerunner*   In-room dining, offering relatively inexpensive pizza, chicken, and desserts.

Bike and watercraft rentals are available. There's a playground and a video arcade game room for the kids, as well as a 1.4-mile jogging path around the lake for adults! Caribbean Beach Resort is located at 900 Cayman Way, Lake Buena Vista, FL 32830-1000. The direct phone is 407-934-3400.

Coronado Springs   Disney's newest moderately priced resort is set on 136 acres, its 1,967 rooms surrounding a picturesque, 15-acre lagoon, called Lago Dorado. The hotel is themed after explorer Francisco de Coronado's travels from Northern Mexico to the American Southwest; the rooms are themed in three different areas: the Casitas, with their colorful plazas and fountains (and closest to the main lobby and registration area); the Ranchos, highlighted by an arroyo (that's Spanish for "creek"); and the Cabanas, with many rooms overlooking a rocky shoreline.

The Seven-Cities-of-Gold-theme extends to the hotel's main pool, with a 46-foot replica Mayan pyramid with water cascading down its stone steps and a water slide. A kiddie pool and three quiet pools are available for those who wish to avoid the crowds at the main pool. There is also a 20,000-square-foot playground nearby.

Restaurants at the Coronado Springs include:

- *Maya Grill*   This full-service, sit-down restaurant features a Mayan decor and a lakeside view. It offers Mayan cuisine for breakfast and dinner, and prepares meats and seafood over an open wood-burning fire. Entrees up to $20. Reservations are suggested.

- *Francisco's*   This casual 200-seat lounge sports an outdoor sidewalk-café atmosphere. Specialties include hors d'oeuvres, snacks, and regional specialties. It features live entertainment on Thursday through Monday evenings.

- *Pepper Market*   This is a food court with an outdoor market atmosphere; serves breakfast, lunch, and dinner from 6:00 A.M. until midnight. Nine food stands offer a variety of options: pasta and pizza, barbecue, Mexican food, hamburgers, hot dogs, spit-roasted and fried chicken, sandwiches, salads, and bakery items. Many entrees under $10.

- *Siesta's*   Located next to the main pool area, this pool bar and grill offers American and regional specialties, including burgers, sandwiches, tacos, and specialty drinks. Most items are below $10, and room delivery is available on many items.

Bike and watercraft rentals are available, and for the athletically inclined, there's a sand volleyball court and a nature walk.

Sneaky Tip: "Are You With the Convention?"

The Coronado Springs Hotel features 95,000 square feet of meeting space (including a ballroom that's the largest hotel ballroom in the United States). For the cheapskate, this means that when a convention is in town, inexpensive rooms once reserved for conventioneers often become available at the eleventh hour due to cancellations. It might be worth your while to do a little research, find out what organizations or corporations are in town during the time of your stay, and when you make your reservation, tell a little white lie and say that you are staying at the hotel for the convention. Don't tell them we told you to do this, but why should businesspeople always get the cheapest rates?!

Coronado Springs Resort is located at 1000 West Buena Vista Drive, Lake Buena Vista, FL 32830-1000. The direct phone is 407-939-1000.

Shades of Green   This hotel is no longer a Disney-operated resort, but we are including it in this section because it is on Disney property—and it's cheap!

Way back when the Magic Kingdom opened in 1971, there were three hotels: the Contemporary, Polynesian, and Golf Resort (so named because it sat in the middle of Disney's Magnolia and Palm golf courses). The Golf Resort wasn't a very lucrative hotel since it never attracted people who didn't play golf. Thus, they tried changing the name to the Disney Inn, but that didn't help to attract guests either. So, in 1994, Disney leased the hotel to the U.S. Department of Defense, which now operates the facility.

If you are active or retired from the military, a member of the reserves or the National Guard, or a Department of Defense civilian, you may be eligible to reserve a very reasonably priced room at the Shades of Green. You'll still enjoy many of the benefits of staying at a Disney hotel—use of their transportation system, early admissions to the parks, package delivery to your room, etc. And since this was one of the original hotels, the rooms are oversized compared to today's standards.

Room rates are dependent upon the military rank of the person booking the room and are really quite cheap. So if you fit the requirements, it's worth giving it a try. But a word of warning: This hotel is now extremely popular because it is so cheap. You should make your reservation as far in advance as possible. And if you find that the hotel is fully booked, try to get an overflow room at one of the other Disney on-site hotels.

Shades of Green is located at 1950 West Magnolia/Palm Drive, Lake Buena Vista, FL 32830-2789. The direct phone to the hotel is 407-824-3400. For reservations, call 407-824-3600.

Start Dreaming

The following on-site hotels may not be in the cheapskate's budget, but someday. . . .

Animal Kingdom Lodge   If you just can't get enough of the exotic animals at Disney's Animal Kingdom, then this is the hotel for you! Styled after a South African game reserve, this 1,293-room resort boasts its own 33-acre private reserve, containing 100 exotic grazing animals and 130 birds. Most accommodations offer a view of the savannah, and the animals roam as close as 30 feet from the guest rooms (we just hope you're not downwind!). As with most of the higher-priced Disney resorts, the architecture—including the five-story oasis—is breathtaking, and it's worth a trip over just to see it. Rates: $199 to $510. Animal Kingdom Lodge, 2901 Osceola Parkway, Lake Buena Vista, FL 32830 (407-938-3000).

Beach Club Resort   Step back in time to Cape Cod of the late 1900s, and these quaint seaside cottages, offering beautifully decorated rooms done in pastel colors, presented on a grand scale. We particularly enjoyed the resort's tremendous attention to detail (e.g., the additional television speaker in the bathroom area). This 500-room resort is the closest to EPCOT. It's actually within walking distance to EPCOT's back entrance at the International Gateway. Rates: $279 to $610. Beach Club Resort, 1800 EPCOT Resorts Boulevard, Lake Buena Vista, FL 32830-1000 (407-934-8000).

BoardWalk Resort   This 378-room resort allows you to step back in time to a 1930s-era seaside resort reminiscent of Atlantic City. The resort is built on a waterfront boardwalk and artistically combines accommodations and lodging with an entertainment complex offering shopping, dining, and a dance hall (see pages 178–181 for more details). Check out the pool—the slide is modeled after the old wooden roller coaster at Coney Island. Rates: $279 to $630. BoardWalk Resort, 2101 EPCOT Resorts Boulevard, Lake Buena Vista, FL 32830-1000 (407-939-5100).

Contemporary Resort   One of the two original Disney World hotels, it was considered a technological marvel at the time it opened in 1971. The tower of the Contemporary Resort is a fifteen-story A-frame structure and the monorails to the Magic Kingdom glide right through the center of the hotel (it's still pretty neat to look at today). Its 1,000 rooms have been updated many times, and this is still a wonderful hotel despite its age. If you're lucky, you might even get a room that looks out onto the Magic Kingdom! Rates: $224 to $505. Contemporary Resort, 4600 North World Drive, Lake Buena Vista, FL 32830-1000 (407-824-1000).

Disney Cruise Line   Once upon a time, Disney had an exclusive partnership with Premiere Cruise Lines, purveyors of "the Big Red Boat." On these combination cruise- (three or four days to the Bahamas) and land- (three or four nights onsite at Disney) vacations, you spent a week vacationing with your favorite Disney characters (who traveled on board with you). Now, Disney has taken it to the next level, launching their own cruise ship line. The itinerary is pretty much the same, a week total in the Bahamas and in Disney World, including a stop at Disney's own 1,000-acre island, Castaway Cay. There are many activities for children of all ages, and half the fun is the ship itself, where hidden Mickeys and other characters abound in the ship's artwork and design (the ship's horn even blows "When You Wish Upon a Star"). However, at prices ranging from $1,300 to $4,300 for the week (depending on which Disney hotel you're staying at), we'd venture a guess that this ship will not be docking in many Cheapskate's harbors. If you win the lottery or rob a bank, call 800-951-3532, or ask your travel agent for more information.

Fort Wilderness Homes/Cabins   It's like camping with all the comforts of home, or as Disney calls it, "Roughing it, Disney style!" Each of these permanent, manufactured homes comes complete with a full-size kitchen, bathroom, living room, and bedroom, plus daily housekeeping. The Wilderness Cabins resemble a log cabin and are Fort Wilderness's latest addition. Each cabin can accommodate six people (if you don't mind the bunk beds), plus one child under three in a foldaway crib. Some have private decks. The Wilderness Homes are actually giant, stationary motor homes and can accommodate between four to six people, but the homes have been at Fort Wilderness for quite a few years and are beginning to show their age. Surrounding the resort are 784 acres of cypress and pine trees that provide a tranquil shelter from the craziness and crowds of the theme parks. Rates: $219 to $299. Fort Wilderness, 4510 North Fort Wilderness Trail, Lake Buena Vista, FL 32830-1000 (407-824-2900).

Grand Floridian Beach Resort and Spa One of the prettiest Victorian-style hotels you'll ever see. Feel the charm and graciousness of an era gone by in this award-winning hotel— Princess Di even stayed here! Even if you can't afford to stay the night (and let's be realistic, who can?), you should get off the Magic Kingdom's monorail and venture into the lobby of this hotel—it's breathtaking. Rates: $314 to $790. Grand Floridian Beach Resort, 4401 Floridian Way, Lake Buena Vista, FL 32830-1000 (407-824-3000).

(If you are curious to see how the other half vacations, stop by the Grand Floridian's Guest Services desk and see if they're offering any of their free, little-publicized guided tours of the resort.)

Old Key West Resort A new name for what was formerly known as Disney's Vacation Club. Originally built as a time-share resort, the Old Key West offers deluxe studios, and one, two, and three-bedroom villas. Staying here can be a good deal if you're traveling with a lot of people—sometimes it's cheaper than renting two rooms in another hotel. But to us it lacks a bit of the charm and appeal of the other resort hotels. It just doesn't have the Disney magic, and if we're going to stay on-site, that's what we look for. Rates: $244 to $349 (studio); $330 to $480 (one bedroom); $459 to $730 (two bedrooms); and from $955 to $1,290 (three bedrooms). Old Key West Resort, 1510 North Cove Road, Lake Buena Vista, FL 32830–1000 (407-827-7700).

Polynesian Resort Experience the beauty of the South Pacific without leaving Florida. This 700-room resort is also one of the original hotels built when the Magic Kingdom opened in 1971, and has also stood the test of time (and been through several renovations). Island decor abounds, and lush tropical gardens create quite an island paradise. And the Poly is just a monorail ride away from the Magic Kingdom. Rates: $289 to $625. Polynesian Resort, 1600 South Seas Drive, Lake Buena Vista, FL 32830-1000 (407-824-2000).

Wilderness Lodge   This 728-room resort, designed like the rustic lodges of the American National Parks, is just spectacular! Natural wood and stone prevail in its decor, and the seven-story lobby is one of the most incredible you'll ever see, with its massive stone fireplace, giant totem poles, and Western-style chandeliers. And don't miss the pool: It starts as a bubbling hot spring in the lobby of the hotel, trickles outdoors into a small stream, drifts into a roaring waterfall, and flows into the swimming pool, which empties into another hot spring and geyser. The geyser, which erupts every hour on the hour, has been named *New* Faithful. Rates: $189 to $475. Wilderness Lodge, 901 Timberline Drive, Lake Buena Vista, FL 32830-1000 (407-824-3200).

The Villas at Wilderness Lodge   This Disney timeshare resort also offers accommodations to travelers, and the theming echoes that of the neighboring Wilderness Lodge. The resort and grounds evoke the grandeur of the Rocky Mountains, circa the 1800s and the rustic heyday of the railroad. Rooms range from studios (with microwaves and mini-refrigerators) to one-bedroom villas (fully-equipped kitchens, washer/dryer, whirlpool, sleeper sofa), to two-bedroom villas (two baths, fully-equipped kitchens, washer/dryer, whirlpool, sleeper sofa). Rates: $264 to $400 (studio); $360 to $525 (one-bedroom); and from $509 to $895 (two-bedroom). The Villas at Wilderness Lodge, 801 Timberline Drive, Lake Buena Vista, FL 32830-1000 (407-938-4300).

Yacht Club Resort   A sister resort/neighbor to the beach Club, the Yacht Club is reminiscent of a Newport, Rhode Island, hotel at the turn of the century. This 500-room resort is also within walking distance of EPCOT. The Yacht Club and Beach club share a pool—Stormalong Bay. Covering over three acres, Stormalong Bay is actually much more than a pool—it's an experience! Swim along with the current and enjoy its whirling waters and bubble jets. You'll see why a day at Stormalong Bay can be as much fun as a day in the parks. Rates: $279 to $615. Yacht Club Resort, 1700 EPCOT Resorts Boulevard, Lake Buena Vista, FL 32830-1000 (407-934-7000).

A La Carte or Meals Included?

If you buy a Disney package deal, you are often given the option of paying for your food at the time you book your trip (often referred to as a Food 'n' Fun Feature). This provides you with breakfast and dinner at a variety of Disney restaurants in the parks and at the Disney-owned hotels, as well as use of recreational equipment (like boats, bikes, tennis lessons, and horseback riding), with all taxes and gratuities included. Sounds interesting and convenient, but at around $60 per person per day, we don't think it's worth it to most cheapskates, unless you plan on using a bicycle until the tires go flat. Save your money and eat what you want, when you want, at the money-saving places we recommend.

(Note: Disney has been toying with the idea of allowing just the adults in a party to add the meal plan option to their ticket. Then, maybe the kids can eat from your plate? It can't hurt to ask while making your trip reservations.)

Recommended Off-site Accommodations

As you might expect, there are so many off-site hotel rooms available in the Disney World area, it would fill a whole book if we were to list every one. Rates vary widely. Some rooms are available for around $35 a night, if you book off-season, while some are more expensive than if you stayed at one of Disney's highest priced hotels. It's up to you what you want to spend, but there are enough rooms to go around for the cheapskate.

For the most part, however, you get what you pay for. If you can swing the $80 a night for Disney's All-Star or Pop Century resorts, by all means stay there. The convenience of being on Disney's property is really worth it in the long run (read on and you'll see what we mean). But if you can't swing a stay on-site, or if the Disney resorts are booked solid, check out some of these off-site hotels.

Contrary to popular belief, Walt Disney World is not in Orlando, Florida, but, rather, in an area about twenty-five miles from the center of Orlando. It is a "city" unto itself, created by Disney, called Lake Buena Vista. The main gate to Disney World borders on the town of Kissimmee, Florida. There are so many hotels located in both Lake Buena Vista and Kissimmee it seems ridiculous to stay anywhere else. Why on earth would you want to stay in Orlando and spend 30 minutes on Interstate 4 in traffic, traveling back to your hotel at night, when you can get a room one mile from the Disney main gate? (One word of caution: When we say main gate, we're talking about Disney's main entrance on US 192. It's still about four miles from the highway exit until you get to the parking lot for the Magic Kingdom—and that four miles is usually spent in bumper-to-bumper traffic.)

Since we've established that there's no reason to stay in Orlando if you're vacationing in Disney World, we've included only those hotels that are located in either Kissimmee or Lake Buena Vista. Kissimmee is probably the best place to stay if you think you will be visiting the Magic Kingdom predominantly, while Lake Buena Vista is closer to the entrance to EPCOT. The hotels in Lake Buena Vista are generally newer than the Kissimmee hotels, because EPCOT opened in 1982, while the Magic Kingdom opened in 1971. They're also more expensive. The hotels in Kissimmee are much cheaper and, for the most part, are more like budget motels than the resorts of Lake Buena Vista. Some hotels have been better maintained than others.

Before making your reservation, call or write to a few of the hotels and ask them to send you a brochure, and look at the pretty pictures. Then you'll be able to make a better decision as to which place looks right for you.

And please note that some of these accommodations are suite hotels, i.e., two or more rooms. They may cost a bit more, but imagine being able to put the kids to bed in one room while watching some TV in the other.

Important notes regarding our off-site listings—

- All of these hotels are within 10 miles of the Disney grounds.

- All feature cable TV and many have in-room movies (what decent hotel doesn't these days?).

- Many offer complimentary continental breakfast—but just because they offer it, don't assume they have a full-service restaurant on site. (Not to worry—it's such a tourist friendly area that you're sure to find eats just steps away.)

- Many offer shuttles to Disney (more than likely to the Transportation and Ticket Center, then you're on your own from there). These shuttles are often available only at scheduled times, and sometimes they're not even free. (Be sure to ask. When we knew they were free, we told you so.)

- In some cases, our listing may not do the place justice—it may actually be a nice, clean, modern hotel but we just couldn't get enough information about it.

- We've listed the toll-free numbers and websites for the major hotel companies serving the Disney area. It's a good idea to check everything ahead of time—these places change hands (and thus amenities) on occasion.

- If you're considering one of these hotels, do your homework and ask for a color brochure before you make a decision.

- Get rates from the web, from the toll-free number, and from calling the hotel direct. Each source may give you a different price and, of course, it's your job to take the lowest one.

- We've mentioned the "average" rates that just about everyone can get—if you're a senior citizen, a member of AARP, AAA, etc., inquire about possible special savings.

- Last but not least—ask about the "rack" rate (not sure what the term means, but whatever it is, it could save you money.)

Kissimmee Area

Best Western Eastgate   403 rooms in tropical setting. Heated outdoor pool and whirlpool. Video game room, large playground, and two lighted tennis courts. Restaurant. Free Disney shuttle—4 miles from gate. Rates: from $42. 5565 W. Irlo Bronson Hwy (US 192), Kissimmee, FL 34746 (407-396-0707).

Best Western Suites and Resort Hotel on Lake Cecile   158 family suites—studio and bi-level—with fully equipped kitchens. Free grocery shopping service. Outdoor pool, poolbar, whirlpool/spa. Barbecue and beach area. Playground, game room, fishing docks. Complimentary continental breakfast. Five miles from gate. Rates: from $100. 4786 Irlo Bronson Hwy, Kissimmee, FL 34746 (407-396-2056).

Clarion Hotel Maingate   198 rooms. Heated pool, hot tub, and poolbar. Game room, restaurant and lounge—kids eat free breakfast with paid adult. Free Disney shuttle 1½ miles to gate. Rates: from $80. 7675 Irlo Bronson Hwy, Kissimmee, FL 34747 (407-396-4000).

Clarion Suites Resort World   311 rooms—all one- and two-bedroom suites and villas, many with kitchens. Heated indoor/outdoor pool, kiddie pool, hot tub, and sauna. Basketball, lighted tennis courts, and playground. Game room, exercise room, restaurant, and bar. Four miles from Disney. Rates: from $117. 2800 N. Poinciana Blvd, Kissimmee, FL 34746 (407-997-5000).

Comfort Inn Maingate South   150 rooms—some with refrigerators and hot tubs. Outdoor pool, hot tub, and game room. Pets okay. Near Interstate—less than 9 miles from Disney. Rates: from $50. I-4 at U.S. 27 (exit 23), Kissimmee, FL 33837 (863-424-2811).

Comfort Suites Maingate   150 rooms with microwaves and refrigerators. Heated pool, kiddie pool, hot tub, and poolbar. Game room. Restaurant—free deluxe continental breakfast. Free Disney shuttle—three miles to gate. Rates: from $90. 7888 W. Irlo Bronson Hwy, Kissimmee, FL 34747 (407-390-9888).

Comfort Suites Maingate East   198 rooms with microwaves and refrigerators. Heated outdoor pool, kiddie pool, hot tub, and poolbar. Game room and exercise room. Restaurant and lounge—free continental breakfast. Free Disney shuttle.

2 miles to gate. Rates: from $125. 2775 Florida Plaza Blvd., Kissimmee, FL 34746 (407-397-7848).

Days Inn Eastgate 200 rooms. Courtyard with pool and picnic area. Restaurant. Kids stay and eat free. Free Disney shuttle—3½ miles to gate. Rates: from $49. 5245 Irlo Bronson Hwy, Kissimmee, FL 34746 (407-396-7700).

Doubletree Guest Suites Orlando—Maingate 150 one-, two-, and three-bedroom two-story villas with two full baths and fully-equipped kitchens. Pool, restaurant, and lounge. Tennis, basketball, playground. Three miles to Disney. Rates: from $119. 4787 W. Irlo Bronson Hwy, Kissimmee, FL 34746 (407-397-0555).

Econo Lodge 99 rooms—many with microwaves and refrigerators. Outdoor pool. Game room and restaurant—free continental breakfast. Four miles to Disney. Rates: from $36. 4669 W. Irlo Bronson Hwy, Kissimmee, FL 34746 (407-396-1890).

Econo Lodge 216 rooms, all with microwaves, refrigerators, and safes. Heated pool and poolbar. Game room and restaurant—free continental breakfast. Pets okay. Free Disney shuttle—four miles to gate. Rates: from $40. 5335 Irlo Bronson Hwy, Kissimmee, FL 34746 (407-396-2121).

Econo Lodge Maingate 445 rooms. Pool and whirlpool, poolside bar. Restaurant and lounge, free breakfast for kids 12 and under. Game room, and children's playground. Pets okay. Free Disney shuttle—just over a mile to the gate. Rates: from $45. 7514 W. Irlo Bronson Hwy, Kissimmee, FL 34747 (407-396-2000).

Four Points by Sheraton Inn Lakeside 651 rooms, each with refrigerators. Three pools and two kiddie pools. Four lighted tennis courts. Restaurant and lounge. Free breakfast and dinner buffet for kids 10 and under. Free Disney shuttle—7 miles from gate. Rates: from $99. 7767 W. Irlo Bronson Hwy, Kissimmee, FL 34747 (407-396-2222).

Four Points by Sheraton Orlando Kissimmee 221 oversized suites, some with refrigerators and microwaves. Heated pool and whirlpool. Restaurant and bar. Fitness room. Free Disney shuttle—7 miles to gate. Rates: from $55. 4018 W. Vine St, Kissimmee, FL 34741 (407-870-2000).

Hampton Inn Orlando/West Disney Maingate 164 rooms. Complimentary continental breakfast. Outdoor heated pool, shuffleboard, basketball and tennis. Just over a mile from maingate. Rates: from $60. 3104 Parkway Blvd, Kissimmee, FL 34747 (407-396-8484).

Hampton Inn Orlando—Disney Maingate West 118 rooms with microwaves and refrigerators. Complimentary expanded continental breakfast. Outdoor pool. Free Disney shuttle—one mile from gate. Rates: from $84—kids under 18 free with parent. 3000 Maingate Ln., Kissimmee, FL 34747 (407-396-6300).

Holiday Inn Kissimmee—Downtown 200 rooms—some with kitchenettes and sofa beds. Pool, whirlpool, and kiddie pool. Restaurant and bar. Fitness center, tennis court, picnic area, grills, and game room. Pets okay. Nine miles to gate. Rates: from $70. 2009 W. Vine St, Kissimmee, FL 34741 (407-846-2713).

Holiday Inn Maingate East 614 rooms (110 suites, many themed for kids). Family oriented. Microwaves, mini-refrigerators, some with kitchenettes. Buffet restaurant, food court. Tennis courts, pools, playground, game room. Free Disney shuttle—3 miles to gate. Rates: from $62. 5678 W. Irlo Bronson Hwy, Kissimmee, FL 34746 (407-396-4488).

Holiday Inn Maingate West 287 rooms. Tropically landscaped courtyard. Free form heated pool plus kiddie pool. Two restaurants and lounge, game room. Free Disney shuttle—just over a mile away. Rates: from $49. 7601 Black Lake Rd., Kissimmee, FL 34747 (407-396-1100).

Holiday Inn Nikki Bird Resort 530 rooms. Two restaurants, lounge, three tennis courts. Free Disney shuttle—one mile from gate. Rates: from $75. Holiday Inn Nikki Bird Resort, 7300 W. Irlo Bronson Hwy, Kissimmee, FL 34746 (407-396-7300).

Homewood Suites 156 one- and two-bedroom suites with fully equipped kitchens. Complimentary continental breakfast. Outdoor whirlpool spa and heated pool, kiddie pool. Cabana with gas grills. One mile from gate. Rates: from $159. 3100 Parkway Blvd., Kissimmee, FL 34746 (407-396-2229).

Howard Johnson   435 rooms. Pool and spa, plus covered heated pool. Basketball, game room, shuffleboard, volleyball, and picnic area. Restaurant/cocktail lounge. Free Disney shuttle—4 miles from gate. Kids stay free. Rates: from $62. 8660 W. Irlo Bronson Hwy, Kissimmee, FL 34747 (407-396-4500).

Howard Johnson Express Inn & Suites   123 rooms (some suites with fully-equipped kitchens) on Lake Cecile. Heated outdoor pool, whirlpool, kiddie pool. Complimentary continental breakfast. Golf, game room, playground, fishing, barbecue grills, picnic area by lake. Free Disney shuttle—3½ miles to gate. Kids stay free. Rates: from $50. 4836 W. Irlo Bronson Hwy, Kissimmee, FL 34746 (407-396-4762).

Howard Johnson Express Inn Parkside   100 rooms. Heated outdoor pool and kiddie pool. Restaurant. Picnic area with grills. Free shuttle to Disney—7 miles from gate. Kids stay free. Rates: from $40. 4311 W. Irlo Bronson Hwy, Kissimmee, FL 34746 (407-396-7000).

Howard Johnson Inn Maingate East   567 rooms. Heated outdoor pool, plus kiddie pool and whirlpool. Restaurant. Two miles from Disney. Kids stay free, kids under 12 eat free. Rates: from $49. 6051 W. Irlo Bronson Hwy, Kissimmee, FL 34747 (407-396-1748).

Howard Johnson Resort Hotel   160 rooms, with microwaves and mini-refrigerators; some themed kids' rooms feature separate private areas for parents. Heated outdoor pool, whirlpool. Restaurant. Bar and grill poolside. Arcade, picnic area with grills, convenience store. Adventurers' Club for kids. Kids stay free. Free Disney shuttle—3 miles from gate. Rates: from $85. 4985 W. Irlo Bronson Hwy, Kissimmee, FL 34746 (407-396-4343).

Kissimmee Eastgate Thriftlodge   80 rooms, some with refrigerators, microwaves; some suites with full kitchenettes. Pool. Two restaurants—free continental breakfast. Free Disney shuttle—five miles to gate. Rates: from $35. 4624 W. Irlo Bronson Hwy, Kissimmee, FL 34746 (407-396-2151).

Kissimmee Main Gate Travelodge Suites   134 suites, all with microwaves and refrigerators. Pool, bar. Free continental breakfast. Free Disney shuttle—5 miles to Disney. Rates:

$50. 4694 W. Irlo Bronson Hwy, Kissimmee, FL 34746 (407-396-1780).

Knights Inn Maingate   120 rooms. Pool and game room. Free continental breakfast. Free Disney shuttle—one mile from gate. Rates: from $45. 7475 Irlo Bronson Hwy, Kissimmee, FL 34746 (407-396-4200).

Main Gate East/Kissimmee Travelodge   446 rooms. Olympic-size pool, whirlpool, sauna, kiddie pool. Restaurant and bar. Free Disney shuttle—5 miles to gate. Rates: from $56. 5711 Irlo Bronson Hwy, Kissimmee, FL 34746 (407-396-4222).

Motel 6 Orlando   347 rooms. Two outdoor pools. Small pets okay. Eight miles to Disney. Kids stay free. Rates: from $30. 5731 W. Irlo Bronson Hwy, Kissimmee, FL 34746 (407-396-6333).

Motel 6 Orlando West Kissimmee   148 rooms. Outdoor pool. Restaurant. Small pets okay. Seven miles to Disney. Kids stay free. Rates: from $30. 7455 W. Irlo Bronson Hwy, Kissimmee, FL 34747 (407-396-6422).

Orlando—Days Inn Kissimmee/Highway 192   226 rooms, some with kitchenettes and Jacuzzis. Large pools, game room. Continental breakfast. Eight miles from gate. Rates: from $39. 4104 W. Irlo Bronson Hwy, Kissimmee, FL 34741 (407-846-4714).

Orlando—Days Inn Kissimmee/West   54 rooms. Outdoor pool. Continental breakfast. Five minutes from gate. Rates: from $38. 9240 Irlo Bronson Hwy, Kissimmee, FL 34711 (863-424-6099).

Orlando—Days Inn Maingate East of Walt Disney World Resort   404 rooms. Four pools (two heated). Children's playground and game room. Restaurant and lounge—kids under 12 eat free. 2½ miles from gate. Rates: from $50. 5840 Irlo Bronson Hwy, Kissimmee, FL 34746 (407-396-7969).

Orlando—Days Inn West of Walt Disney World   333 rooms. Olympic-sized swimming pool. Game room, laundry, and fitness center. Restaurant. Free Disney shuttle—2½ miles from gate. Rates: from $53. 7980 Irlo Bronson Hwy, Kissimmee, FL 34747 (407-997-1000).

Orlando—Days Suites Maingate East of Walt Disney World Resort   300 rooms. Family resort complex of apartment style suites with full kitchens. Four pools, game rooms, playground, and barbecue and picnic areas. Restaurant and cafeteria on-site. Free Disney shuttle—2½ miles from gate. Rates: from $170. 5820 W. Irlo Bronson Hwy, Kissimmee, FL 34746 (407-396-7900).

Orlando/Kissimmee East Gate Orange Travelodge Suites   157 suites, all with microwaves and refrigerators. Outdoor heated pool and Jacuzzi, kiddie pool. Playground and game room. Restaurant and bar. Free Disney shuttle—5 miles to gate. Rates: from $66. 5399 Irlo Bronson Hwy, Kissimmee, FL 34746 (407-396-7666).

Orlando/Kissimmee Travelodge Hotel Maingate   298 rooms. Restaurant and lounge, free breakfast buffet for kids. Safe in rooms. Two pools, including kiddie pool. Game room. Adjacent to Disney—Free shuttle. Rates: from $66. 8600 W. Irlo Bronson Hwy, Kissimmee, FL 34747 (407-396-0100).

Orlando Knights Inn Maingate East   64 rooms with safe deposit boxes. Pool. Free continental breakfast. Free Disney shuttle—four miles from gate. Rates: from $39. 2800 N. Poinciana Blvd., Kissimmee, FL 34746 (407-396-8186).

Quality Inn   131 rooms. Outdoor pool. Seven miles to Disney. Rates: from $40. 4156 W. Vine St., Kissimmee, FL 34741 (407-870-7374).

Quality Inn Lake Cecile/World Center   222 rooms. Outdoor pool, restaurant. Beach, jet ski, water ski. Free Disney shuttle—four miles to gate. Rates: from $45. 4944 W. Irlo Bronson Hwy, Kissimmee, FL 34746 (407-396-4455).

Quality Inn Maingate West   198 rooms—some with microwaves and refrigerators. Heated pool, picnic area, playground. Restaurant—free continental breakfast. Free Disney shuttle—1½ miles to gate. Rates: from $40. 7785 W. Irlo Bronson Hwy, Kissimmee, FL 34747 (407-396-1828).

Quality Suites Maingate East   All-suite hotel: 225 one- and two-bedroom, 2 bath suites with kitchenettes. Free continental breakfast. Outdoor heated pool, kiddie pool, hot tub, poolbar, playground. Free Disney shuttle—less than 2 miles from gate. Rates: from $79. 5876 W. Irlo Bronson Hwy, Kissimmee, FL 34746 (407-396-8040).

Radisson Resort Parkway   718 rooms in lushly landscaped

setting. Pool with waterfall and waterslide; two whirlpool spas, sauna, additional heated pool and kiddie pool. Restaurant and lounge. Playground and game room. Two lighted tennis courts, volleyball, horseshoes, and jogging. 1 ½ miles from gate. Rates: from $79. 2900 Parkway Blvd, Kissimmee, FL 34747 (407-396-7000).

Ramada East Gate Fountain Park   402 rooms and suites on private lake. Heated pool, hot tub, and kiddie pool. Lighted tennis courts, putting green, game room, basketball court, shuffleboard. Restaurant and lounge—kids eat free with paid adult. Free Disney shuttle—four miles away. Rates: from $67. 5150 W. Irlo Bronson Hwy, Kissimmee, FL 34746 (407-396-1111).

Ramada Inn Resort Maingate   391 rooms. Two heated swimming pools, kiddie pool. Lighted tennis and basketball courts. Exercise room with sauna. Restaurant, lounge, and deli. Kids eat breakfast and dinner free with paid adult. Free Disney shuttle—½ mile to gate. Rates: from $75. 2950 Reedy Creek Blvd, Kissimmee, FL 34747 (407-396-4466).

Ramada Plaza Hotel-Inn Gateway   500 rooms, some suites. Refrigerators, some with microwaves. Two pools, one heated. Fitness center, bar/lounge, restaurant. Free shuttle to Disney—1 mile from gate. Rates: from $59. 7470 Irlo Bronson Hwy, Kissimmee, FL 34747-1743 (407-396-4400).

Red Roof Inn Kissimmee   102 rooms. Outdoor heated pool. Small pets allowed. Free Disney shuttle—5 miles to gate. Rates: from $45. 4970 Kyng's Heath Rd., Kissimmee, FL 34746 (407-396-0065).

Renaissance Worldgate Hotel   566 rooms. Two outdoor pools and whirlpool. Two restaurants, lounge. Lighted tennis, volleyball, and basketball courts. Exercise room. Less than one mile from Disney. Rates: from $75. 3011 Maingate Ln, Kissimmee, FL 34747 (407-396-1400).

Rodeway Inn Maingate   125 rooms—some with refrigerators. Outdoor pool, game room, picnic area, restaurant. Free coffee and donuts. Five miles to Disney. Rates: from $32. 4736 W. Irlo Bronson Hwy, Kissimmee, FL 34746 (407-396-0400).

Sleep Inn Maingate   104 rooms—all with microwaves, refrigerators, and safes. Outdoor pool. Restaurant—free deluxe continental breakfast. Free Disney shuttle—four miles to gate. Rates: from $50. 8536 W. Irlo Bronson Hwy, Kissimmee, FL 34747 (407-396-1600).

Super 8 Maingate   Reportedly the largest Super 8 in Florida: 281 rooms. Restaurant and pub. Large swimming pool, sun deck, and children's playground. Game room. Free Disney shuttle—one mile to gate. Rates: from $45. 7571 W. Irlo Bronson Hwy, Kissimmee, FL 34747 (407-396-7500).

Super 8 Motel—Orlando/Kissimmee/Lakeside   126 rooms, many with kitchenettes. Pool. Free continental breakfast. Four miles from Disney. Rates: from $50—children free. 4880 W. Irlo Bronson Hwy, Kissimmee, FL 34746 (407-396-1144).

Super 8 Motel—Orlando/Kissimmee/Maingate   60 rooms. Pool. Free continental breakfast. One mile from Disney. Rates: from $40. 5875 W. Irlo Bronson Hwy, Kissimmee, FL 34746 (407-396-8883).

Super 8 Motel—Orlando/Kissimmee Suites   83 standard rooms and suites (suites have two bedrooms, full kitchens, and can sleep up to 6). Pool. Free coffee and donuts. Nine miles from Disney. Rates: from $45. 1815 W. Vine St., Kissimmee, FL 34741 (407-847-6121).

Lake Buena Vista Area

Note: The seven hotels marked with "*" are considered to be in the Disney Hotel Plaza. They are non-Disney hotels located within Disney, near Downtown Disney. While they are high quality hotels, and may be cheaper to stay in than Disney hotels, they are not Disney properties and, therefore do not offer Disney ambiance and charm. However, they do offer guests free Disney transportation (i.e. bus service), advance dinner reservations, and multi-day passes.

*Best Western Lake Buena Vista Resort Hotel   325 rooms. Outdoor heated pool and playground. Game room. Restaurant and lounge. Free Disney shuttle. Rates: from $99. 2000 Hotel Plaza Blvd., Lake Buena Vista, FL 32830 (407-828-2424).

Clarion Suites Lake Buena Vista 60 rooms, all one- or two-bedroom villas with full kitchens—reportedly the largest vacation villas in Lake Buena Vista. Heated pool, whirlpool. Lighted tennis and basketball courts, billiards, workout room, playground. Free continental breakfast, delivered to room. Five miles from gate. Rates: from $114. 8451 Palm Pkwy, Lake Buena Vista, FL 32836 (407-238-1700).

Comfort Inn Lake Buena Vista 640 rooms, all with refrigerators and microwaves—some suites feature separate kids area. Outdoor heated pool. Game room, playground. Restaurant and lounge—kids 11 and under eat free with paid adult. Pets allowed. Free Disney shuttle—3 miles from gate. Rates: from $50. 8442 Palm Pkwy, Lake Buena Vista, FL 32830 (407-239-7300).

*Courtyard by Marriott 323 oversized rooms. Two heated outdoor pools with whirlpool, kiddie pool, fitness room. Restaurants and lounge. Free Disney shuttle. Rates: from $89. 1805 Hotel Plaza Blvd., Lake Buena Vista, FL 32830 (407-828-8888).

Courtyard Lake Buena Vista @ Vista Centre 222 rooms, 86 suites. Outdoor heated pool and whirlpool. Playground. Gift shop and game room. Restaurant, lounge, and deli. Two miles from Disney. Rates: from $69. 8501 Palm Pkwy, Lake Buena Vista, FL 32830 (407-239-6900).

*Doubletree Guest Suites 229 suites with fully-equipped kitchens. Outdoor heated pool, whirlpool, and kiddie pool. Tennis, sand volleyball, playground, and game room. Restaurant and lounge. Free Disney shuttle. Rates: from $129. 2305 Hotel Plaza Blvd., Lake Buena Vista, FL 32830 (407-934-1000).

*Grosvenor Resort at Walt Disney World Village 630 rooms. Heated pools, spa, tennis. Playground. In-room refrigerators and coffee makers. Three restaurants and two lounges. Rates: from $109. 1850 Hotel Plaza Blvd., Lake Buena Vista, FL 32830 (407-828-4444).

*Hilton at Walt Disney World Village 814 rooms and suites. Two pools, Jacuzzi. Health club. Seven restaurants. Free Disney shuttle. Rates: from $149. 1751 Hotel Plaza Blvd., Lake Buena Vista, FL 32830 (407-827-4000).

Holiday Inn Family Suites Resort, Lake Buena Vista 800 suites with kitchenettes—some themed, some with whirlpools. Two outdoor pools, one with water park theme, hot tub. Poolside fitness facility, ping pong, mini-golf, game room. Restaurant and cocktail lounge: Kids 12 and under eat free, all guests can eat free breakfast buffet daily. Free Disney shuttle—one mile from gate. Rates: from $129. 14500 Continental Gateway, Orlando, FL 32821 (407-387-5437).

Holiday Inn Sunspree Resort 507 rooms (231 suites)—some are kid-themed KidSuites. All with mini-kitchenettes. Heated pool, heated kiddie pool. Twin whirlpool spas. Playground, game room, basketball. Full fitness center. Two restaurants: Kids eat free. Pets allowed. Free Disney shuttle—one mile from gate. Rates: from $99. 13351 SR 535, Lake Buena Vista, FL 32821 (407-239-4500).

*Hotel Royal Plaza 394 rooms. Heated outdoor pool, therapy pool. Sauna. Lighted tennis courts. Fitness center. Game room and gift shop. Restaurant, coffee shop, and lounge. Free Disney shuttle. Rates: from $129. 1905 Hotel Plaza Blvd., Lake Buena Vista, FL 32830 (407-828-2828).

Orlando Days Inn Hotel, Lake Buena Vista 203 rooms. Outdoor pool. Playground and game room. Restaurant and lounge—kids eat free breakfast and dinner with adult. Free Disney shuttle—one mile from gate. Rates: from $65. 12799 Apopka-Vineland Rd., Lake Buena Vista, FL 32830 (407-239-4441).

*Wyndham Palace Resort & Spa 1,014 rooms. Three pools, sauna, and health club. Three lighted tennis courts. Gift shop and boutiques. VCR/rental store. Five restaurants, three lounges. Free Disney shuttle. Rates: from $169. 1900 Buena Vista Dr., Lake Buena Vista, FL 32830 (407-827-2727).

How to reach the major motel chains

Best Western: bestwestern.com; 800-780-7234

Choice Hotels (Clarion, Comfort Inn/Suites, Econolodge,

Quality Inn/Suites, Rodeway Inn, Sleep Inn): choicehotels. com; 800-4-CHOICE

Courtyard by Marriott: marriotthotels.com; 888-840-7829

Days Inn: daysinn.com; 800-544-8313

Doubletree: doubletree.com; 800-222-TREE

Hampton Inn: hamptoninn.com; 800-HAMPTON

Hilton: hilton.com; 800-774-1500

Holiday Inn: holiday-inn.com; 800-HOLIDAY

Homewood Suites: homewood-suites.com; 800-CALL-HOME

Howard Johnson: hojo.com; 800-406-1411

Knights Inn: knightsinn.com; 800-418-8977

Motel 6: motel6.com; 800-4-MOTEL-6

Radisson: radissonsas.com; 800-333-3333

Ramada Inn: ramada.com; 888-298-2054

Red Roof Inn: redroof.com; 800-REDROOF

Sheraton (4 Points): sheraton.com; 888-625-5144

Super 8: super8.com; 800-800-8000

Travelodge (also ThriftLodge): travelodge.com; 800-835-2424

Wynhdam: wyndham.com; 877-999-3223

Off-site Cheap Eats

Considering this is the world's most popular vacation destination, you're sure to find literally hundreds of eating choices off-site—ranging from popular fast-food (Dairy Queen, Taco Bell, Subway, etc.), to popular chain restaurants (IHOP, Red Lobster, Outback Steakhouse, etc.) and even Mom-and-Pop-type places. If you're staying off-site, you shouldn't have to go far to find something inexpensive to munch at any meal.

The On-site versus Off-site Argument

It used to be you could hardly call a stay at one of Disney's on-site hotels a bargain. Years ago, only a chosen few—those who had money to burn—could afford such "luxury." That all changed in 1988 with the opening of the Caribbean Beach Resort, Disney's first budget-priced hotel. Disney finally realized that the average family couldn't spend $200 a night on a hotel room.

Since the Caribbean opened, several more Disney hotels have sprung up to appeal to the cheapskate's pocketbook—first, Port Orleans and its neighbor, Dixie Landings (now known as Port Orleans Riverside). And with the opening of the All-Star Sports and Music Resorts in 1994, the All-Star Movies Resort in 1999 and the Pop Century Resort in 2001 with their nearly 8,000 budget-priced rooms, there's really no reason not to at least entertain the thought of staying on-site. (Isn't it ironic that when the All Star Sport and Music Resorts opened, the per-night price of the other Disney "economy" hotels—the Caribbean Beach Resort, Port Orleans, and Dixie Landings—went up? Very interesting. . . .)

We won't lie to you: You can stay somewhere for less per night than you would at even a budget Disney hotel. Your room may even be larger, especially if you stay in an off-site suite. But we think it's worth the extra cost when you consider the convenience and time savings that can be gained.

Benefits of On-Site Accommodations True, you can probably pay around $35 per night off-site if you're willing to go off-off-season and you do your homework (see our recommendations). But staying on-site means never having to get behind the wheel of a car your entire vacation. Disney transportation is available to take you anywhere you could possibly want to go. For example, monorails drop you at EPCOT, boats can take you to the Disney-MGM Studios, and it's just a short bus ride to Blizzard Beach (or any other Disney destination) from your hotel.

Disney's transportation system is one of the world's most impressive, comfortable, and efficient, and it can be a fun part of the adventure of visiting the parks (though it can also cause delays during busy seasons). Disney transports about 200,000 passengers a day: The mass transit systems of America's largest cities could take a lesson from Disney's fleet of boats, buses, trams, and monorails. If you stay at a Disney hotel, you can ride 'em all, free, as often as you want. If you want, you can have breakfast at the Magic Kingdom, an afternoon of shopping at Downtown Disney, lunch at the Disney-MGM Studios, a snack at Blizzard Beach, dinner at EPCOT, then cap off your day with clubbing at Downtown Disney. (And if you can do all that in one day, you've got the strength and stamina of an Olympic athlete!) There's no faster way to get from here to there than the Disney transportation system—unless you hitch a ride in Dumbo's chapeau! (Imagine waking up in the morning and being whisked away to the Magic Kingdom just by stepping onto a monorail car.)

Now imagine spending fourteen hours in a crowded theme park. By then the kids have fallen asleep in your arms. Which of the following scenarios would you choose? You stand in a long line waiting for the monorail or ferry boat to take you to general parking, board a tram to take you to the *vicinity* where your car is parked, walk to your car, load the kids in, fight the maze of traffic out of the lot, and drive to your hotel, another twenty-five minutes away (without the traffic). And we won't even talk about the huge delays you'll experience during your *morning* commute to the park.

Or, you stand in a short, resort-guests line (after all, there are still more people who stay off-site than on-site) and have the monorail or any of Disney's other vehicles drop you directly at your hotel. Yes, Disney hotels can be pricey, but by staying on-site you won't lose the "Disney magic" after you leave the parks. Disney applies the same special touches to their hotels that they do to their attractions. Each Disney hotel is themed and the attention to detail is incredible.

A stay at a Disney resort can be a vacation in itself. If time permits in your itinerary, we recommend visiting one of the higher-priced Disney resorts. Maybe have lunch in their restaurant and dream of your next Disney vacation.

It is important to remember when staying at any on-site Disney resort that an off-season stay will afford the best value for your money. Check with reputable travel agencies for specials, and also contact the Disney Club for their best deal. (If you are not a member of the Disney Club, consider buying a membership—$65 for two years. It could be worth more in savings than the cost of the membership (see chapter 11 for a rundown of the many Disney Club Card benefits).

Another bonus for staying on-site is that Disney resort guests are allowed early admission into the parks. Generally speaking, the theme parks open at 9:00 A.M. (except for the Animal Kingdom, which usually opens at 8:00 A.M.). But each day of the week, a different park (except Animal Kingdom) opens a section at 8:00 A.M. For the exclusive use of resort guests. By getting to the park early, you can finish more rides in this extra hour than you could in two or three hours once the crowds enter.

The current schedule for early admission is:

Sunday	Disney-MGM Studios
Monday	Magic Kingdom
Tuesday	EPCOT
Wednesday	Disney-MGM Studios
Thursday	Magic Kingdom
Friday	EPCOT
Saturday	Magic Kingdom

Not all of the rides open at 8:00 A.M., but enough of the popular attractions do to make it worth your while to get there early! By seeing the most popular rides before the crowds enter the park, you'll have the rest of the day to enjoy the rest of the attractions at a more leisurely schedule.

The following is the current schedule of rides that open early:

Magic Kingdom

- Alien Encounter
- Astro Orbiter
- Buzz Lightyear's Space Ranger Spin
- Cinderella's Golden Carrousel
- Dumbo the Flying Elephant
- It's a Small World
- Mad Tea Party
- The Many Adventures of Winnie the Pooh
- Peter Pan's Flight
- Snow White's Adventures

- Space Mountain
- Tomorrowland Light and Power Company
- Tomorrowland Speedway
- Tomorrowland Transit Authority

EPCOT

- Body Wars
- Spaceship Earth
- Test Track

Disney-MGM Studios

- The Great Movie Ride
- Rock 'n' Roller Coaster
- Star Tours
- The Twilight Zone Tower of Terror

Call 407-824-4321 to confirm the early admissions schedule.

(Note: Most Disney transportation begins regular operations at 7:30 A.M., with resort buses and the Magic Kingdom monorail starting at 7.) This may change off-peak, so call to confirm.

More On-site Advantages:

- Parking in the Disney resort lots is free to Disney hotel guests; other visitors are charged about $5. And, if after driving forty-five minutes and sitting in traffic, you show up at the parking lot too late, the attendant can turn you away if the lot's full. (Note: If this happens to you, drive to the EPCOT lot, one of the World's largest, and grab a bus to wherever it was you were going.)

- Guest Services—Take advantage of Disney's pampering assistance with dining and show reservations; have purchases you made in the parks shipped directly to your room, etc. Those are some of the special touches you receive from Guest Services when you stay on-site.

- Midday Break—Beat the heat and the crowds, rest those weary dogs, and get refreshed by taking a midday nap in

your room; swim in your hotel's pool, grab a bite to eat, etc.
Your room's proximity—and Disney's free transportation—
make these often welcome diversions possible. (And even if
you don't leave for a midday break, many vacationers will,
which will lessen the crowds in the parks.)

- You can charge meals from hotel restaurants and fast food
operations to your hotel room, as well as items purchased
from the many gift shops within the park. When you check
in, you're issued a plastic credit card that serves as a Disney
AmEx during your stay!

- You can buy theme park attraction tickets right at your hotel
and save a few valuable minutes.

- In-room baby-sitting service—True, most of us wouldn't feel
confident leaving the kids with a stranger. But come on now,
you gotta know Disney's only gonna hire trustworthy, kid-
loving baby-sitters to watch yours, right in your room! (See
the special baby-sitting section in chapter 9 for more details.)

On-site Disadvantages   Yes, it is more expensive to stay
on-site than off. Compare the cost per night at Disney's All-
Star Resort with our least expensive off-site choice, taking into
account the advantages we've already discussed. Now, here are
the disadvantages:

- Since you won't be parking in the main lot, you won't enjoy
the privilege of hearing the parking lot tram operator an-
nounce, after you board the tram, "You are parked in
Goofy."

- You won't experience the joy of sitting in bumper-to-
bumper traffic on Route 192—that doesn't include the
backup on Disney's World Drive!

Can you guess where our preference lies? Staying in a Disney hotel is like enjoying the Disney magic 24 hours a day,
with the fun going on long after you've left the parks' attractions. Simplify your trip—stay on-site. If you're like most peo-

ple, your Disney vacation will be one of the most expensive trips you'll ever take. Due to its tremendous cost, you may be hard-pressed to ever go to Disney again. Save up the few extra dollars and stay in a Disney resort.

But if your finances simply forbid your on-site stay, we won't hold it against you. And you'll still have a real good time (if you don't count the traumatic "getting there" part!).

Try These Money-Saving Ideas

- Book the cheapest room in whatever hotel you choose. Then, when you arrive to check in, ask about the possibility of an upgrade. You can often get a better room at the same price.

- When you call Walt Disney World reservations, be knowledgeable. The operators are instructed not to give you the cheapest rates, not to offer unasked-for information and money-saving tips, and to only answer the questions posed to them. If you know that cheaper rates exist, ask for them; then they'll answer. Sneaky, huh?

No Matter Where You Stay, Before You Go

Make your lunch and dinner reservations (which can be made up to sixty days in advance) before you leave for Florida at whatever sit-down places you decide to eat, especially if you're vacationing during one of the busier times of the year (read on for our restaurant recommendations). That way you're assured of eating where you want, when you want (and you'll be better able to stick to our itinerary). Call the Disney restaurant reservations line 407-WDW-DINE.

And lately it seems that each of the Disney hotels is competing against its Disney counterpart to fill its rooms. This means that some of the less busy hotels are offering often unadvertised specials to sell more rooms. Make sure to ask the operator if any hotels are offering deals—sometimes the savings can be as much as 30–50%.

- Ask for the corporate room rates when you call. Often, depending on the whim of the hotel clerk, all you need is a business card to receive discounted business rates when you check in.

3

What's It All About, Mickey?

BACKGROUND INFORMATION ON WALT DISNEY WORLD

The sheer size and scope of the Walt Disney World entertainment complex is enough to overwhelm even the well-heeled traveler. Here are the facts:

- Walt Disney World, at 47 square miles (30,500 acres), is roughly the size of San Francisco, or twice the size of Manhattan Island.

- The Magic Kingdom itself, which opened in 1971, is 107 acres, with a parking lot of 125 acres (by comparison, Disney's grandmother of all resorts, Disneyland, is just 80 acres).

- Disney's second Florida attraction, EPCOT Center (Future World and World Showcase combined), which opened in 1982, clocks in at around three hundred acres (which includes the forty-acre lake, World Showcase Lagoon). Incidentally, it's a 1.3-mile circuitous route around the lagoon.

- Disney-MGM Studios, which opened in 1989, is set on 154 acres.

- Disney's Animal Kingdom, which opened in 1998, covers over 500 acres and is Disney's largest theme park to date.

- There are currently 28 resort hotels on Disney property, with nearly 25,000 places in which to lay your head (be it a hotel room, a campsite, or a private villa), more than 60 swimming pools, 23 wading pools, five lakes surrounded by white sand beaches, three romantic lagoons, and three splashy water theme parks.

- You'll find 150 different places to eat on-site, of which over 65 are table-service restaurants.

- Over fifty thousand cast members (that's Disney's term for "employees")—from garbagemen and painters to costumed characters and ride attendants—are on-hand to help you have the greatest vacation ever.

It's easy to be intimidated by Walt Disney World. That's why you'll need to read this book before your trip, then refer to it while you're in Florida.

We'll go park by park, discussing the ins and outs of the attractions, the shops, the food, and the fun. But first, you've got to buy your way in. . . .

TICKETS, GET YOUR TICKETS!

If you want to play, you've got to pay (Mickey's guard dog, Pluto, doesn't take too kindly to people hopping the fence). The variety of tickets available can boggle the mind—from tickets worth one day's admission to passes good for unlimited admissions for one year. Generally speaking, the tickets offering longer lengths of admission are the best bargains. And since such tickets are good forever, it might be worth purchasing a longer, multiday passport and saving the unused portion of the ticket for a return trip.

The prices quoted were accurate as we went to press, but are subject to change at any time . . . and the way Disney has been raising their prices over the last few years, we recommend checking for the most recent pricing (either call the trusty Disney information line at 407-824-4321, or check with one of the staff at your local Disney Store) Tax not included. Please note that children under three are admitted free.

(Special savings of around 10 percent are offered to Disney Club members. If you plan on doing some serious Disneying, we definitely recommend your joining the club. See chapter 11 for more details.)

One-Day One Park Only Pass

This admission ticket is good for one day only and can be used for admittance to just one park. You cannot park-hop with this ticket.

The Four Major Theme Parks
Adult: $48
Child (3–9): $38

Blizzard Beach and Typhoon Lagoon
Adult: $29.95
Child (3–9): $24.00

River Country
Adult: $15.95
Child (3–9): $12.50

Downtown Disney Pleasure Island
Adult: $19.81
(18 and over)

Wide World of Sports (general admission)
Adult: $8.70
Child (3–9): $6.81

Park-Hopper Pass

This ticket allows you unlimited admission to the 4 theme parks, and lets you hop from one park to another as often as you'd like. (Note: Unused park hopper days don't expire.)

4-Day Park-Hopper
Adult: $192
Child (3–9): $152

5-Day Park-Hopper

Adult:	$217
Child (3–9):	$172

Park-Hopper Plus Pass

This ticket allows you unlimited admission to the 4 theme parks, lets you hop from one part to another as often as you'd like . . . plus adds admissions to Disney's "lesser" attractions (as indicated)—Pleasure Island, the water parks, and Disney's Wide World of Sports.

5-Day Park Hopper Plus (includes 2 visits to the "lesser" parks)

Adult:	$247
Child (3–9)	$197

6-Day Park Hopper Plus (includes 3 visits to the "lesser" parks)

Adult:	$277
Child (3–9)	$222

7-Day Park Hopper Plus (includes 4 visits to the "lesser" parks)

Adult:	$307
Child (3–9):	$247

If you can manage the additional cost, we advise you to buy passes for extra days (e.g. if you're staying at Disney for six days, buy the seven-day hopper). Since there's no expiration date, you can use your unused day(s) the next time you go and not have to pay for the (inevitable) price increase.

Length of Stay Pass

Includes unlimited admission to the Magic Kingdom, EPCOT, Disney-MGM Studios, Animal Kingdom, Blizzard Beach, Typhoon Lagoon, River Country, and Pleasure Island for your entire stay—from the moment you check in to your hotel until the end of day on the day you check out. The only hitch is that you must be a Walt Disney World resort hotel guest. It is easiest to reserve your length of stay pass when you reserve your room, that way, when you check in you will be handed your admission ticket and you won't need to wait in any ticket lines. Always remember to use your Disney Club card, if you have one, when you make your reservations.

WDW Resort Length of Stay	Per Adult (tax included)	Per Child tax included)
1 night/2 days	$120.85	$ 96.48
2 nights/3 days	163.26	130.40
3 nights/4 days	221.55	177.04
4 nights/5 days	263.96	210.95
5 nights/6 days	297.88	238.51
6 nights/7 days	331.81	265.02

Annual Pass

Affords unlimited admission to the magic Kingdom, EPCOT, Disney-MGM, and Animal Kingdom for a period of one year. Also includes free parking and use of the Disney transportation system.

Adult: $349
Child (3–9): $297

Annual Waterparks Pass

Affords unlimited admission to all three water parks for a period of one year. Also includes free parking and use of the Disney transportation system.

Adult: $99.95
Child (3–9): $80.50

Annual Downtown Disney Pleasure Island Pass

Affords unlimited admission to Downtown Disney Pleasure Island for a period of one year. Also includes free parking and use of the Disney transportation system.

Adult: $54.95
(18 and older)

(Annual passes also available for Disney Quest, Cirque de Soleil. Inquire within.)

Premium Annual Pass

Pass is good for unlimited admission to all the major and minor parks for a period of one year; including free parking and unlimited use of Disney transportation system.

Adult:	$469.00
Child (3–9)	$399.00

Many passes can be purchased in advance at your local Disney Store. Purchasing tickets in advance will save you from standing on the ticket line at the Walt Disney World Resort, and after a trip to Disney world, you'll be pleased with each line you don't need to stand on. And remember, the Disney Stores also accept the Disney Club card. You may also purchase tickets in advance by calling 4-7-WDISNEY. And, if you're into the Internet. You can purchase tickets online at www.disneygo.com/vacations/travel/tickets.html.

Many Disney vacation packages offer park passes. Be sure to check the fine print of which passes are being included, and you'll be able to see if it's more economically feasible for you to purchase all the components of your trip—park admissions, room, airfare, transfers, etc.—separately.

Your last resort should be to buy passes to the park the day of your visit. This can cause unnecessary delays and the loss of valuable vacationing time!

FASTPASS

Without a doubt, this is the most fantastic thing to ever come to Disney World. It beats any ride that's ever opened at the park. It's better than any parade. But, you ask, what is *FAST-PASS?*

FASTPASS is a way of reserving your spot in line at one of the popular attractions at the theme parks. In other words, you get to reserve a time to ride, for example, Space Mountain, then you go ride another Tomorrowland attraction. When you come back to Space Mountain, you bypass the lines and basically walk right onto the ride.

This is how it works—when you approach one of the popular attractions, you will now see three lines. One is the *FAST-PASS* distribution line, one is the *FASTPASS* return line, and the last is the standby line. You first want to receive your *FAST-PASS* ticket on the distribution line. There is a bank of machines where you will be asked to insert your admission pass to the park. A ticket will print out with an assigned time for you to return to the attraction. There is typically a one-hour spread in the time that you are assigned—in other words, your ticket will tell you to return, for example, sometime between 10:20 A.M. and 11:20 A.M. Then you are free to go to any other attraction you feel like, and when your designated time approaches, you return to your *FASTPASS* ride, enter the *FAST-PASS* return line, and go straight to the front of the line. Of course, if you like to spend your time standing in lines, you can always wait in the standby line with the herd of people who don't understand the importance of being able to skip as many lines as possible.

Now, we know there are some of you who are thinking, "Wow, this is great—I'll just go around the park grabbing as many *FASTPASSes* as I can and then go back and do the attractions." Well, Disney thought of you when they designed this system. Remember when we told you that you would have to insert your theme park admission pass into the *FASTPASS* distribution machine to get a ticket? That's because your ID is entered into their main computer and you will be blocked from getting a second *FASTPASS* until the first one is used or the time printed on the ticket expires.

At the entrance to each *FASTPASS* attraction, there will be a sign showing the estimated waiting time on the standby line, and the time you would be assigned with the next *FASTPASS*. This is a great help because sometimes the wait for the ride isn't long at all, and you can save your *FASTPASS* for the next attraction. The following attractions currently offer *FAST-PASS:*

Magic Kingdom	Buzz Lightyear's Space Ranger Spin
	Haunted Mansion
	Jungle Cruise
	Many Adventures of Winnie the Pooh
	Peter Pan's Flight
	Space Mountain
	Splash Mountain
EPCOT	Honey, I Shrunk the Audience
	Test Track
	Maelstrom
Disney-MGM Studios	Indiana Jones Epic Stunt Spectacular
	Rock 'n' Roller Coaster
	Star Tours
	Tower of Terror
	Voyage of the Little Mermaid
	Who Wants to be a Millionaire
Animal Kingdom	Dinosaur
	It's Tough to be a Bug
	Kali River Rapids
	Kilimanjaro Safaris

More attractions will be added to *FASTPASS*. *FASTPASS* has been in existence since the year 2000, and it has worked very well since its inception. In our opinion, whoever thought this up deserves a bonus the size of Michael Eisner's!

DISNEY WORLD TOURS

Back when the Magic Kingdom opened in 1971, everyone knew about the extensive service tunnels, called utilidors, located under the park that allowed for the seamless movement of employees and services. Each land has secret passages to the utilidors, which is why you will never see a cast member dressed in a Tomorrowland costume walking through Frontierland. But, in the beginning years of the park, Disney did everything in their power to stop you from seeing the utilidors. They were considered "backstage" areas and they thought it would ruin the show if guests were allowed backstage.

Now, in their continued quest for the almighty buck, Disney has begun to sell escorted tours to their previously "off-limit" areas. And, although you do sort of get a rude awakening when you first walk backstage and see drab and dreary atmosphere where most of the background action goes on, it is an absolutely fascinating experience. So if your pocketbook permits this extracurricular activity, and/or you've been to Disney World a few times and are looking to do something different, we would recommend taking one of the following tours:

Keys to the Kingdom   This tour takes approximately 4½ to 5 hours, and includes only the Magic Kingdom. You'll learn a little about the initial construction of the park along with some history of the Disney Company. Then, you'll duck behind one of those doors marked, "Cast Members Only," and enter the backstage of the park. After a tour of the utilidors and costuming areas, you'll venture to the Parade Production Center to see where the floats are stored. Currently, the price for this tour is $58 and includes lunch at the Columbia Harbor House.

Backstage Magic   This tour takes 7 hours to complete, and covers the Magic Kingdom, EPCOT, and the Disney-MGM Studios. In the Magic Kingdom, you'll go underground to the utilidors and DACS (the acronym for their computer control room). You'll learn how computers control almost every aspect of the shows in the park—whether it's the rides or parades. At EPCOT you'll go behind the scenes at the Living Seas, and at the studios you'll go backstage at Fantasmic! You'll be taken backstage at numerous rides where you'll learn the nuts and bolts workings of the attractions. You'll also enjoy a very nice lunch at Mama Melrose's at the Disney-MGM Studios. This tour is pretty pricey at $199, but we truly enjoyed taking it.

You can reserve a tour by calling 407-WDW-TOUR, and it is suggested you book your tour at least two months in advance. They offer many other tours, but we feel that these two are the best. Of course, elements of the tours are subject to change at any time. And please realize that the tours involve a good deal of walking, so make sure that you wear comfortable shoes and clothes. Also, bear in mind that while you are backstage, Disney will not allow you to take any pictures. If you decide to book a tour, discounts are given to Disney Vacation Club members, annual passport holders, Disney Club members, and American Express card holders, so make sure you let them know if you fit any of the above.

4

The Magic Kingdom

Just reaching Mickey's secluded fiefdom is an adventure in itself! When Unca Walt built Disneyland, it was surrounded by lush orange groves on acres of land. As the park caught on, however, the oranges were flattened, parking lots and competing attractions sprang to life, and the real world closed in on Disneyland. Walt vowed never to let that happen again, and protected his new resort in Florida by buying up thousands of acres of land surrounding it. And in order to make a trip to the Magic Kingdom seem like a trip to a far-off, other world, he made it literally an ordeal to get to the park. There's no simple, quick way to get there. You must either take a ferryboat or a monorail from the Transportation and Ticket Center (although if you stay on-site, you have more transportation options, like a bus, or, from many hotels, a water launch). You should expect it to take anywhere from thirty minutes to an hour from the time you leave your car to the time you set foot on Main Street, so plan accordingly.

The Magic Kingdom was Walt Disney World's first park, opening in 1971, and it's the park most people think of first when they think of Disney World. It's a veritable kid's mecca, but people of all ages will find something to love there.

The Magic Kingdom is made up of six distinct lands surrounding a central hub, in which Cinderella Castle represents the park's centerpiece. These lands, clockwise beginning at the nine o'clock position, are Adventureland, Frontierland, Liberty Square, Fantasyland, Mickey's Toontown Fair, and Tomorrowland. But before you can get to any of Disney's "neighborhoods," you'll have to step out onto Main Street, the thoroughfare that runs between the entrance turnstiles and the Castle.

Note Regarding Cheap Eats in the Magic Kingdom

The Magic Kingdom is not known for its great table-service restaurants, so it might be best to "fast-food it" on the day you're there. In each "Land" we've mentioned only the most inexpensive restaurants and the maximum price you'll pay. You can choose a more fancy-shmancy place, but trust us, they're not worth it (at least not in the Magic Kingdom, anyway).

Remember: Make your big meal of the day lunch and avoid the rush by eating at off-peak times (plan on lunching around 11:00 A.M. and having dinner or munchies around 4:30 P.M.). While the rest of the world is munching at peak hours, you'll be enjoying the best attractions with shorter lines!

Note: In the past, we would have urged you to make reservations immediately upon your arrival in the Magic Kingdom for the lunchtime show of the Diamond Horseshoe Saloon Revue. Now Disney has decided to inconvenience you further by making the seating at this exceptional show available on a first come, first served basis. So, get to the theater at least forty-five minutes before the 12 P.M. lunchtime show. Read on for more details.

How to Get There

The Magic Kingdom can be reached by ferryboat and monorail from the Transportation and Ticket Center (TTC). (The monorail also connects to the Grand Floridian, the Polynesian, and the Contemporary resorts, and, at the TTC, to EPCOT.) Water launches service the Magic Kingdom from Fort Wilderness, the Grand Floridian, the Polynesian, River Country, and Wilderness Lodge. Disney World buses reach the Magic Kingdom from all the theme parks and Disney resorts.

Visitors arriving by car park in the lot at the TTC; the lot is free to Disney hotel guests (others: $5).

Key Magic Kingdom Landmarks

- Baby Needs/Changing Station—Baby Center, next to the Crystal Palace (on the central hub toward Adventureland)
- Banking Services—There's an ATM machine under the railroad station
- Disney Dollars (Disney's souvenir gift certificates, which work the same as cash in the parks and in Disney Stores)—Available at City Hall and Guest Services
- First Aid—Next to the Crystal Palace
- Information—City Hall
- Lockers—Under the Main Street Railroad Station
- Lost and Found, Lost Persons—City Hall
- Stroller Rentals—Strollers are available for $6 per day ($5, plus $1 deposit), and it's a bit awkward getting kids in and out of them. Save money (and time waiting on the rental line) and bring your own.
- Wheelchair Rentals—To the right of main turnstiles, before you reach the Walt Disney World Railroad Station; $6 ($5, plus $1 deposit)

MAIN STREET

This is the first area that opens in the morning and the first you'll encounter as you pass through the park's turnstiles.

There are no attractions, per se, on Main Street; just rows of quaint shops and restaurants leading to the central hub and what is essentially the symbol of the Magic Kingdom, Cinderella Castle (which is part of Fantasyland). But don't be tempted to stop in the shops immediately upon entering the park—that's what everybody else will be doing, silly! Instead, come back in the afternoon when Main Street's less crowded.

Your time in the A.M. will be better spent heading for a specific destination (see the itineraries in chapter 10), thus seeing the most popular attractions while everybody else is dillydallying.

Step out from under the Walt Disney World Railroad platform and into a picture-perfect world. Main Street resembles what might have been a turn-of-the-century street in small-town America, or at least what Walt Disney envisioned small-town America to look like, with its quiet, spotless streets. Vehicles from yesteryear progress up and down the street. You will see finely manicured lawns and shrubs, and workers touching up paint, but you will never see a piece of garbage on the ground for more than thirty-two seconds.

What You'll See

City Hall   More for information than entertainment. One of the first buildings you'll pass, it's to your left as you enter Town Square. Stop in and pick up maps, entertainment and character visit schedules and locations, parade times, park hours, and other pertinent information to help you plan your day.

The Walt Disney Railroad   These real steam-turned-diesel trains take you on a one-and-a-half mile tour around the park without walking, which is especially effective in busy times. Problem is, busy times also mean there's a backup waiting for the train. The train stops here at Main Street, in Frontierland (the busiest station, for some reason), and at Mickey's Toontown Fair. Trains leave about every five minutes, and the whole circuitous trip is said to take about twenty minutes, but that doesn't include the time you'll spend on line waiting for the next train—valuable time you could be spending elsewhere. Unless your timing's perfect, or you're a real train buff, you're probably better off walking it at a brisk pace.

Note: No strollers are allowed on the train.

(We also recommend that you forego rides on the Disney firetruck, and in the complimentary horse-drawn carriages, antique cars, and the like. Although they're interesting, quaint, and all that, they're not worth the wait. You can get from point A to point B faster by hoofin' it.)

Where You'll Eat

Sit-Down

Plaza Restaurant   Grilled sandwiches, cold sandwiches, hamburgers, ice cream, sodas, and milk shakes. Prices up to $11. One of the Magic Kingdom's higher priced, table-service restaurants. Given the choice, however, we'd take Tony's (see below) or the Liberty Tree Tavern (in Liberty Square, natch) over this place.

Tony's Town Square Restaurant   Fashioned after the Italian restaurant at which the Lady and the Tramp share a plate of spaghetti, this real-thing offers a good selection of Italian dishes. It's one of the most expensive restaurants in the Magic Kingdom, but it also has the best food. So decide for yourself whether it's for you. If you do decide to spend the extra bucks here, we recommend eating lunch, rather than dinner, as the menu is relatively the same and the prices are somewhat cheaper (breakfast to $8, lunch $16, dinner entrees $23).

Cafeterias/Food Courts

The Crystal Palace   A self-service buffeteria in an impressive all-glass, air-conditioned, greenhouse-like building, offering beef, chicken, pasta, barbecue pork, and fish. If you're going to eat at this attractive, buffet-service restaurant, why not share your meal with a Disney character? Check the Character Dining section in chapter 9 for more information.

Fast-Food/Counter Service

Casey's Corner   All-beef hot dogs, soda, and more, with a baseball theme. Located at the top of Main Street. Prices up to $4.

Snacks/Drinks

Main Street Bake Shop   Baked goods, drinks, and ice cream. Prices up to $3. This is one of the busiest places in the park during the first few hours after opening. Everyone stops by for a quick breakfast bite on the way to the fun. If you know us by now, you know we recommend that you avoid the crowd and either eat breakfast before you get to the park or bring a light breakfast snack with you. However, one of the best afternoon snacks can be found here—a block of vanilla ice cream wedged between two fresh-baked cookies (you even get to pick the type of cookie).

When you step outside the bake shop, take a big whiff of air and savor the smells of the freshly-baked cookies being prepared inside. *Surprise!* What you're smelling isn't the cookies baking—it's the manmade scent of artificial cookies being pumped into the air from canisters located below the sidewalk! It doesn't matter because it still smells good, and the cookies (the real ones, not the artificial ones) taste good, too! Hope we didn't spoil your fun!

Main Street Wagons   Throughout the Main Street area (especially on East Center Street), you'll find these old-fashioned wagons selling everything from espresso to soda, baked goods to fresh fruit. Prices up to $3.

Plaza Ice Cream Parlor   Take a guess what you can eat here! Frozen confections up to $3.

Where You'll Shop

Main Street's shops stay open one-half hour after the rest of the park closes. Don't shop first, as soon as you enter the Magic Kingdom, but don't go here the very end of the day either. Try to pass through in the afternoon while you're on the way to somewhere else. And if you don't want to carry your packages onto the rides for the whole rest of the day, Disney will hold them for you. Just tell the cashier you want to arrange for the packages to be held for later pickup. And if you're staying on-site, you can arrange to have the items shipped directly to your room!

The Chapeau   As the name implies, this is where you can buy every hat imaginable, especially the mouse ears (monogramming is free) that everybody buys, but no one wears after returning home.

Crystal Arts   This store is presented by Arribas Brothers, not Disney, so don't expect to find many Disney-related products here. Glassblown figures and glassware are available, as well as glass etching to personalize your purchases.

Disney & Co.   This shop offers a good selection of Disney character products for the home. It's the place to go if you've always wanted a Mickey Mouse shower curtain or a set of Mickey dinnerware. But bear in mind that this store changes its merchandise line very frequently, so there's almost no telling what you might be able to buy here during your visit.

Disney Clothiers   The perfect place to pick up an embroidered Mickey shirt. This shop offers a nice selection of better quality character fashions for kids and adults, and also has nice quality Disney jewelry and accessories.

The Emporium   This is the ultimate Disney department store. Here you'll find every Disney souvenir you could possibly think of—from tee shirts to hats, from stuffed animals to that souvenir button you just have to have. You can do most of your shopping here and save yourself from having to schlepp everything through the park.

A little-known fact is that the Emporium carries a stash of over-the-counter drugs. You won't see them displayed anywhere, but if you ask one of the store clerks, they can go to the back room and get the cure for what ails ya!

Firehouse Gift Station   Plenty of Mickey souvenirs with a fireman theme, presented in the Main Street Firehouse, of course. Also, the best source for *101 Dalmations* merchandise. Get it? Firemen, dalmations??

Harmony Barbershop   If your do's looking a little shabby, why not get your ears lowered at this little-known shop. It's a real, old-fashioned barbershop, albeit a littler pricier than what you pay at the neighborhood chop shop (one of those famed harmonic quartets even warbles a tune here on occasion!). Call 407-824-6550 for an appointment.

Kodak Camera Center   This shop has film, cameras, and accessories. Two-hour film developing (oh yes, you'll pay extra for such speediness!), and they'll even deliver your pictures to your on-site hotel. The center also stocks a nice selection of Disney videos.

Main Street Athletic Shop   Sports-related gifts and clothes—the place to go for that much-needed set of Disney golf club covers. Have your "team's" photo taken here against a variety of Disney backgrounds.

Main Street Cinema   Once upon a time, they used to show old-time Mickey Mouse cartoons here. In fact, they paid homage to the Mouse who started the Kingdom by continuously showing his first cartoon feature, *Steamboat Willie*. But, alas, showing cartoons for free doesn't do much for the Disney bottom-line, so they have turned this theater into a store, where you can pick up stuffed animals and other cha-cha from the latest Disney video releases. If you've read this far, you shouldn't be surprised by this turn of events.

Main Street Confectionery   Watch peanut brittle being made fresh while you take in the smells of this old-time candy store. Lots of delicious chocolates to tempt you, but remember that chocolate does not enjoy the Florida heat. They also sell fresh cotton candy.

Main Street Gallery   Fine quality Disney collectibles—statues, plates, sculptures, figurines, etc.—and an extensive collection of limited-edition animation art and production cels and lithographs. Make it a point to win the lottery before you enter this store, the prices make this place seem more like a museum to a cheapskate than a real shop.

Main Street Market House   This shop stocks old-time hard candy and a variety of Mickey kitchen gadgets. If you've been looking all over for that Mickey-shaped cake pan, lollipop mold, or waffle maker, you'll find it here.

Newsstand   This is the place to pick up various sundries, souvenirs, and film, but don't expect to find the daily newspaper here. This is undoubtedly because Walt wanted to keep the

Magic Kingdom an "unreal" place, free of all the doom and gloom of the outside world—the kind of doom and gloom you read about in the papers!

The Shadow Box   You can watch the artists at work as they make a cut-out silhouette of your kids.

Uptown Jewelers   This shop has a nice selection of character figurines and music boxes, and one of the largest collections of Mickey Mouse watches on-site.

ADVENTURELAND

Located to your left as you face Cinderella Castle with Main Street at your back, this land has a rustic/Polynesian/South Seasian feel to it, with its plethora of thatched roofs and lit tiki torches dotting the landscape. Home to two of the Magic Kingdom's best attractions.

What You'll See

The Enchanted Tiki Room   In the tiki-tiki-tiki-tiki-tiki room, in the tiki-tiki-tiki-tiki-tiki room—you know that song that has grated against all of our nerves at some point (it's right up there with "It's a Small World"). In the 1960s, this attraction was surely thought of as being a marvel of modern technology, watching a room full of birds singing their hearts out, but of late, it was looking a little old, and dare we say, boring. The folks at Disney, never willing to sit on their haunches for long, have recently redesigned the attraction and have placed it under new "management." The Enchanted Tiki Room is now run by Iago and Zazu, those fine, feathered stars of *Aladdin* and *The Lion King,* respectively. Although the new "owners" add a few laughs—even poking fun at the dull reputation of the previous show—you'll still see the same flock of birds that have inhabited their perches since the room first opened.

Even if it's not the most thrilling attraction at the park, it is cool inside, and seats are provided. Since long lines are definitely not a problem at the Tiki Birds, you've always guaranteed a seat here!

Jungle Cruise   Undoubtedly inspired by John Huston's classic film *The African Queen,* the Jungle Cruise allows you to explore faraway lands by boat, Disney style. Around every bend in the river, there are new and exotic flora (actual plant life native to the river regions your boat is supposedly plying, uprooted and brought in; these plants often have to be warmed by heaters to accommodate them during the sometimes-cool Florida winters) and fauna (lifesize robotic rhinos, hippos, elephants, zebras . . . even headhunters!) to face. You'll travel through re-creations of a Southeast Asian jungle, the Nile River Valley, the African grasslands, and the Amazon rainforest. The only real hazards you'll face on your journey will be the silly, tired jokes told by your captain/tour guide. In fact, the amount of fun you have on the trip depends a lot on the demeanor of your guide. If guides are noticeably sick of telling guests the same corny jokes over and over again, their hearts will just not be into it, and they may talk so fast that you miss half the punchlines (hey, maybe that's not so bad after all!) Don't worry, the guide can't take a bad day out on you by crashing your boat, your vessel rides on an underwater track. And if you haven't ridden the Jungle Cruise lately, you should try it now, it's been recently refurbished and expanded.

Three things to bear in mind regarding the Jungle Cruise: 1) You may get wet, since hippos, elephants, and waterfalls come close to dousing your boat; 2) the line can seem deceptively short, since a small waiting area when you first enter the line hides a weaving, packed queue as you get closer to the boatloading area; and 3) the ride and its waiting area (although shaded in most spots) are entirely outside. If you wilt easily in the heat, and the waiting time is long, you just may want to avoid this ride. Ask—if the wait is more than 15 minutes, come back later and try again.

Shades of World Motion's "It's Fun to be Free" attraction: Rumors abound that this ride might be closing soon. It is one of the original rides from the 1970s (actually designed in the 1960s, and a Disneyland favorite before its Florida counterpart opened), and some people (i.e. those who make the Disney decisions) feel the ride is a bit out of date. After all, they say, who wants to see Audio-Animatronic elephants frolic when you can see the real thing on the safari ride at Animal Kingdom? But we kind of like this ride, outdated as it may be, and hope that it remains in Disney's plans for the future. Let's stage our own unique protest: To everyone reading—Blitz this ride; ride it several times during your visit to show Disney that it's still popular and the fans want it to stay. *Don't Miss This! FASTPASS!*

The Magic Carpets of Aladdin   Fly high above Adventureland on your own four-passenger magic carpet! Well, not *exactly:* Sixteen "carpets" are connected to an enormous genie bottle. You control the movement of the carpet—up, down, pitching forward or backward—as a giant camel periodically spews water at you.

At the time of the writing of this book, this ride was still under construction. However, it appears that it will be very similar to Dumbo in Fantasyland, and is probably suited more for the younger members of your group.

Pirates of the Caribbean   Ride a mini-pirate galleon through sets depicting a pirate raid on a village. Cannon balls "fly" overhead, fire licks ransacked buildings, "gunshots" whiz by, flower pots explode (then reassemble themselves for the next guests), dogs howl—you smile! Look around and be aware of the small details—yes, that *is* hair on that robot's pirate's leg! In these politically correct times, Disney has recently updated this ride. Originally, while raiding the town, the pirates chased the village women, as pirates are wont to do, but this apparently upset some folks. So now, the women chase the pirates. One of the original gags was lost in the translation, but we guess most people won't even notice. But you will *now*, right cheapskate?!

Warning: This ride sports a small flume-type drop and there's a possibility you may get wet. And don't let those pirates fool you! While there may seem to be no line on this ride when you first approach, the line winds around inside the building. So plan on waiting awhile, even if it seems like there's no line outside. But it's worth it. It's nice and cool inside (unlike the Jungle Cruise's line), and it's one of Disney's best rides. And remember rule number 1: The shortest line for this attraction is usually the one on the left. *Don't Miss This!*

Shrunken Ned's Junior Jungle Boats   Navigate a remote-controlled miniature version of the Jungle Cruise through a myriad of obstacles, sans the "witty" repartee of the larger attraction. At $1 a "voyage" for this pretty much run-of-the-mill arcade game, we can think of better ways of spending your money and time at the Magic Kingdom.

The Swiss Family Treehouse   Remember that ole Swiss family, the Robinsons? Here's a faithful re-creation of the dwelling from Disney's 1960 movie, *The Swiss Family Robinson.* Actually, it's a fake Disney tree (the only thing living is the Spanish moss) that sports three hundred thousand plastic leaves and concrete roots that extend forty-two feet into the ground, but don't let us spoil your fun. Anyway, those Robinsons have thunk up some interesting inventions for making life in the jungle a little easier, and they're all on display here (how does running water in every room grab ya?). The attraction is more meaningful if you've read the book or watched the movie, since it discusses some of the film's plot points. Even if you haven't seen the film, take the time to check out the details here and read all the plaques describing the family's life in their tree. The treehouse is worth seeing if you've never seen it before, but it may be an attraction you want to avoid if you've seen it before, or if the line is too long. The good news is that the line moves constantly, although it wanders all the way up and down the tree. The bad news is that it remains outside for its entire length.

Where You'll Eat

Fast-Food/Counter Service

Egg Roll Wagon   Only in Disney! Many varieties, including pork, shrimp, vegetable, pizza, and oriental cheese. About

$2. (Why do they call them egg rolls, anyway? There's nary an egg in 'em!)

El Pirata y el Perico Across from Pirates of the Caribbean. Tacos, nachos, salads, and hot dogs. Up to $5.

Snacks/Drinks

Aloha Isle Pineapple, fruit drinks, and frozen treats, most under $3. Try the supercalifragilistic Dole Whip!

The Oasis In the center of Adventureland. Sodas and snacks, most under $3.

Sunshine Tree Terrace Behind the Tiki room. Cold drinks and light snacks; frozen yogurt, desserts, and shakes. The best, most refreshing deal is the Citrus Swirl, a frozen orange juice swirled with nonfat vanilla frozen yogurt. Up to $3.

Where You'll Shop

Bwana Bob's This shop has a cute collection of cuddly stuffed animals and brightly colored toys. Film and camera accessories are also available.

The Crow's Nest This is where you'll find film, cameras, and accessories. There's also a drop-off for speedy film processing (but you'll pay more!).

Elephant Tales This shop features clothes and accessories with a jungle theme for men and women, plus stuffed animals and more.

House of Treasure The place for gifts with a pirate theme (What did you expect? It's located next to Pirates of the Caribbean!). The selection includes toy buccaneer guns, felt pirate hats, and Jolly Roger flags.

Island Supply This is the place to buy gifts for the environmentally conscious consumer, and for those who just wish to get back to nature. You'll find tee shirts and gifts, many of which will appeal to the gardener on your list, as well as natural sunscreen products.

Laffitte's   The shop for all the essential gear for the littlest pirates, including toy swords, pistols, felt hats, and the all-important plastic hook to replace one's hand . . . plus candy.

Plaza del Sol Caribe Bazaar   This outdoor bazaar sells clothing with a tropical island theme, sold in the plaza near the exit to Pirates. It's the place where you'll find much-needed straw bags, piñatas, and giant floppy sombreros.

Tiki Tropics Shop   Dudes looking for surfing duds should look no further. You'll find tee shirts and baggies, even way-cool shark-tooth jewelry.

Traders of Timbuktu   This is the stop for gifts and jewelry imported from Africa. You'll find inexpensive trinkets and carved wooden animals as well as dashikis.

Treasure Chest   Toys, toys, more toys, and sunscreen.

Zanzibar Shell Company   If you forgot to pick up souvenirs at Animal Kingdom, here's another chance. There's a large selection of tee shirts, stuffed animals, and knickknacks from the other Disney "Kingdom."

FRONTIERLAND

Disney's Old West-themed land (complete with clapboard sidewalks and hitching posts), sandwiched between Adventureland and Liberty Square.

What You'll See

Big Thunder Mountain Railroad   A roller coaster that races up, around, and through Disney's manmade mountain, just fast enough to offer a thrill, but slow enough that you won't lose your lunch. This coaster is pretty racy for Disney, but tamer than Space Mountain. As you zip around turns and down hills, try to notice the Audio-Animatronic chickens, donkeys, possums, goats—even an old forty-niner—as well as the authentic tools and equipment that litter the area surrounding the ride and the party going on in the saloon. Pay close attention to the mining town, the falling rocks, and the earthquake effects. (Note: they say the last car feels the bumps and turns the most, so choose your seat wisely.)

Try to ride once during the day and once at night (when it will be less crowded). The line can be deceptive (it weaves around inside the building) but it moves fast. Kids must be forty inches tall to ride. *Don't Miss This!*

Country Bear Jamboree   These twenty life-size Audio-Animatronic bears who sing, play instruments, and tell dumb jokes in Grizzly Hall have felt the wrath of many a critic and travel writer over the years, but we still like them. It's all great fun and exuberance, especially if you've got kids in your group. Don't be bashful: Clap your hands! Pay attention to everything around you in the theater—the trophies on the wall are even part of show, and you'll see them again on your way out. The show changes seasonally, and many of the "performers" have been updated. The lobby waiting area fills up before they let you into the air-conditioned theater. If you join the line just as the lobby is getting filled, you'd better try again later because you'll have a long wait: It's eighteen minutes between each show.

Diamond Horseshoe Saloon Revue   This is a free, albeit scaled-down version of Disney's immensely popular Hoop-Dee-Doo Revue show (which is held nightly in Fort Wilderness's Campground Pioneer Hall, to the tune of almost $40 a head). But the show at the Diamond Horseshoe is very popular, too, and the price is right. There are six shows daily. We recommend seeing the 12:00 P.M. lunchtime show, but you must show up early. Read on for all the details.

Frontierland Shootin' Arcade   An electronic version of your basic carnival shooting gallery. A great way for Disney to sucker your spare change away from you! The special Disney touch? The little marksmen shoot real buffalo rifles, but blast infrared beams, not bullets. Don't waste too much time aiming—you get a specific number of shots or an allotted shooting time, whichever expires first. We agree that there are better ways to spend your time at Disney world.

Splash Mountain   This ride is one of the Magic Kingdom's most popular and tells the *Song of the South* story—you remember, all those "Brer" critters (rabbit, bear, fox, etc.). It features the most elaborate (and numerous) Audio-Animatronics in the park, but it's too bad almost all of it is overshadowed by the splashes. This one's worth going on a few times (if you don't mind the lines!) just to pay closer attention to the story details you might have missed on the half-mile ride through gardens, swamps, and caves. Oh yeah, and to thrill again to the 52-foot, 40-miles-per-hour final plunge. This is one of those rides that fills up early and maintains a long line throughout the day, so we recommend making it one of the first attractions you see, if you're so inclined. Note: If you want to get wet, sit in front and on the right side. Kids must be 44-inches tall to ride. *Don't Miss This! FASTPASS!*

Tom Sawyer Island   Walk in the footsteps of boyhood pals Tom Sawyer and Huck Finn. Take a raft across Rivers of America to an island with hills to climb, a working windmill, and two bridges—one's a swinging suspension bridge, the other a barrel bridge you can bounce on. Kids can also explore Fort Sam Clemens, featuring a guardhouse with Audio-Animatronics animals as well as a second-floor shooting gallery (extra charge). The island's cave is almost too realistic, and its pitch-black, claustrophobic labyrinth can scare even adults (take it from us!).

The island offers a reprieve from the structured lines and occasional mayhem of the rest of the World. All of us could use a moment to breathe, but the island is best enjoyed by kids (boys, more so than girls), ages 6 to 12. We recommend you put a time limit on your visit to Tom's place, or you'll waste all day when you could be experiencing attractions you can all enjoy. And if you are traveling without kids, this attraction may be worth skipping. But don't wait too long to explore Tom Sawyer Island—the area closes at dusk.

Little known secret: Be on the lookout for paint brushes Tom Sawyer might have left behind when he finished his chores. If you find one, take it to a Cast Member and you'll get a nice surprise!

Walt Disney World Railroad The steam train picks up passengers from Frontierland, with stops at Mickey's Toontown Fair and Main Street. Note: This Frontierland station is often the railroad's most crowded one.

Where You'll Eat

Fast-Food/Counter Service

Aunt Polly's (on Tom Sawyer Island) Sandwiches, fried chicken, soft ice cream, cold drinks, most items under $7. A nice, fairly unknown (read: quiet and remarkably uncrowded) place. Nothing beats the quiet solace of kicking back and sipping a lemonade on Aunt Polly's porch.

Diamond Horseshoe Saloon Revue Disney's popular Western show, serving relatively inexpensive counter-service sandwiches, snacks, and beverages, most everything under $6. Shows are scheduled at 10:45 A.M., 12 P.M., 1:15 P.M., 3:30 P.M., and 4:45 P.M. (We recommend the 12 P.M. lunchtime show.) Admission is on a first-come, first-served basis. Show up early or you'll miss the fun.

Pecos Bill Tall Tale Inn and Café Burgers, hot dogs, chicken wraps, chicken salad, vegetable salad, and more, served in a Western-themed restaurant. This is one of the largest fast-food joints in the park, serving a nice variety of foods. Up to $7.

Snacks/Drinks

Turkey Leg Wagon Only in Disney (the sequel): If you see people walking around like modern-day King Henry VIIIs, gnawing on unsuspecting turkey appendages, then you must be near the Turkey Leg Wagon! Grab one for under $5. Located across from the Country Bears.

Westward Ho Across from the Mile Long Bar. Cookies, pretzels, chips, and drinks. Up to $3.

Where You'll Shop

Big Al's   A store named after the Country Bear Jamboree's favorite character. You can even find the popular stuffed animal version of ol' melancholy Al here. Toys and sunscreen. And, if you feel like playing Davy Crockett, this is the place to pick up a coonskin cap.

Briar Patch   Located near the exit to Splash Mountain, here's where you'll find the traditional "I survived Splash Mountain" tee shirts and other logo items. They also stock Winnie-the-Pooh clothing and collectibles, and a variety of country crafts.

Frontier Trading Post   Clothing, Western-style jewelry, leather goods, belt buckles, film, and moccasins. For the little ones, they have sheriff's badges, tom-toms, toy horses, and other Western gear. We especially recommend the mini-cowboy hats and Native American headdresses to hang from your car's rearview mirror.

Frontier Wood Carving   This is the place to go if you want your name—or anything else, for that matter—scrawled into a block of wood.

Prairie Outpost and Supply   Saddlebags full of yummy candy and gourmet kitchen gadgets. Why not bring a Mickey hot plate home to the one you love?

Trail Creek Hat Shop   Hats and western-style leather goods. Buy a cowboy hat here—or, if you're politically correct, an authentic reproduction of a Native American headdress.

LIBERTY SQUARE

This is not really a "land," but rather, the small colonialesque area that separates Frontierland from Fantasyland.

What You'll See

The Hall of Presidents   A "living" history lesson that some might consider boring, especially the younger kids (maybe they'll fall asleep, if you're lucky). But at least it's air conditioned! The show is made up of life-size robots of each of our presidents, who are assembled to hear Abraham Lincoln give a speech (the show has changed somewhat as of late, now George Bush also speaks, while Lincoln rattles his notes, waiting his turn). As you watch the show, pay attention to all the presidents in their authentic garb as they move and fuss about, just like the real chief executives! Shows start on the hour and half hour and last about twenty-two minutes. If you approach the theater and there seems to be a long line, don't be discouraged: The theater can hold up to 700 people.

The Haunted Mansion   Board your Doom Buggy (get it?!) for a visit with hundreds of Grim Grinning Ghosts (999 to be exact, and there's room for one more. Any volunteers?). It's not real scary, but there are enough surprises and things jumping out at you to keep you on your toes (the scariest thing is really the happy shrieks you'll hear from the people riding just ahead of you). The ride can be very dark at some points and scary for young children. The line moves constantly, even though there may appear to be a line outside. (Those are the people waiting to enter the pre-ride area, the somewhat hokey stretching room. The nearby Riverboat and Hall of Presidents attractions might have just disgorged their 1,200 people.) Advice for photographers: Don't use a flash, use high speed film. (And don't bother videotaping, because it's too dark inside for anything to come out. We already tried and wasted film.) Watch for Disney's famous details, like the raven that appears again and again throughout the ride, door knockers that knock themselves, a ghostly teapot pouring tea, and dancing ghosts. The fun begins even before you walk through the front door: Notice the humorous inscriptions on the gravestones as you approach. Each one denotes the name of one of the original ride designers. *Don't Miss This! FASTPASS!*

A bit of trivia: the singing statues in the graveyard (the one on the ride, that is) were based on a singing group from the 1950s called the Mello Men. One member of the group, Thurl Ravenscroft, was the man who did the voice for Frosted Flakes's Tony the Tiger ("They're Great!") and sang the theme for *The Grinch That Stole Christmas.*

> ### Secret Tip—How to Get on the Haunted Mansion Ride First
> When you're ushered into the portrait room, stand under the portrait of the lady holding the parasol, riding a unicycle. Once the pre-show is over, you'll be the first to exit the portrait room and the first to get on the Doom Buggy.

Liberty Square Riverboat   A fifteen-minute cruise around Rivers of America. The ride is slow and not terribly exciting, but it can provide a nice break on a hot afternoon and affords you great views (and photo opportunities) of Splash Mountain and the Haunted Mansion. The best seats are all the way in the front or the back, where you're able to see both sides of the river. Boats leave on the hour and half hour.

Liberty Tree   Not really an attraction, but more of a conversation piece. This 130-year-old tree was transplanted from the other end of the sprawling Disney acreage. (Check out the round plugs in the tree—those weren't naturally formed. Holes had to be drilled into the tree and huge dowels inserted in it to transport it to Liberty Square.) It's called the Liberty Tree because thirteen lanterns hang from its branches symbolizing the original thirteen American colonies.

Mike Fink Keelboats   Smaller, faster boats that follow the same basic route as the big paddlewheel riverboats. If you must go on a boat, choose one or the other, not both—one round-trip ride is sufficient for anyone, thank you. And be sure to tell everyone back home that you rode on a keelboat.

> ### One of the Quietest Areas in the Magic Kingdom—for Those Who Just Need It
> Rest in the quiet area just behind Ye Olde Christmas Shoppe.

Where You'll Eat

Sit-Down

Liberty Tree Tavern   More expensive, sit-down restaurant featuring an Early American menu of chicken, steak, sausage, seafood, pot roast, New England clam chowder, roast turkey with all the trimmings, and more served in a Colonial setting. If you must pick a sit-down place, it might as well be this one, and the meal you should eat here is lunch (since it's less expensive than dinner for the same fare, up to $15 per entree lunches versus $20 per entree dinners). After 4:00 P.M., this restaurant becomes a character dining location. See chapter 9.

Fast-Food/Counter Service

Columbia Harbour House   Across from Ichabod's Landing. Seafood (fried fish, clam chowder served in a bowl fashioned from a loaf of dark bread), sandwiches (smoked ham, smoked turkey), chicken fingers, salads, and desserts. Up to $7.

Snacks/Drinks

Fruit and Vegetable Wagon   A farmer's-market-type wagon located behind the Columbia Harbour House, featuring apples, grapes, pickles, and more, for up to $3.

Liberty Square Wagon   Baked potatoes with all the toppings, plus beverages. Up to $3. Located near the pickle and fruit stand.

Sleepy Hollow   Offers chocolate chip cookies, cookie ice cream sandwiches, brownie sundaes, cobblers à la mode, and fresh-made caramel popcorn. Up to $4.

Where You'll Shop

Heritage House   If you've always wanted a necklace crafted out of a coin, then you've come to the right place. This shop also stocks a variety of presidential, Civil War-related merchandise, and a wide variety of Early American reproductions for the home. These include pewter knickknacks and candlesticks, ceramic mugs, and glassware.

Ichabod's Landing   THE place to replenish your supply of fake vomit, magic tricks, gags, and expensive masquerade materials.

Liberty Square Portrait Gallery   Artists are on hand here to create that one-of-a-kind, hand-drawn portrait of you and your family.

Mme Leota's Cart   More magic tricks and masks. Located (appropriately enough) at the exit to the Haunted Mansion.

Patriot's Cart   Everything Yankee Doodle Dandies could ever want in red, white, and blue: windsocks, flags, shirts, etc.

Silhouette Cart   If you'd like a silhouette portrait created of yourself and your family, saddle up to this cart.

The Yankee Trader   Disney and non-Disney kitchen accessories, along with a selection of gourmet food and snacks. Anyone in the mood for pasta shaped like everyone's favorite mouse? They also stock a nice selection of Coca-Cola collectibles; and if you're a cookbook connoisseur, check out the store's excellent selection.

Ye Olde Christmas Shoppe   Who can think of Christmas while baking under the Florida sun? But it's easy to get in the holiday spirit in this cozy shop. It's the place to go year-round for that special Disney Christmas ornament. They also offer a nice variety of non-Disney Christmas items, too. They'll even wrap your purchase so it survives Space Mountain!

FANTASYLAND

At least as far as the kiddies are concerned, this is the most magical place in the Magic Kingdom. Since there are more kids per square foot here, you're also more likely to run into more costumed characters here than in any other land.

If you're traveling with kids—or this is your favorite "land" too—we think it's best to visit during the 3:00 P.M. parade when most of the other kids will be distracted, then catch the parade another time or day. Or hit Fantasyland very early in the day.

What You'll See

Ariel's Grotto   For years, Disney has been trying to figure out what to do with the former 20,000 Leagues Under the Sea attraction. They're still toying with some ideas on how to best use the space. For now, it just affords you the opportunity to have a picture taken in a very natural setting with the Little Mermaid.

Cinderella Castle   Not a ride or attraction, but the center-piece of the park, and the site of much of Disney's outdoor diversionary entertainment (diversionary, meaning entertainment that diverts you from the rides, thus making the lines shorter!). The castle is the home of Cinderella's Royal Table, a place too dear for the cheapskate's wallet (for a laugh, check out the prices on the posted menu). Anyway, the castle's at least worth a walk-through on your way to Fantasyland and parts beyond. (Notice the tile mosaics that tell the story of Cinderella and her evil siblings. Yes, that's real, solid 24 karat gold inlaid in the mosaics!)

Cinderella's Golden Carrousel   It's a real carnival carousel, built around 1917 and discovered by Disney researchers in New Jersey. No two of the ninety hand-carved animals on the ride are the same. While you're riding, look around at the ceiling and the hand-painted Cinderella scenes, and enjoy the musical Disney selections played by the ride's Italian pipe organ.

If the line is long, save the carousel for another time when you can just walk right on.

Dumbo the Flying Elephant   For some reason, every little kid loves this ride, and it's the cause of some major traffic jams. A fresh coat of paint has been added recently, along with six more Dumbos so more people can ride at one time. But it's still a huge wait (people have been known to wait an hour for this one-and-a-half-minute ride). But just try denying your toddler a ride! The riders can control their own up and down movement. And check out Timothy Mouse, who occasionally pops up in the middle. If you're traveling with a child three to eight years old, who loves Dumbo, or who doesn't know

Dumbo but loves flying around in circles, it may be worth making this ride your first stop, riding it before anything else in the Magic Kingdom. Or come late in the day when most kids have tuckered out. That's how bad the line can get.

It's a Small World This ride, populated by relatively hokey wooden dolls warbling that familiar refrain, "It's a world of laughter, a world of tears . . ." is very slow, and the incessantly repeated song gets old real fast. But kids love it, and it features a welcome blast of air conditioning. The song just won't get out of your head, but the line's usually not too bad, so go on, ride it again! You *know* you want to. To make the time fly by, pay close attention to the native garb the children/dolls are wearing. And check out the smiles on your real kids' faces! It's all worth it, after all!

The Legend of the Lion King Animation, life-size puppets, special effects, and music combine to bring the story of Simba and his jungle friends to life in the place that was formerly known as Magic Journeys (now known as the Fantasyland Theater).

Due to its popularity, we suggest you come early or late or during the early parade to enjoy this superior 28-minute show. It's one of the best live shows in all of Disney World, but beware: At times it's a little loud and scary, and may be too much for very small children. Keep an exit in sight and try to avoid sitting on the sides or in the first three rows of the theater— you won't be able to get a good view of all the action. *Don't Miss This!*

Mad Tea Party Inspired by *Alice in Wonderland,* and featuring Alice and several of the characters from that classic cartoon, this is still just your run-of-the-mill teacups ride that can be found at every traveling carnival. If you're a person who doesn't enjoy spinning until you feel queasy or waiting in line for a ride that can be found anywhere, then this is one "attraction" that's worth avoiding.

The Many Adventures of Winnie the Pooh Hop into your own Hunny Pot vehicle and join Pooh and his friends, Piglet, Eeyore, Tigger, Rabbit, Owl, Gopher, Kanga, and Roo on a journey through the Hundred Acre Wood. Bounce along with Tigger as you follow Pooh through several scenes from his best-loved stories. You'll even get to play a part in Pooh's dream with the Heffalumps and Woozles.

This ride replaces Mr. Toad's Wild Ride, which we will miss merely because it was one of the original attractions at Disney World to open on opening day. Mr. Toad actually had quite a following among Disney fanatics, and on the day that the ride closed, demonstrators were on hand to protest its closing. But this new ride rates a "10" on the cuteness scale, so it's definitely worth seeing. *Don't miss this! FASTPASS!*

Peter Pan's Flight "Fly" over London and Neverland aboard flying pirate ships with Peter and his friends. The boats are suspended from the ceiling, so at times it seems like you're really flying. This is one of the more entertaining rides in Fantasyland for both kids and adults. *FASTPASS!*

Snow White's Adventures Formerly known as Snow White's Scary Adventures, this ride might have been too scary for its young riders. So a "scaryotomy" was done to it recently. The ride has been updated, with the scariest scenes of the witch (who used to jump out at you from nearly every turn) having been removed, and the fair Ms. White herself (who only showed up occasionally) added to more scenes. But it's still very dark and a little scary. A little tip: What prepares you for the frights is that you can often hear the people in the car in front of you reacting to the scary parts, so you can be ready when it's your turn.

Where You'll Eat

Sit-Down

Cinderella's Royal Table If your little daughter insists that you must dine with Cinderella in her castle, save your shekels, and choose a lunch here when it's less expensive (up to $17, as opposed to dinner, up to $25). This is the most popular character meal on Disney property, so don't disappoint your little princess. Be sure to make your reservations exactly

60 days in advance by calling 407-WDW-DINE. It's guaranteed that the character dining will sell out on that day. Start calling at 7 A.M. when the reservation line opens. Cinderella's is also the only restaurant offering a bird's-eye view of the Magic Kingdom. It serves prime rib, chicken, and seafood. (Character Breakfasts are also offered here—see chapter 9 for more information.)

Fast-Food/Counter Service

Lumiere's Kitchen   Located near Winnie's. Corn-dog nuggets, foot-long hot dogs, French fries. Up to $6.

The Pinocchio Village Haus   Next to Small World. A nice variety of salads, chicken wraps, cheeseburgers, and hot dogs. Up to $7.

Snacks/Drinks

Enchanted Grove   Slushes, soft-serve ice cream, and strawberry swirls (frozen strawberry juice swirled with vanilla ice cream). Up to $3.

Hook's Tavern   Next to Peter Pan's Flight (appropriately enough), so while you're basking in the glow of a ride with Peter and the gang, enjoy snacks, coffee, and hot chocolate, most under $3. Could we interest you in a soda served in a commemorative cup? You know, the kind of plastic cup you pay an extra dollar for?!

Mrs. Potts' Cupboard   Ice cream cones, sundaes, floats, and shakes, most under $4.

Scuttle's Landing   Beverages and shaved ice, most around $2–3.

Where You'll Shop

(In all of Fantasyland's shops, the focus is on Disney-character merchandise.)

Fantasy Faire   This is the place to find all of those princess gowns for the little princesses in your life.

Film Kiosk   Film, accessories, and photo-developing drop-off. Again, we repeat, buy your film at home, and wait until you get back to do your developing.

Information Kiosk   Character souvenirs and FREE information. (You won't see the word "free" used too often at Disney, so excuse our momentary exuberance.)

The King's Gallery   Gifts based on characters from the animated classic, *Cinderella*. But what else would you expect from a store located right inside Cinderella's Castle? Watch as artisans create beautiful jewelry by using gold wire and steel. And where else in the world could you buy a life-size suit of armor? (A bit uncomfortable under the Florida sun, however.)

Seven Dwarfs Mining Company   Gifts and clothing styled after the Disney classic cartoon *Snow White and the Seven Dwarfs*. Stuffed animals, hats, tee shirts, and sweatshirts. We'd bet even Grumpy smiled when he saw his first royalty check from this shop.

Sir Mickey's   Disney character clothing, accessories, and hats. One of the best collections of tee shirts in the park, plus Disney statuettes, videos, and souvenirs.

Tinker Bell's Treasures   Disney character clothing for infants and kids, and toys for your little prince or princess. A beautiful selection of Madame Alexander dolls, some made exclusively for Disney World. They also handle stroller and wheelchair rental replacements (in case you blow a tire or something).

MICKEY'S TOONTOWN FAIR

Once upon a time (actually, 1989) this area opened as Mickey's Birthdayland, in honor of the rodent's sixtieth birthday. It was such a hit with kiddies that the Disney folks adapted it, renamed it Mickey's Starland, and kept it open. Set in the little hamlet of Duckburgh, USA, it has been revamped once again. Perhaps it's to tie it in with a future Walt Disney Worldland modeled after the Disneyland version on the West Coast, Toontown? Let's wait and see.

Pretty sedate entertainment fare, probably more intriguing to kids than adults, but any Mickey fan will love it.

What You'll See

Donald's Boat A climb-on/walk-through attraction that lets your kids burn up some pent up energy racing around Donald's boat. But watch out for the squirting water! You can get wetter here than on Splash Mountain.

Goofy's Barnstormer A relatively mild roller coaster designed for the under 40-inch crowd (that's all those kids who are too small for Disney's other coasters). Adults are welcome to ride as well.

Mickey's Country Home Walk through Mickey's home and look for all the little Disney touches, like "Mickey ears" on the tomatoes growing in the garden. Don't forget to meet Mickey himself in the tent in his garden.

Minnie's Country Home Check out Minnie's home. Be sure to notice the small details, like the cake rising in her oven, and while you're there, pop some popcorn in Ms. Mouse's microwave.

Toontown Hall of Fame Your opportunity to meet Mickey's friends (i.e., costumed characters), up-close and personal.

Walt Disney World Railroad Next stop, Main Street. If you time it right, and get to the station when there's no line, and you're headed to Main Street anyway, jump on the train and take a shortcut.

Where You'll Eat

Snacks/Drinks

Toontown Farmer's Market Fresh fruit, canned juice, hot and cold beverages. Up to $3.

Where You'll Shop

County Bounty Disney character toys, souvenirs, and more toys.

Funny Photos Stand in front of a blue screen and have your family's photo superimposed on a variety of Disney backgrounds.

TOMORROWLAND

This land was originally conceived as a celebration of the future. But around ten years ago the Disney people realized their view of the future was beginning to appear very outdated. So, in 1995, they completed a major renovation of this whole land. Today it resembles a unique city of the future. Disney has essentially looked back to look forward: Now the whole area has a timeless Buck Rogers-esque theme, and is presented as an Interplanetary Convention Center (kind of a stretch, but it works . . . usually!).

What You'll See

Astro Orbiter Formerly StarJets, here's Tomorrowland's answer to Fantasyland's Dumbo ride, although this one is somewhat higher and faster than its elephantine counterpart. And since this ride lacks the charm of the Fantasyland ride, it's nothing more than your typical amusement park ride, and thus worth skipping (especially if the kids already made you waste half the day waiting to ride Dumbo!). Not worth waiting on a line for this one.

Buzz Lightyear's Space Ranger Spin Travel with Buzz "to infinity and beyond" in this fun interactive trip. Team up with everybody's favorite space ranger as he tries to save the universe from his nemesis, the evil Emperor Zurg. Spin your way through several scenes from Buzz Lightyear's adventures while you take aim at moving targets with a laser gun. You get to ride in the same vehicle with a friend, who also has control of a laser gun. You score with each hit of the targets, and your score is recorded throughout the trip. It's great fun for all of you competitive types out there! If you've got kids taggin' along who are *Toy Story* fans, then *Don't Miss This! FASTPASS!*

Carousel of Progress We refuse to accept that they've

closed this charming attraction, which was a nostalgic look at progress, set in an unusual rotating theater. We hope the head Disney honchos rethink this and reopen this classic experience. (You guys listening?)

The ExtraTERRORestrial Alien Encounter Disney calls this a sensory thriller, and it's far and away the Magic Kingdom's scariest ride. The scene is the Tomorrowland Interplanetary Convention Center, and you're on hand to see the newest innovation from a company called X-S Tech: the X-S Series 1000 Teleportation System. To showcase the new technology, demonstrators are attempting to teleport the company's chairman, but something goes terribly wrong with the experiment, and there's a horribly deformed alien on the loose. Worst of all, you're strapped into your seat with no means of escape!

Legend has it that when Disney chairman Michael Eisner testrode this one, he deemed it too tame, so it was sent back to the drawing board for six months of retooling. Think twice before taking the little ones along—they must be 44 to 48 inches tall to ride in any case, and children will be shown a preview video ahead of time to see if they still want to ride.

This ride replaces the much-less-scary-and-terribly-outdated Mission to Mars (which had replaced the even more outdated Voyage to the Moon). Note: The ride is somewhat interactive, so if you stay quiet and keep a low profile, you can see others get attacked instead of you. But if you want to really enjoy the attraction to the fullest, try to get a seat in the back row, because the special effects seem better from back there. *Don't Miss This!*

Galaxy Palace Theater Mickey and his friends present a show that's called "out of this world." Check the entertainment schedule for show times, but remember: This is an outdoor show. You will want to avoid seeing it in the middle of the day when the Florida sun is at its strongest.

Space Mountain Catch a rocket for the thrill of a lifetime. This is one of the most popular rides in the park—an exciting roller coaster ride in the dark (or maybe it's exciting because it's dark), with stars and meteors "flying" overhead. If the ride were outside, it would seem relatively tame (with its top speed of twenty-eight miles per hour), but thanks to some neat special effects (not to mention the overall lack of light!) Space Mountain is sure to thrill even the diehard coaster fanatic. Don't let the lack of a line outside deceive you, the line weaves back and forth almost incessantly *inside* the mountain and it's almost always crowded. It's best to see Space Mountain very early or very late in the day, or try during dinnertime. By the same token, don't let a long outside line fool you: The line inside may be short and the Disney staff is just trying to discourage you from entering the line at the end of the day. Be sure to ask them how long the wait will be. It's never what they say, but at least it gives you a bit of a reference point. At least the pre-ride show (making you feel like you're embarking on an intergalactic journey) has been improved somewhat.

A few words of advice: Don't go on Space Mountain right after you eat; don't bring any prized souvenirs onboard your spaceship and be sure to secure your glasses, pocketbook, and other loose belongings. Ride tips: Put more weight in the front of your rocket and the faster it will go; the last car of the rocket feels the bumps and turns the most; the left track has sharper curves, while the right side has deeper dips.

For those who enter the building, then think better of riding, there's a chicken-out line, which leads out of the building to an arcade, the Tomorrowland Power and Light Company. Kids must be forty-four inches tall to ride. *Don't Miss This! FASTPASS!*

The Timekeeper   A unique movie experience, which originally debuted at Disneyland Paris, presented here in the Transportarium (formerly the American Journeys Theater). Jeremy Irons and the voice of Robin Williams (as the voice of Timekeeper) join you on a film adventure, shot in Circle-Vision 360. That's Disney's unique nine-camera mechanism that allows viewers to see nine views of the same scene at the same time simply by looking around the room. You'll travel to the past and witness the future, while meeting visionaries Jules Verne and H. G. Wells.

We miss the patriotic American Journeys travelogue film

that was shown here previously, but this new one's a winner. However, if the line's coming out the building, come back later; and bear in mind that this theater-in-the-round has no seats. *Don't Miss This!*

Tomorrowland Light and Power Company   This is the fake power station for this fanciful world of the future, located at the exit of Space Mountain. It also features a video arcade.

Tomorrowland Speedway   Is this what progress hath wrought: loud cars belching their pollution into the air? Sad to say, the kids line up to ride this one in droves. Maybe that's because it's nothing more than a carnival go-cart track and the kiddies feel like they are controlling the action. Four parallel tracks are available, about a half-mile each. Parents: It's safe. Even though the kids steer, the cars can't go off the center-rail track and their speeds don't exceed seven miles per hour. Let's hope Disney brings this ride into the future with electric (quiet, pollution-free) cars.

Tomorrowland Transit Authority   Formerly known as the WEDWAY People Mover, most of the novelty of this ride is the vehicle itself: You're treated to an aerial view of Tomorrowland on a car with no moving parts (it's propelled by opposing magnets in the car and on the track). You'll get to peek at the Space Mountain line. At its best, this ride is a place to sit down and the line is usually relatively short; at its worst, the ride is probably too long.

Where You'll Eat

Fast-Food/Counter Service

Cosmic Ray's Starlight Café   The largest fast-food spot in the Magic Kingdom. Soups, salads, burgers (including vegetarian), sandwiches, and chicken for up to $7. Since the restaurant is large, you've got a good chance of finding a table even if you insist on eating during peak times. (Formerly the Tomorrowland Terrace.)

Lunching Pad at Rockettower   (Lunching pad, get it?!)

The newest Disney food craze: smoked turkey legs and other snacks and beverages, most around $6 or $7. Located near the Astro Orbitor.

The Plaza Pavilion   Between Main Street and Tomorrowland. Pizza, sandwiches (Italian hoagie, chicken parmesan), salads, and ice cream. Up to $7.

Snacks/Drinks

Auntie Gravity's Galactic Goodies   Located at the base of the Astro Orbiter ride. Juice, snacks, frozen yogurt, and fresh fruit. Up to $4.

Where You'll Shop

Geiger's Counter   The place for Disney character hats, with free monogramming available. This is also one of those terribly expensive photo developing drop-off sites. At night they break out those tacky glow-in-the-dark light sticks and fancy flashlights that you'll just love to waste your money on.

Merchants of Venus   Unusual clothing and souvenirs, as well as a robotic tee shirt painting machine that creates customized shirts. This is the place to find official Alien Encounter merchandise—it's the only place in the world this stuff is sold.

Mickey's Star Traders   Disney character clothing and souvenirs. Carries most of what you'll find in Main Street's huge emporium, but Mickey's is often less crowded and has shorter lines at the cash registers.

Ursa Major Minor Mart   Candy, clothes, and gifts. And guess what? More Disney souvenirs. And if your sweet tooth's talking to you, you can pick up some candy here.

Did You Know . . . ?
Probably the least crowded bathroom in the Magic Kingdom is behind the outdoor market at the exit of Pirates of the Caribbean. Sshhhh! Keep this to yourself!

E-TICKET RIDE NIGHTS

If you really dislike lines, here's a great opportunity for you to avoid waiting for some of the Magic Kingdom's most popular attractions. However, this is only available if you have a multi-day admission ticket and you are an on-site Disney resort guest (another reason for staying on Disney property!).

On certain nights, several times a month, a limited number of guests are allowed to remain in the park three hours after closing and the most popular rides remain open exclusively for them. You must purchase a ticket in advance at the guest services desk at your hotel. Then, after 4:00 P.M., you will be able to exchange your ticket for a wristband at locations throughout the Magic Kingdom. The ticket currently costs $10, but it's like you've got the park to yourself, so we believe it is well worth the additional charge—especially during off-peak periods of the year, and especially if you can stay the entire three hours.

The following rides remain open on E-ticket night:

- Alien Encounter

- Astro Orbiter

- Big Thunder Mountain

- Buzz Lightyear's Space Ranger Spin

- Country Bear Jamboree

- Haunted Mansion

- Space Mountain

- Splash Mountain

- Timekeeper

Some food, beverage, and merchandise concessions will be open on E-Ticket Nights, and the Disney characters are also available for photo ops. Sounds great to us!

FREE AT THE MAGIC KINGDOM

Check the park's daily Entertainment Schedule for more details.

The Diamond Horseshoe Saloon Revue   Free Frontierland show reminiscent of those performed in Old West saloons (see page 73 for the details).

Electrical Water Pageant   The Electrical Water Pageant is one of the oldest "parades" in operation at Disney World. It debuted on October 26, 1971 and consists of a number of barges, over one thousand feet long in total, decorated with thousands of twinkling lights, traveling across Bay Lake and the Seven Seas Lagoon. Watch as King Neptune, the Loch News Monster, an octopus, and other aquatic creatures come to life to the sound of synthesized music. And leave it to Disney to end with a star-studded salute to America!

We list it here, under the Magic Kingdom, because it's easier to catch the pageant on a night you're at the Magic Kingdom since it's so close.

The nightly pageant stops at each of the resort hotels, and can be seen at the following times: 9:00 from the Polynesian Resort, 9:15 from the Grand Floridian, 9:35 from Wilderness Lodge, 9:45 from Fort Wilderness, and 10:05 from Contemporary Resort.

Note the following: The Water Pageant takes place only during busy seasons. Check the Magic Kingdom entertainment schedule; it is canceled at the slightest indication of inclement weather.

Fantasy in the Sky Fireworks   Presented nightly when the park is open late, this spectacular fireworks show over Cinderella Castle includes more than two hundred shells that are blown off within five minutes. And if you're relatively close to the castle, you just might see Tinker Bell fly by!

Feature Parade   Held daily (times depend on the season; check the entertainment schedule for times), this parade usually centers around Disney's timeless and beloved animated characters or on a current or upcoming feature film release, which means the show, combining elaborate floats, singers, special effects, and music, changes periodically. Grab a spot early—one of the best places to see the parade is from the Walt Disney World Railroad platform on Main Street, or along the sidewalk in Liberty Square.

And, great news for those who couldn't care less about parades: Take advantage of the fact that all the gawkers are watching the show go by to see some of the Magic Kingdom's best attractions while they are less crowded. While the crowds are watching the parade, you can be screaming down Splash Mountain!

SpectroMagic Parade This dazzling nighttime spectacle—utilizing holograms, 60,000 lights, special effects, and a state-of-the-art sound system—winds it way down Main Street USA twice each night during busy seasons. If you want to see the parade, line up at the curb at least 45 minutes before the starting time. Best viewing spots are in Frontierland where less of a crowd will gather (everyone wants to see the parade from Main Street). Before you choose your final viewing spot, check with a cast member to see which direction the parade will be coming from (it changes with each showing). Then look around and make sure your view isn't blocked by parade crosswalks, lightposts, etc. In other words, sometimes you'll find that your view may be better from the other side of the street!

We'll miss Ye Olde Main Street Electrical Parade, but this one is pretty cool, too!

Hot, Time-Saving Magic Kingdom Tip:

Get to Disney's Contemporary Resort (by bus, car, whatever), then walk to the Magic Kingdom. It's a bit of a hike, but it avoids all the time wasted in long lines taking a ferry or monorail ride from the Transportation and Ticket Center. And, when the park is closing, you'll zip past the crowds on your way home.

5

EPCOT

EPCOT, which stands for Experimental Prototype Community of Tomorrow, Disney World's second major resort park, opened in October 1982. Originally envisioned by Walt to be a real town of the future, it has instead evolved into a combination futuristic theme park and permanent World's Fair. EPCOT tends to appeal more to adults, although Disney has added more and more attractions and sites to appeal to children.

EPCOT Center is made up of two distinct areas, FutureWorld and World Showcase. FutureWorld's eight pavilions, focusing on a futuristic/technological theme, include Journey Into Imagination, the Land, the Living Seas, Spaceship Earth, Test Track, the Universe of Energy, and Wonders of Life. The mirror-image Innoventions East and West buildings round out the offerings in FutureWorld, the first area you reach as you pass through the main entrance turnstiles.

World Showcase celebrates the culture and people of eleven different countries: Canada, China, France, Germany, Italy, Japan, Mexico, Morocco, Norway, the United Kingdom, and the United States. Visitors can reach World Showcase by proceeding from the EPCOT main entrance, through FutureWorld, or via the International Gateway, located near the United Kingdom.

Disney World travel veterans might notice some changes

'round here, in part because Disney's 10-year sponsorships with major companies expired in 1992 and many did not renew. And sadly, several of our favorite attractions have closed, but hopefully not forever!

To stay on top of—and often ahead of—technology, EPCOT has expanded and renovated in recent years, added a new fountain show, and much more. At roughly twice the size of the Magic Kingdom, you'll need at least a day and a half or more to see it all. If you've got young children in tow, it may not take you as long-there are only so many "rides" that they'll enjoy.

Note Regarding Cheap Eats in EPCOT

To save money, we recommend fast-food snacks and dinners, but try to set money aside for at least one nice lunch at one of World Showcase's world-famous restaurants. Lunches often offer the same entrees as dinners at a lower price. Such lunches might be a little bit more expensive than a cheapskate can usually afford, but save your pennies because the food is definitely worth it!

How to Get There

EPCOT Center can be reached by monorail from the Transportation and Ticket Center (TTC), the Grand Floridian, the Polynesian, and the Contemporary Resorts. Disney World buses reach EPCOT from all the theme parks, Disney resorts, and the Transportation and Ticket Center. EPCOT can also be reached through World Showcase, via the International Gateway; water launches from there connect to the Dolphin, Swan, Yacht Club, Beach Club, and BoardWalk resorts. Visitors arriving by car park in the large EPCOT Center lot; the lot is free to Disney hotel guests (others: $5).

Key EPCOT Landmarks

- Baby Needs/Changing Station—Located to the right of Test Track, near what was formerly known as the Odyssey restaurant, which is closed to the general public. (It is currently used for private parties and special events.)

- Banking Services—There are ATMs to the left of Spaceship Earth (as you enter through the park's main gate), and between the countries of Germany and Italy in World Showcase. Personal checks up to $25 can be cashed at Guest Relations in the Innoventions East pavilion.

- Camera Center—At the Entrance Plaza. To save money, we recommend bringing your film, camera, and other supplies with you and waiting until you get home to have your pictures developed. As you would expect, you'll pay more for these products and services at Disney.

- Disney Dollars (Disney's souvenir gift certificates, which work the same as cash in the parks and in Disney Stores)— Available at Earth Station.

- First Aid—On the World Showcase side of the now-closed Odyssey restaurant.

- Lockers—At the Entrance Plaza and at the International Gateway in World Showcase.

- Lost and Found—At the Entrance Plaza.

- Message Center—In the Innoventions East pavilion. You can leave and receive messages for people, whether they're visiting EPCOT, the Magic Kingdom, the Disney-MGM Studios, or Animal Kingdom.

- Package Pickup—At the Entrance Plaza.

- Tour Window—At the Entrance Plaza. Stick with us, and save the added expense of slow-paced, guided tour, which is what you'll get here.

- Wheelchair and Stroller Rentals—Outside the Main Gate, and at the International Gateway in World Showcase.

- WorldKey Information Service—EPCOT's interactive information and reservation system has terminals located in the Innovations East pavilion of FutureWorld, and near Germany in World Showcase. Use the touch screen to make meal reservations (unless you've already done them in advance), plus get detailed information about all of EPCOT's shows, events, and exhibits.

FUTUREWORLD

This is the first area you'll encounter as you enter EPCOT's main gates, which is why it can get crowded early in the morning. Since the Disney execs have decided to inconvenience you in an effort to save some money—as they forego the opening of World Showcase every morning until 11:00 A.M.—FutureWorld is the *only* EPCOT area open first thing in the morning.

FutureWorld Traffic Report

At times, you may encounter ridiculous crowds when you approach a ride. This may be because a neighboring building just disgorged 500-plus guests. You can either come back in a few minutes, or join the line (because the attraction you're about to go on might be able to easily accommodate a huge crowd). Apply this technique throughout Disney World.

What You'll See

The Innoventions Pavilions

Formerly known as Commuicore, the two crescent-shaped buildings that lie just beyond Spaceship Earth and flank the new Fountain of Nations, are now called Innoventions. Visitors can try futuristic video games, computers, and other inventions, many so new they're not yet available for sale and may never be. While the old Communicores seemed to be static, dull, and often overlooked, you can spend hours (if you wanted to) fiddling with the products at Innoventions (though half of that time might be spent fighting the crowds and waiting for a chance to use them).

Innoventions East With your back to Spaceship Earth, the building on the left, Innoventions East, exhibits tomorrow's consumer goods. This four-acre pavilion has been called a cross between a futuristic arcade and a science lab. First see the multimedia show starring Bill Nye the Science Guy to learn what Innoventions has to offer. Visitors can try the latest time-saving appliances and gadgets, virtual reality, interactive media, and more—new inventions are brought in every three months. (Beware: The virtual reality exhibit costs extra, and it can get expensive.)

At the Imagineering Laboratory, witness Disney's Imagineers at work on future attractions. There's also a WorldKey Information kiosk here.

Innoventions West Across the fountain from Innoventions East, here you'll find hands-on exhibits of the latest technology in personal entertainment and communications systems. For example, you can try out wireless digital musical instruments and sound systems, computer and voice recognition systems, virtual travel, and wrist phones, as well as educational and entertaining high-tech gadgets. Sega showcases its latest in mindless video game fun—so beware of these games swallowing up your young ones. All the exhibits here change frequently.

Also in Innoventions West EPCOT Discovery Center—For those inquiring minds who simply have a "need to know" about everything, here is your source for information surrounding the exhibits in EPCOT and Walt Disney World. Whatever your question or interest, you should be able to find an attendant here who has access to a Disney databank on that specific topic.

Resources for Teachers—Teachers will find information here to enhance their knowledge. Much literature, software and collateral material are provided, as well as the ability to interact, via computer, with other teachers throughout the world.

Walt Disney Imagineering Labs—Disney's creative masters use this design laboratory at night, and try out their inventions on you during the day.

Journey Into Imagination Pavilion

This is the strikingly futuristic building that lies beyond the brilliantly colored waterfall and the erratically dancing Leap Frog Fountains.

Honey, I Shrunk the Audience   This Magic Eye Theater is the site of an exceptional 3-D film based on the popular Disney films *Honey, I Shrunk the Kids* and *Honey, I Blew Up the Kid*. Watch what mayhem follows when Professor Wayne Szalinski (Rick Moranis) demonstrates his incredible shrinking machine at the Inventor of the Year Awards ceremony. In this case you, the audience, are the ones who get accidentally shrunk, and thanks to well-produced 3-D effects, you'll get "attacked" by mice, a lion, and a snake.

The film's effects may be too realistic, and booming sound too frightening for smaller kids. If you do decide to see it, we suggest attempting to arrive early in the day or late in the afternoon; and avoid the first few rows where the effects are less realistic. *Don't Miss This! FASTPASS!*

Image Works   You'll walk through this high-tech playground as you exit the Journey Into Imagination ride. These hands-on activities, involving lasers, electronic paintboxes, and the like, appeal mostly to kids. Although many of the exhibits can be fun, don't waste a lot of time here.

Journey Into Imagination   Once upon a time, this was a cute little ride for the young folks. The bewhiskered imp Dreamfinder, and his little friend, Figment, took you on a tour of your imagination. It was a little hokey for adults, but it was one of the few attractions in Epcot that small children could enjoy.

Well, Disney has recently revamped the ride, and tried to make it a ride for older kids. Figment is still around, but Dreamfinder bit the dust. The ride is pretty strange at times and at times may be too intense for young children.

This isn't the most informative or the most rewarding ride. The line is usually negotiable, but if it's not, it's not worth waiting for. Come back later in the day, if for no other reason that to catch some A/C, or skip it.

Leap Frog Fountains These arcing random streams of water outside the Journey Into Imagination building are an attraction unto themselves (although we can't imagine why so many people want to spend valuable attraction-seeing time trying to "catch" the shooting water streams). If you stand in the right place, you just might get wet!

The Land Pavilion

The attractions and exhibits in this huge, round greenhouse-type building deal with one of everybody's favorite things: food.

Circle of Life Located in the pavilion's Harvest Theater. In this new 70-mm film, combining live footage and the animated *Lion King* characters Simba, Timon, and Pumbaa, visitors learn the importance of living in harmony with nature and protecting the environment.

Entertaining, yet informative, and often there's not much of a line. *Don't Miss This!*

Food Rocks A musical review offering a lighthearted message about good nutrition and a balanced diet, starring such notable Audio-Animatronic rock musicians as Pita Gabriel, Chubby Cheddar, and the Peach Boys.

Formerly known as the Kitchen Kabaret, this revamped show is mainly for little kids—if you can get past the characters' names, you just might have a good time, maybe even learn something! (Warning: The music is a bit loud.)

Greenhouse Tour A walking tour, leaving every half hour from 9:30 to 4:30, which begins where the Living With the Land boat ride leaves off. This tour tells much of the same information as the Land boat ride, and it costs $6 ($4 for kids), so you may want to avoid it, unless you're really into agriculture (but who isn't these days?). Reservations required—make them at the Greenhouse Tour Desk.

Living With the Land Located on the lower level, this is a boat ride through simulated rain forest, desert, and prairie environments, and the history of agriculture is discussed along the way. You'll see the latest technological advancements used in growing plants in different environments. Much of the produce and fish raised in these greenhouses is served in the building's Garden Grill Restaurant.

Recently renovated, this is one of Disney's longest rides . . . or maybe it just seems that way. It's fairly interesting, but it might be too serious (read: boring) for younger kids and impatient adults. So, unless the line is short, or you've just got to know how plants grow in outer space, you can safely skip it.

Living Seas Pavilion

Before you enter, check out the crashing surf sign out front (how do they do that?).

Caribbean Coral Reef Ride   After viewing a short film about the sea, you'll descend in your hydrolator (a fancy name for an elevator that really only moves down less than two inches) and ride a Seacab to Sea Base Alpha, a research facility and the world's largest aquarium (that's 5.7 million gallons of water in there). At Sea Base Alpha, take a closer look at more than five-thousand sea creatures, although none are too menacing. If you're lucky, there may be a diver in the tank giving a lecture—maybe even Mickey himself! If not, there's usually a marine biologist on hand to provide information and answer your questions.

The attraction's hands-on exhibits are neat, but don't waste a lot of time in this area: There's usually a backup at the diving suit exhibit, and after you wait, you'll be sorry you did, because it's nothing great. You can hang around Sea Base Alpha as long as you like—in fact, it may be worth nosing around the gift shop awhile till the crowd dies down, affording you a better view of the creatures and exhibits. And don't forget to visit the manatees—many once believed these creatures were mermaids, but none of them (not even the little guy born recently at EPCOT) bears any resemblance to Daryl Hannah. (Incidentally, if you get caught in one of those incredible central Florida downpours, this is a great place to stay dry.) *Don't Miss This!*

Spaceship Earth

Yes, EPCOT's symbol, that giant 180-foot-high silver golf ball, does house a ride. Sci-fi writer Ray Bradbury and Disney's imagineers present the history of communications. To a narration by esteemed actor Jeremy Irons, you'll travel in a "time machine," proceeding from the days of Cro-Magnon man and the origins of language, to the satellite networks of the future. Lifelike Audio-Animatronics and carefully constructed dioramas tell the story in one of EPCOT's longest and best rides, mainly geared to adults and older kids. Don't miss all the small Disney details (real hieroglyphics on the Egyptian temple walls, a real Greek play being recited, and more!).

Spaceship Earth is most crowded first thing in the morning. As a rule, everybody walks through the main gate and right into this ride, but's continuously loading (all the cars are connected in one big ring throughout the ride), so the line moves pretty quickly. We recommend getting on immediately upon entering the park (providing you take our advice and get to EPCOT an hour before its scheduled opening!), or try mid-afternoon, or just check on the length of the line throughout the day. *Don't Miss This!*

Like most Disney attractions, it seems this one has been recently updated with new music, narration, and ending. And whereas you once exited the ride into Earth Station (an EPCOT information center), you now find yourself in the AT&T Global Neighborhood, filled with interactive communications displays of the not-too-distant future. Spend some time checking out these neat hands-on exhibits, especially the mini flight simulators that ring the exhibit area. It's like controlling your own personal Body Wars ride!

(Disney Veterans: Remember those fun restaurant reservation lines in Earth Station, on which you made your meal reservations with a Disney employee you watched on the TV screen while he or she watched you? Well, they're gone! So make your meal reservations up to sixty days before you leave for your Disney trip, or from your room on the night before you reach the park. Call 407-WDW-DINE.)

Test Track Pavilion

Test Track   If you've ever wanted to make like a crash test dummy and take a lap around General Motors's Proving Grounds in Michigan, here's the next best thing! Take a six-passenger electric test vehicle for a ride around what is being billed as Disney's longest (5 1/2 minutes) and fastest (reaching speeds of 65 MPH) attraction ever. Along the way, your car will climb a three-story hill, go through numerous antilock braking and handling tests, and experience hot and cold tests in special environmental chambers. You'll even simulate a 25 MPH crash!

Test Track opened years after its original announced launch date due to incessant mechanical problems. Disney still has problems with this ride and it is occasionally shut down. It takes an hour for the ride to reset itself each time they shut it down. And, even though we've been on the ride on numerous occasions, it has only operated at full speed on one trip.

Here's an important tip! There are two lines for this ride: one for groups traveling together, and one for singles. If you aren't concerned about your group sitting next to each other in the vehicle, take the single line: there's rarely more than a five-minute wait, and usually you'll walk right onto the next car.

If and when they finally get the bugs worked out this will be an exciting ride, with 34 hairpin turns and cornering banks that are steeper than the final drop at Splash Mountain. But we'll never fully endorse Test Track because it replaces one of our favorite attractions, It's Fun to Be Free, which was a fun journey through the evolution of transportation and very rarely was *inoperable!* Still, it is fun to go 65 MPH around the outside track. Kids must be 40 inches tall to ride. *Don't Miss This! FASTPASS!*

Test Track Exhibits   The latest GM vehicles (and futuristic prototypes) are on display here, as well as arcade-type games in which you can test your driving skills. Enter at the side of the building, but we wouldn't spend a lot of time here.

Universe of Energy

Ellen's Energy Adventure   In this pyramid-like, mirrored building, you'll discover how energy (solar, nuclear, and fossil fuel) is created. It's in an innovative moving theater that combines lifesize Audio-Animatronic dinosaurs with short, informative films, featuring comedienne Ellen DeGeneres. If you walk in and it seems crowded, don't be discouraged because the theater seats about 600 people.

The movies may be a little too long for kids' patience (especially the one you'll see at the end of the ride), but once the theater seats separate and you get to dinosaurland, brought to you in real-life smell-o-vision (you got it: they pump in musty, swampy, tropical, sulphury smells in order to make the attraction more lifelike!), you'll win them back over. All kids love dinosaurs! (If they're bored, with any luck, they'll take a nap. If yours is one of the six kids in the world who doesn't like dinosaurs, you may not want to go on this ride because it may be too scary.) Shows run every 17 minutes. *Don't Miss This!*

Wonders of Life Pavilion

Exhibits and attractions regarding health and the inner workings of the human body.

AnaComical Players   Actors and comedians periodically put on an improvisational comedy show in the small open theater near the Fitness Fairgrounds, often involving audience members in the fun. If you're lucky and you happen to time it right, check it out—but it's not worth waiting for.

Body Wars   This is a very rough, bumpy flight-simulator ride through the human body. You are miniaturized and injected into a human body to bring back a technician who has been investigating a splinter (sounds dumb, but it's pretty lifelike). Along the way, your ship gets sped through the circulatory system, attacked by infection-fighting white blood cells, and more high jinks.

Body Wars is similar to Star Tours in the Disney-MGM Studios, but much rougher and the graphics are more intense. One word of advice from someone who tried. Don't videotape in here if you are subject to motion sickness (on second thought, even if you're not). You can get pretty banged up even without a camera to your eye, and you may come close to losing your lunch. *Don't Miss This!*

Those chickens who won't go on the ride can explore the rest of the attractions in the Wonders of Life pavilion. . . .

Cranium Command   Through cartoons and a humorous multimedia presentation, you'll be introduced to an elite corps of brain pilots who are trained to run the human body. Then you become the pilot of a 12-year-old boy during a typical, frenzied school day.

Many people miss this Audio-Animatronic ride, not knowing it's tucked away there in the back of the theater, but it's definitely worth seeing, especially if there's no line. Don't miss the pre-show cartoon or you might not know what's going on. The show runs every 15 minutes. *Don't Miss This!*

Fitness Fairgrounds   A large collection of hands-on activities and exhibits examining lifestyles and fitness. Ride the Wonder Cycles, step into the Coach's Corner (where tennis, golf, and baseball swings are analyzed), and more—but don't waste too much time here.

Goofy About Health   A cartoon starring everybody's favorite dim-witted dog (he is a dog, isn't he?!),, it can be found in the Wonders of Life pavilion.

The Making of Me   A humorous movie discussing the facts of life, presented Disney style, so you know all the gory details will be gently glossed over. But there are some surprising details, as well as a funny turn by comedian Martin Short—use your parental discretion.

The lines are often long here because the theater is small. It's fun, but not worth a long wait.

Where You'll Eat

As with all EPCOT restaurants, we recommend spending more on a delicious (early) lunch, then grabbing some fast-food for dinner and snacks. But the better eating establishments are located in World Showcase, with most of the FutureWorld eats being of the nothing-special variety you can find in any Houlihans/Bennigans/Olive Garden/Denny's-type place. Best to walk the extra feet into World Showcase. But, if you just can't wait to fill your face . . .

Sit-Down

The Garden Grill (The Land) A pleasant restaurant serving typical American food (chicken, fish, steak), served all-you-can-eat, family style. The unique touch here is that the restaurant slowly revolves to give you a pretty good view of the varying ecosystems featured in the Living With the Land attraction. So, if you're faced with long lines for the attraction, eating at the Garden Grill might be a good alternative. This restaurant now offers character dining, so if your kids insist on eating with Mickey, this could be the place. See chapter 9 for more details. Other than that, the restaurant is nothing special and not really worth a special trip . . . or the extra expense. If you're going to pay these prices (most dishes around $20), you might as well walk a little father to one of the World Showcase establishments.

(Interesting Note: All the fish and vegetables served here are actually grown and raised in The Land pavilion.)

Coral Reef (Living Seas) If you seek a nice place (albeit more expensive than most, as far as cheapskates are concerned) to sit down with the family for a decent meal in FutureWorld, we recommend this restaurant, offering seafood, chicken, beef, and pasta. When you arrive, you receive information on what fish you might see swim by in the huge Living Seas' aquarium—one entire wall of the restaurant is a window into the aquarium. (They should also give you postcards of which of these fish you will be *eating*, but we digress.) The seating is multileveled tiers so all can get a good view. The kids will sit still, with their eyes glued to the divers and fish swimming in the tank—we promise.

If you're looking for one good sit-down meal in FutureWorld, this is the place to visit. Ask for a table next to the window—it's worth a shot, although all of the tables will afford you a pretty good view. Lunch and dinner are served, but again, eat lunch here because the prices will be cheaper for similar fare (up to $17 for lunch, over $20 for dinner). Reservations are required and should be made up to 60 days in advance. Call 407-WDW-DINE.

Cafeterias/Food Courts

Sunshine Season Food Fair (The Land)   This food court offers a variety of selections for any appetite—from barbecue to pasta, from salads to ice cream. Up to $8. Usually mobbed, especially by cheapskates.

Fast-Food/Counter Service

Electric Umbrella (Innoventions East)   A counter-service restaurant, serving burgers, chicken sandwiches, hot dogs, salads, and frozen yogurt. Seating can be found indoors (for air conditioning) or out (for people watching). Less expensive than a typical EPCOT sit-down place, open for lunch and dinner, with most entrees under $7.

Pasta Piazza Ristorante (Innoventions West)   A counter-service spot offering all-day dining, although those stopping by to grab a breakfast bite may face a considerable wait early in the day (better to eat breakfast before you arrive in EPCOT; see our itinerary for details). Enjoy everything from an omelet or a pastry to pizza, pasta, and more. You can sit indoors or out here. Less expensive than a typical EPCOT sit-down place (most items under $7); open for breakfast, lunch, and dinner.

Pure and Simple (Wonders of Life)   Across from the Ana-Comical Players' stage. Sandwiches, salads, waffles, fruit, frozen yogurt, juices—all with good nutrition in mind (you know, low fat and all that). How about a tasty beta-carotene salad? Most items under $7.

Snacks/Drinks

Fountain View Espresso and Bakery (Innoventions West)   Offers early to late light dining options: from a cappuccino and a pastry to a glass of wine, most offerings under $5. As its name implies, this place offers you a pretty good view from its outdoor terrace of the water shows at the Fountains of Nations. But you can expect many other visitors will have the same idea, so check the entertainment schedule when you enter the park and pick a good viewing locale at least a half hour before showtime.

Ice Station Cool This isn't exactly a counter-service restaurant, rather a chance to sample exotic flavors of sodas from around the world produced by Coca-Cola. We'll admit most flavors are a little too weird for our liking, but the ginger ale and—believe it or not—watermelon flavor, aren't too bad. But the best part is that it is free, so if you feel like wetting your whistle, it's worth stopping by. To get to the sampling room you will walk through a corridor with walls reportedly made out of ice, and just doing *that* on a hot summer's day is a treat in itself.

Where You'll Shop

The Art of Disney EPCOT (Innoventions East) An art gallery selling Disney animation art and other high-priced collectibles. A nice place for the cheapskate to visit, but you wouldn't want to shop here!

MouseGear (Innoventions East) One of the best and largest stores in all of Walt Disney World, the MouseGear sells books, videos, and other sorts of Disney merchandise and EPCOT souvenirs, on many levels. You'll also find one of the largest selections of tee shirts and sweatshirts in the parks. It's a great place to kill some time during the occasional downpour.

Camera and Film (Journey Into Imagination) Film and camera accessories and a large collection of Figment character merchandise.

Green Thumb Emporium (The Land) Chef Mickey strikes again. This time you'll see his likeness on a wide variety of kitchen accessories and gadgets. Gardeners can also find some imaginative gifts in this shop.

Sea Base Alpha (Living Seas) Gifts with a marine theme. Whales, dolphins, and manatees abound in all sorts of incarnations—from statues to key chains to refrigerator magnets.

Gateway Gifts (Spaceship Earth)   Disney character souvenirs. Your last chance before leaving the park to pick up that tee shirt you've been mulling over all day.

Camera Center (Spaceship Earth)   Film, cameras, and accessories; video camcorder rentals. Complimentary video camera battery recharging (that's nice); photo developing (that's not nice, that's expensive).

Well and Goods (Wonders of Life)   Sports-themed merchandise with Goofy as the star player. This is the place to buy a soccer shirt with—you guessed it—our favorite goofball's likeness. Sports items range from golf balls to water bottles to sweats.

Most Deserted FutureWorld Rest Rooms

- the Land pavilion, next to the Garden Grill
- The Living Seas, near the entrance to the Coral Reef restaurant

---

WORLD SHOWCASE

Disney's version of a permanent World's Fair, with 11 "countries" located along the one-and-a-quarter-mile-long promenade that surrounds the World Showcase Lagoon. This area is more for adults than kids, with much more to see, than to do or participate in. Young families can go through World Showcase faster than most, because there are fewer kiddie rides here. But *all* of the countries, with their unique shops, charm, and architecture (inspired by notable buildings and styles around the world), are worth a visit, if for no other reason than to share the culture of the people who work in the different countries—yes, the people you encounter in each country really live in that country most of the year. Every EPCOT employee we've ever met has been fun-loving and cordial, and each has had an interesting story to tell.

Once upon a time, smart Disney vacationers used to run to World Showcase as soon as the EPCOT gates first opened, thus bypassing the swarming crowds who stopped at the first attractions they came to (i.e., FutureWorld). This would afford those in World Showcase almost no lines in practically any country. By the time the crowds made their way to World Showcase, those who were there early had seen everything they wanted to see, and could make their way to a less-crowded FutureWorld.

Alas, the Disney brass caught on to our ploy, and now they don't open World Showcase until 11:00 A.M., some two hours after FutureWorld opens. God knows why they did this—maybe it saves money on salaries. However, these savings have not been passed on to ticket buyers! So, when you arrive, grab an entertainment schedule and see when World Showcase opens. Check our itinerary for tips on touring and making the most of this dumb Disney policy.

Traveling Tip:

The FriendShips that ply the water of World Showcase may look tempting, but you're better off walking. The time you spend waiting for the next ship to arrive could be time well spent touring World Showcase.

If you find yourself captivated by culture, architecture, and people of the "countries" you visit, why not plan a trip to see the real thing? Each World Showcase pavilion includes an information center/tourism office.

A variety of live performers from the different countries

This may make kids appreciate World Showcase more

If your children aren't real big on learning about the different countries and cultures of World Showcase, maybe you can trick them into having a good time. Buy each kid an EPCOT passport, available just about everywhere in the park. This passport includes a set of stamps for each country in World Showcase. As you see the world around the lagoon, have a cast member stamp the passport and write something in his or her native language. Who knows, your kid may actually learn a thing or two about other cultures!

entertain throughout the day in the World Showcase. Check out the entertainment schedule for show times. While we wouldn't make a special trip to see them, if you're in the area and a show is about to begin, it might be worth a few minutes of happy diversion.

What You'll See

The American Adventure

As host country to this Disneyesque World's Fair, this pavilion is the centerpiece of World Showcase and the site of one of EPCOT's most entertaining and informative attractions.

The American Adventure   Housed in a building reminiscent of Philadelphia's Independence Hall, built of 110,000 handmade bricks, this is Disney's most realistic Audio-Animatronics show. And at thirty minutes, it's one of the longest— which is great, since it's so entertaining.

Mark Twain and Ben Franklin are your guides on a patriotic journey through America's rich history, from the landing of the Mayflower to World War II. Guest stars include George Washington, Theodore Roosevelt, Susan B. Anthony, and many others in a multimedia spectacular combining robots, authentic props, film, slides, music, and more. Again, check the attention to details, including Twain's smoking cigar, Will Roger's spinning lasso . . . and just how in the world do they get Ben Franklin to climb steps?!

If you can, catch the pre-show entertainment, the Voices of Liberty, an a cappella group singing timeless patriotic classics. Check the entertainment schedule for times.

The American Adventure is a timeless Disney classic that was already great, even before recent updates and enhancements. *Don't Miss This!*

The American Gardens Theater   This lagoon-front theater offers live entertainment throughout the day, including concerts featuring traditional American music, folk dances, and frequent celebrity appearances. Check your entertainment schedule for all the details.

Canada

From the towering totem poles to the craggy landscape of the Canadian Rockies, step into Canada and you'll feel like . . . you're in Canada! The Caledonia Bagpipe Band performs regularly throughout the day—check your entertainment schedule.

O Canada! A sweeping eighteen-minute film that travels across the country that lies to the north and brings a Circle-Vision 360 camera along for the memorable ride. Enjoy Canada's beautiful unspoiled scenery and cosmopolitan cities. Again, there are no seats in the theater; and, as mentioned earlier in the description of Tomorrowland's Timekeeper attraction, to best enjoy the film, look around you periodically to check all the different views of the same scene. It's the next best thing to being there.

China

The centerpiece of this exhibit is the half-scale model of Beijing's Temple of Heaven, surrounded by exotic gardens and landscaped pools with traditional Chinese music piped in. Make sure you stop in as you leave the theater at the Chinese art exhibition in the House of the Whispering Willows.

Wonders of China This fast-paced film presents the people and culture of China, as narrated by an actor portraying poet Li Po of ancient China. There are no seats inside, as the eighteen-minute film is shot in Circle-Vision 360—with screens surrounding the audience portraying different views of the same scene. (To get the most of the movie, don't forget to look all around you while the film is playing.)

The film is enlightening and entertaining . . . but probably more so for parents than kids.

France

No, that's not the real Eiffel Tower, but an incredible simulation, along with the rest of France, with authentic architecture, landscaping, shops, and food. Check your entertainment schedule—you might be able to catch a performance by a mime or an act by "The Living Statues."

Impressions de France   Not quite Circle-Vision 360, this attractive eighteen-minute film, which celebrates the landscape, culture, and people of France is set to the lilting music of legendary French composers and is shown on a 200-degree semicircular screen. Sure, bring the kids, get 'em some culture. The worst they can do is fall asleep, and you'll enjoy the movie. And *this* theater has *seats!*

Germany

No attractions here to speak of, aside from some typical Bavarian architecture, shops, and eats (read on for our descriptions and recommendations). But if you time your visit just right, you'll hear the cool clock in the town hall chime.

Italy

No attractions or rides, but plenty of classic architecture: Check out the re-creation of the Venetian Campanile and the Doges' Palace, as well as the Fontana de Nettuno (many pose for pictures here).

Japan

A red *torii* gate graces the shore of World Showcase Lagoon at the entrance to this, one of EPCOT's most beautiful countries, made up of peaceful gardens, fish ponds, wind chimes, a classic Japanese pagoda, and more. Check your entertainment schedule for live traditional music and dancing performed several times daily. And don't miss the performance by Miyuki, who sculpts mythical creatures from unassuming blocks of sugar candy—sometimes even while blindfolded.

Mexico

One of the most unique pavilions at EPCOT. You enter what appears to be a Mayan temple (check out the Mexican and pre-Colombian artifacts as you pass through), and find yourself looking down at the cool, perpetually nighttime scene of a Mexican open-air market, with shops, villas, and a smoking volcano in the distance. It's like being outside, but you're *inside* and it's air conditioned!

El Rio del Tiempo This charming boat ride, reminiscent in some ways of Magic Kingdom's It's a Small World, is the closest thing Disney World has to a Tunnel of Love ride. It's pretty tame—without the bells, whistles, and technology of some of the other rides you encounter—and it's among the least crowded rides in EPCOT. So steal a smooch with a loved one, even if the ride is pretty simplistic.

Morocco

Enter this faithfully constructed replica of a Moroccan town, with sites and architecture reminiscent of the mysterious Northern African country. Be sure to visit the "Treasures of Morocco" exhibit and view the handiwork of Moroccan craftsmen.

Norway

The Old World charm of Norway comes through in the architecture and sights of this little "town." There are replicas of a fourteenth century fort and a medieval church, among other quaint buildings that surround a cobblestone courtyard.

Maelstrom As of this writing, this is World Showcase's only thrill ride, and way too short for our money. Ride a Viking ship through Norway, past and present, replete with special effects, lighting, and Audio-Animatronics (including a sometimes-too-scary-for-kids three-headed troll that attacks the boat several times. Warning: you may get wet!). *Don't Miss This!*

Being one of EPCOT's most thrilling rides, its line can often be long—especially if the neighboring Wonders of China has just let out. If there are people waiting well into the courtyard, you might consider coming back later because there's also a huge serpentine line inside the building. And again, bear in mind that this one is quite dark and somewhat scary for small children.

Something to do while you're waiting on this often long line: Look for the hidden Mickeys on the mural where you board your boat. We'll give you a hint—look closely at the helmets the Vikings are wearing. The other two are a little harder to find!

Go to church and get cool

A lot of people don't realize it but you can go inside the wooden church and escape for a minute from the Florida sun and heat. Check it out!

United Kingdom

An authentic British street, replete with traditional and varied architecture (even one with a "thatched" roof!), shops, gardens . . . even those funny red phone booths! Check your entertainment schedule to see when the street comedy troup will be performing.

Where You'll Eat

Sit-Down

We recommend trying at least one of the ethnic restaurants you'll find in World Showcase, but remember: You will pay more (more than $20 per meal, in many cases). But hey, you can't eat fast food every day (your arteries will never let you forget it)! Check the menus at each place to make sure you can find something you like. And, if possible, make your reservations early (up to sixty days before your visit, or at least from your hotel room the night before your visit).

Le Cellier Steakhouse (Canada) If you're looking for a good ol' juicy hunka red meat, this is about as good as you can get in the World Showcase, although this steakhouse also offers some fish and poultry dishes. The dining room resembles an old wine cellar—very dark and cool—and is a nice escape from the hot Florida sun. Le Cellier was once an uncrowded cafeteria, but now offers full waitress service. Lunch to $15, dinner $15 and up.

Nine Dragons (China)   Nothing real exotic or out of the ordinary, merely traditional, exceptional Chinese meals, served in a huge, formal Chinese dining room, with selections that reflect the varied cuisine of all the Chinese provinces, including Mandarin, Cantonese, Hunan, and Szechuan.

For our money (most dishes are less than $15), this is the best Chinese food this side of the Great Wall.

Les Chefs de France (France)   EPCOT's most expensive restaurant, and not recommended for the cheapskate. Unless you like Jerry Lewis like many natives of France, or you're a connoisseur of all things French, we believe you'll find much more for your money at one of the many other World Showcase restaurants.

L'Originale Alfredo di Roma Ristorante (Italy)   The finest Italian food you ever ate . . . or *will* ever eat! The owners of this restaurant (which has branches in New York city, Miami Beach, and Rome) claim to have thunk up the pasta delicacy known as fettucini Alfredo (thus, the dish's name). We don't know if that's really true, but if you order the dish, they just may make a believer of you. If you're a fettucini Alfredo fan, it's the best you'll ever have. Other pastas, as well as chicken, veal, and seafood, are also available.

Strolling musicians and singing waiters periodically entertain diners throughout the restaurant at dinnertime. Lunch to $20, dinner over $15.

Tempura Kiku (Japan)   At this often-overlooked, small restaurant located near the Teppanyaki dining area, you sit around a tempura grill. If you're familiar with and enjoy this unique form of battered Japanese chicken, seafood, beef, and vegetables, plus sushi, you should be able to pick up a relatively quick bite here. Many items under $15.

Teppanyaki Dining Room (Japan) A unique dining experience: Disney's version of Benihana. You sit at a large communal table that surrounds a stainless steel grill. Soon a Japanese chef takes his place and prepares your food while you watch (and, because he is a maestro of the knife, fork, and seasoning, his preparation methods are something to watch!). Selections include beef, chicken, seafood, and vegetables, all stir-fried fresh, while-u-wait. Lunch to $15, dinner over $15.

San Angel Inn Restaurante (Mexico) Arguably EPCOT's most romantic eating place: The setting is a large, outdoor café (really, indoor and air-conditioned, so there's nary a bug in sight), situated between El Rio del Tiempo and the Mexican market. Under the pavilion's "evening sky" (painted ceiling!), you'll enjoy round-the-clock candlelight at your table, along with some pretty good (if mild) Mexican dishes of seafood, beef, chicken, chilies, rice, and more. Lunch to $15, dinner over $15.

Restaurant Marrakesh (Morocco) One of World Showcase's least crowded restaurants, probably because most timid vacationers have never eaten Moroccan food and are afraid to try it. That's too bad, because if you bypass this place, you're missing some of the best food in all of EPCOT (actually, that's *not* too bad, because then there's more room in the restaurant for the rest of us!).

In an exotic dining room, you'll enjoy traditional Moroccan dishes—featuring beef, lamb, fish, and chicken concoctions—as well as free entertainment provided by musicians and belly dancers. (Note: the show typically starts twenty minutes after the hour, so plan your meal accordingly.) If you've never tried Moroccan food before, why not be adventurous? This may be the only chance you'll get to experience it. Check the menu out front; we're sure you'll find something on it that you'll like. Lunch to $15, dinner over $15.

Rose and Crown Dining Room (United Kingdom) Authentic English delicacies—steak and kidney pie, prime rib, fish and chips, bangers and mash, Yorkshire pudding—offered in a traditional English pub setting. If you choose to eat here, we recommend trying to get a table outside on the terrace over-looking World Showcase Lagoon, a spot that offers excellent views of the fireworks and laser shows, IllumiNations. Lunch to $15, dinner over $15.

Cafeterias/Food Courts

Biergarten (Germany)   If you want to sample some excep-tional, authentic German cuisine—wursts (that's German for sausage), sauerbraten, spaetzle, potato salad, red cab-bage—we suggest you stop in here. The buffet-style restau-rant's decor is that of an outdoor Bavarian town square (but, of course, it's indoors and air conditioned). You are seated at large communal tables, so socializing is encouraged.

You might as well arrange to eat your meal during the time they have scheduled short performances. These include tradi-tional dancers, yodelers, and musicians, who give you a taste of Octoberfest every day, and the shows (although relatively short) won't cost you extra. Check the schedule at the door. Lunch to $15, dinner $15 and up.

Restaurant Akershus (Norway)   If a hot and cold all-you-can-eat buffet of fish, poultry, meats, salads, vegetables, and cheeses floats your Viking boat, then check out this un-crowded Norway establishment, set in a medieval fortress din-ing room. Lunch buffet $13, dinner $19.

Fast-Food/Counter Service

Liberty Inn (American Adventure)   Typical fare you can get in any American burger joint, i.e., burgers, hot dogs, chicken breast sandwiches, fries, fruit, ice cream, and good old American apple pie. Up to $7.

Lotus Blossom Café (behind Nine Dragons) (China) Sweet-and-sour and stir-fry dishes, egg rolls, soup. Up to $7.

Sommerfest (Germany)   Bratwurst sandwiches, soft pret-zels, apple strudel, black forest cake, and more, are served in an outdoor café. Up to $5.

Yakitori House (Japan)   Brochettes (a fancy name for small shish kebabs) of shrimp, beef, or chicken, and actually quite a tasty snack. Up to $7.

Cantina de San Angel (Mexico)   An outdoor Mexican café overlooking World Showcase Lagoon. This one is *really* outside under the blazing Florida sun, so find a table with an umbrella. Burritos, tortillas, tacos, tostados, churros, nachos, and frozen margaritas. Up to $7.

Kringla Bakeri og Kafe (Norway)   A nice outdoor café offering open-faced sandwiches, pastries, waffles, and more. Up to $5.

Rose and Crown Pub (United Kingdom)   Snacks and ales offered in a traditional English pub setting. Many items from $7 to $10. Same-day reservations are necessary (make them at the usual places: WorldKey information booths or at the restaurant itself).

Snacks/Drinks

Refreshment Port (Canada)   Frozen yogurt, cookies, fruit, and more, most under $7.

Boulangerie Patisserie (France)   A traditional French bakery, serving all those rich goodies, like pastries, croissants, eclairs, chocolate mousse, and strong coffees, most around $5.

La Maison du Vin (France)   (That means House of Wine, for all you uncultured readers!) Sample fine wines, but chances are, if you're a cheapskate, you'll choose to bypass the place!

Weinkeller (Germany)   No food, just wine, but no seats.

Matsu No Ma Lounge (Japan)   An often-overlooked second-floor cocktail lounge with a nice view of World Showcase. It offers traditional Japanese drinks (sip that sake before it grows cold!), as well as sashimi and sushi, most items under $9.

Refreshment Outpost (Between Germany and China)   Frozen yogurt, fruit, vegetarian treats, and ice cream, most under $6 or $7.

Where You'll Shop

One of the favorite pastimes of Disney vacationers is shopping in World Showcase. Where else can you find souvenirs from all over the world and never leave Florida?

The American Adventure

Heritage Manor Americana and antique reproductions, including a large collection of Coca-Cola memorabilia. Homemade crafts with a country theme, including dolls, wall hangings, and wreaths.

Canada

La Boutique des Provinces Authentic Canadian merchandise, with a predominantly French theme, and more refined than those items featured at Northwest Mercantile.

Northwest Mercantile Canadian merchandise with the rustic outdoors in mind. Indian artifacts, toy tomahawks and moccasins, miniature teepees made from tree bark (now who wouldn't want one of these!), lumberjack shirts—just perfect for a hot Florida day.

China

Yong Feng Shangdian Shopping Gallery Located at the exit of the China exhibit, this large shopping plaza offers an extensive collection of goods from China, from silk robes to paper fans. Good assortment of very reasonably priced gifts and small toys for the little ones.

France

Galerie des Halles Located at the exit to Impressions de France, this indoor French market changes its stock periodically.

La Signature Expensive French perfumes and bath products. If you're smart you'll just stand at the door and enjoy the scent for free.

La Maison du Vin (*Vin* = wine, for all you unwashed masses out there.) Fine (i.e., expensive) French wines, brought to you by Barton and Guestier. Cheapskates will want to stick with the homegrown variety available at their local liquor stores.

Plume et Palette This store is definitely not for the cheapskate! Fine porcelain and miniatures from Limoges, France; tapestries fit for a castle; and original oil paintings by well-known French artists. Just look, but don't buy!

Germany

Der Bucherwurm Quaint bookstore that has a nice assortment of books (written in English, of course) dealing with German culture and architecture.

Der Teddybär As the name suggests, this toy store sells adorable teddy bears made by Steiff and Hermann, as well as LGB trains and beautiful German dolls. We can't afford any of them, but they do have an assortment of reasonably priced toys, too.

Die Weihnachts Ecke Beautiful collection of Christmas ornaments and collectibles, all made in Germany. Items vary from inexpensive blown glass and wooden ornaments to collectible nutcrackers that sell for hundreds of dollars.

Glas und Porzellan Glass and porcelain made by Goebel, the company that manufactures Hummel figurines. In fact, if you time it right, you might actually see a Goebel artist here demonstrating how the figurines are made.

Suessigkeiten Junk food, German style. Butter cookies, chocolate cookies, and a variety of goodies to quell your sweet tooth, made by Bahlsen (they're all real good!). And who could pass up that chewy German delicacy—Gummi Bears!

Volkskunst A vast array of cuckoo clocks and German beer steins. We particularly like the handpainted eggs done by a German-born artist, painted with an assortment of Disney characters. Worth looking at, but too expensive for us, we're afraid.

Weinkeller   This wine store stocks 250 varieties of German wines, and wine tastings are held daily.

Italy

Delizie Italiane   Another place to calm your sweet tooth with chocolates and cookies made by Perugina.

Il Bel Cristallo   Armani porcelain collectibles and figurines. Some of the figurines are taken from scenes straight out of the Disney classic movies. But you'll have to break the bank before you can buy one.

La Cucina Italiana   Gourmet foods and wines from Italy.

Japan

Mitsukoshi Department Store   As the name implies, this is a real department store, stocking a variety of items from silk kimonos to chopsticks. You can even buy an oyster here and have them open it in front of your eyes. Each one is guaranteed to have a pearl, which they then clean and will fashion into a piece of jewelry for you (for an additional charge!).

Mexico

Artesanias Mexicanas   Handblown glass giftware presented by Arribas Brothers. Glass etching can be done to personalize your gifts.

El Ranchito del Norte   Gifts and souvenirs from the northern region of Mexico.

La Familia Fashions   Mexican clothing for women and children, some featuring beautiful examples of Mexican embroidery. This shop also has an assortment of silver and turquoise jewelry.

Plaza de los Amigos   If you ever wondered where those large sombreros come from, this is the place. The "outdoor" market also has a large variety of Mexican goods that's reasonably priced, including pottery, wooden toys, and piñatas.

Morocco

The Brass Bazaar If it's made of brass, there's a good chance you'll find it here, along with a nice selection of planters and pots.

Casablanca Carpets Hand-knotted Berber carpets and Rabat carpets, designed with bold, brightly colored mosaics—most will not fly, we suspect. Handwoven bedspreads and throw pillows are also for sale.

Marketplace in the Medina Leather goods (sheepskin wallets and handbags) and straw hats and bags. Handwoven baskets and bamboo furniture, straight from Marrakesh.

Medina Arts and Berber Oasis A variety of authentic Moroccan merchandise. More handcrafted brasswork and baskets, and leather items.

Tangier Traders If you're looking for a fez, look no further! This store also carries an assortment of Moroccan clothing and accessories such as leather sandals and belts.

Norway

The Puffin's Roost This long row of several continuous stores features many items that are way out of the range of your average cheapskate (unless you don't mind shelling out $100 to $300 for Norwegian wool sweaters). But it's still fun to window-shop. The stores also feature items that are less astronomically priced, including Lego sets (Aren't they manufactured in Denmark? Just wondering.), hand-carved trolls of varying sizes (Norway, after all, is the land of the trolls), plus jewelry and knickknacks. Visit the Christmas corner and add a little Scandinavian flavor to your next holiday celebration.

United Kingdom

The Crown and Crest Everything you need when it comes to pubware—if for some reason you need to stock a pub! And if you wish to check the history of your family name, they may be able to help here.

The Magic of Wales   Gifts and handcrafted items made in Wales. The prices here are very reasonable compared to the other stores of the United Kingdom.

Pringle of Scotland   Lambswool and cashmere apparel brought to you by the UK's most famous maker of fine woolen goods. Sweaters, kilts, and scarves; all too rich for a cheapskate's blood!

The Queen's Table   Presented by Royal Doulton, this store has a vast array of figurines known as the Royal Doulton ladies. These porcelain figurines are beautifully crafted and can sell for as much as $12,500.

The Tea Caddy   Brought to you by R. Twinings & Co., Ltd., this authentic-looking tea house has a selection of fine teas offered in a variety of flavors, sold by the box or tin. It also sells teapots and tea strainers.

The Toy Soldier   Fine British toys and pastimes. Teddy bears, Corgi cars and trucks, children's books, and an array of collectible dolls.

International Crossroads

Showcase Gifts   A small souvenir stand that offers a limited selection of Disney character items. It primarily serves as the package pickup depot for those guests exiting via International Crossroads.

World Traveler   The usual assortment of Disney merchandise—shirts, figurines, and souvenirs. There's a large selection of Mickey watches and clocks.

Miscellaneous

Disney Traders (east side of Showcase Plaza)   Disney character merchandise with an international theme. Sunglasses and film are also available.

Port of Entry (west side of Showcase Plaza)   Christmas gifts and decorations from around the world and a large collection featuring your favorite Disney characters.

FREE AT EPCOT

Check the park's daily Entertainment Schedule for more details.

IllumiNations   EPCOT's exceptional fireworks-music-laser-water show, which takes place in and around World Showcase Lagoon. Even if you've seen it before, see it again. In fact, see it every time you come to Disney World (check EPCOT's entertainment schedule for times). We recommend grabbing a good viewing spot along World Showcase Lagoon at least forty-five minutes ahead of time, and choosing a spot in Mexico or Canada, or along the promenade between the United Kingdom and France (if you're leaving via the International Gateway), because once the show is over, everybody (read: tens of thousands of people) heads for the exit, and at least you'll have a head start on most of the crowd.

And be sure to check the wind direction in advance. You don't want to be standing in the smoke residue from the fireworks of this 14-minute show.

If you're already seen IllumiNations, and contrary to our suggestion, have no interest in seeing it again, take advantage of the crowd's distraction and check out the most popular rides in the park.

Hot, Time-Saving, Getting to EPCOT Tip:

Get to Disney's Beach Club Resort, then enter EPCOT/World Showcase through the less-crowded International Gateway entrance.

6

Disney-MGM Studios

Disney World's third major entertainment complex, Disney-MGM Studios, captures both the glamour of Hollywood's Golden Age and the nuts and bolts of a working studio. Opened in 1989, the park was designed to compete with the soon-to-be-opening Universal Studios in Orlando (which has since opened). During its first year, Disney-MGM was, frankly, rather small. With a little luck—and a well-thought-out itinerary—you could see most of the studio in just a few hours.

All of that has changed. Disney-MGM Studios has more than doubled in size since its opening, with more than thrill rides, interesting restaurants, and some of Disney's most worthwhile live stage shows (you'll actually *enjoy* the shows, thinking little of the attractions you may be missing). Now it will take you most of one entirely enjoyable day to see it all. And toward the end of that day, the park becomes less crowded as people who have seen their fill head out.

We've broken the park up into its different areas: Hollywood Boulevard, Sunset Boulevard, Hollywood Hills, Animation Courtyard, Mickey Avenue, New York Street, and Commissary Lane/Echo Lake. Although these "neighborhoods" are not as clearly defined as, say, the lands in the Magic Kingdom, discussing the park this way will make your planning easier and your sightseeing virtually hassle-free.

Note Regarding Cheap Eats in Disney-MGM Studios

Disney-MGM Studios offers inexpensive fast-food and snacks, plus some of Disney's most interesting themed restaurants. In order to get more bang for your entertainment buck, we recommend a sit-down, themed restaurant for lunch and, if you're still in the park, a fast-food dinner or snack. As with all Disney sit-down places, we recommend you make your reservations early: either up to 60 days before your visit, or from your room the day before. Call Disney Dining Reservations at 407-WDW-DINE.

How to Get There

Disney World buses serve the Disney-MGM Studios from all the theme parks and Disney resorts. You can reach the park by boat from the Dolphin, Swan, Yacht Club, Beach Club, and Board Walk resorts. Visitors arriving by car park in the lot at the Disney-MGM Studios; the lot is free to Disney hotel guests (others: $5).

Key Disney-MGM Studios Landmarks

- Baby Needs/Changing Station—Next to Guest Services at park's entrance

- Banking Services—There is an ATM located outside the park's Entrance Plaza. Personal checks can be cashed at Guest Services, also near the Entrance Plaza.

- First Aid—Next to Guest Services, at the park's Entrance Plaza

- Information—Guest Services

- Lockers—Located at Oscar's Classic Car Souvenirs on Hollywood Boulevard

- Lost and Found, Lost Persons—Guest Services

- Message Center—Leave and retrieve messages for other guests here via Disney's computer that links all three parks. Located in Guest Relations.

- Production Window—Stop by to see if there are any shows or films being taped on the lot during your visit.

- Stroller Rentals—Strollers are available for $6 ($5 plus $1 deposit) per day for a single, or $11 for a double. Save money (and time waiting on the rental line) and bring your own.

- Wheelchair Rentals—At Oscar's Classic Car Souvenirs on Hollywood Boulevard

If you've visited Disney-MGM before and you're back for another fun visit, odds are you won't recognize the place. Now under new management, the studios have undergone many gazillions of dollars worth of renovations, expansions, and improvements as of late, and there are many more changes to come. Chances are, by the time you read this, what you're reading is outdated. If so, we're sorry; please let us know what's changed, and we'll correct future editions.

HOLLYWOOD BOULEVARD

This is the first thoroughfare you step onto as you enter the park. It is made up mainly of shops and information areas, but also has one of Disney's best attractions. Strange costumed characters of the Hollywood variety roam the street periodically—you may run into a starlet looking to be discovered, an up-and-coming movie director, a ragtag band dressed in unusual attire, and others. Don't let them distract you from your mission: to see as much as you can as quickly as possible!

What You'll See

The Great Movie Ride Housed in a full-scale replica of the famous Grauman's Chinese Theater in Hollywood—right down to the hand- and footprints in the cement courtyard out front—this is arguably the Studio's most enjoyable entertainment experience. You'll literally ride right through some of the most famous scenes from some of the most memorable movies of all time. You're part of the action in intricately detailed, true-to-the-original scenes from *Singin' in the Rain, Mary Poppins, Alien, Casablanca, The Wizard of Oz, Raiders of the Lost Ark,* and more. There's some hokey repartee between your guide and some of the movie characters (Audio-Animatronic robots), but we can overlook that. Your guide's mood—more specifically, just how sick he or she is of repeating these same lines seventy-three times a day—can affect your ride, but the guides we've had have all had a lot of enthusiasm, so that helps.

The Great Movie Ride is one you can go on again and again and see something new and enjoy it every time, although sometimes a huge line can deter you from doing so (it's best to go early in the day—see our itinerary later in this book for details). Kids will appreciate the ride more if they're familiar with the films. But, even if they're not, they can appreciate a well-thought-out, no-expense-spared attraction when they see one.

Pay attention to the pre-ride show (i.e., to the exhibit of movie memorabilia interspersed throughout the snaking ride line), as well as to the movie trailers shown on the big screen right before you enter the boarding area. They don't make movies like that anymore! *Don't Miss This!*

Where You'll Eat

Sit-Down

The Hollywood Brown Derby Re-creates Hollywood's famous restaurant of the same name, right down to the caricatures on the wall and the famous Cobb (turkey) salad. It also serves grilled beef, lamb, pork, roasted chicken, pasta, and seafood. Check the prices (lunches under $20, dinners over $20), chances are this place is out of your price range. But don't sweat it; there are more exciting and less expensive places elsewhere in the park.

Snacks/Drinks

Starring Rolls Bakery Fresh-baked goods, pastries, pies, most under $5. A great place to grab a quick breakfast.

Where You'll Shop

As with the rest of the Disney parks, the most important thing to do first is to see the attractions. Save your shopping—especially the first shops you reach on Hollywood Boulevard—until later in the day, before you are ready to leave. If you do buy some things during the day and you don't want to carry your packages onto the rides, Disney will hold them for you. Just tell the cashier you want to arrange for the packages to be held for later pickup. If you're staying on-site, you can arrange to have the items shipped directly to your room!

Celebrity 5&10   Tee shirts, mugs, keychains, and buttons—typical theme park souvenirs, all with the Disney-MGM Studios logo.

Cover Story   Have your picture superimposed over a variety of major magazine covers, such as *Sports Illustrated.*

Crossroads of the World   This circular store is located right in the middle of the entrance plaza, as soon as you walk into the park. It's small and offers the basic souvenirs, film, and ponchos.

The Darkroom   A camera store with film, disposable cameras, and accessories for sale. Kodak video cameras are for rent here at $25 a day. However, you must leave a $300 deposit to rent a camera (which can be charged to a major credit card). Bring your video camera from home!

Keystone Clothiers   Better quality Mickey character clothing for men and women. Most of it is beautifully embroidered instead of cheesily printed. A good selection of jewelry, accessories, and watches.

L.A. Prop and Storage   A children's clothing store, featuring character merchandise from some of Disney's most recent animated movies: *Toy Story, Mulan,* and a variety of merchandise starring the Disney princesses.

Mickey's of Hollywood, Pluto's Toy Palace, Disney & Co.   These stores all run into each other and basically carry all the souvenirs, tee shirts, and Mickey stuff you could ever want. This is the place to go for all your Disney-MGM Studios logo items—keychains, bumper stickers, and buttons.

Oscar's Classic Car Souvenirs   This neat shop, done up like a post-World II service station, complete with a vintage-era car and old-time pumps out front, reminds us of a bygone era when gas stations were spotless, and the nattily dressed folks who worked there delivered service with a smile. However, in this station you can't buy gas, or even windshield washer fluid, but, rather, a wide selection of collectibles, souvenirs, and memorabilia dealing with cars. Worth visiting, if for no other reason than to appreciate Disney's famed attention to detail.

Sid Cahuenga's One-of-a-Kind   Authentic movie memorabilia is for sale in this tacky Hollywood-style store. Autographs of the stars, movie posters, and collectibles worn or used by the actors are offered. It's almost a museum in itself.

Sweet Success   All kinds of delectable candy are available at this shop. Hard candy sold in Disney-decorated tins makes a great gift to bring back to your friends.

SUNSET BOULEVARD

Enter the world of postwar Hollywood as you stroll down the Boulevard. This area features an outdoor theater, with a fabulous stage show, and many shops, but no real attractions. Its basic purpose is as a thoroughfare to Hollywood Hills, home of the park's best thrill rides.

What You'll See

Theater of the Stars   This shaded outdoor amphitheater is a reproduction of the famous Hollywood Bowl, and periodically changing live shows take place here throughout the day. Check the entertainment schedule—the show as of this writing was *Beauty and the Beast Live on Stage*. The characters come to life in a musical show based on the hit film. Some youngsters complained that the songs are not in the same order as the movie, i.e., "Be Our Guest" is sung first.

Since this 20-minute show is presented in an outdoor theater, don't go in the middle of the day in the summer, unless you want to know what it feels like to be an egg frying on the pavement. And bear in mind that the intent of live shows such as this is to distract you from the real attractions so the lines become smaller. So if the show is one you're really not interested in, then skip it, and maybe the lines on your favorite ride will be shorter.

Where You'll Eat

Sunset Ranch Market An outdoor food court, reminiscent of a farmer's market. Pick up hot dogs, fruit, snacks, and frozen yogurt while a small nearby stage boasts performances throughout the day. It includes:

Fast-Food/Counter Service

Rosie's Red Hot Dogs Hot dogs, sandwiches, and those famous smoked turkey legs, most items under $6.

Snacks/Drinks

Anaheim Produce A variety of fresh fruit, along with pickles (you remember, the ones that used to sit in those huge barrels at your favorite deli), cotton candy, and a selection of cold drinks. Prices to $3.

Catalina Eddie's Soft-serve frozen yogurt (located near the Tower of Terror), most items under $5.

Where You'll Shop

Once Upon a Time Disney character merchandise and a nice selection of collectibles and figurines. tee shirts, toys, and souvenirs.

Planet Hollywood All the items in this shop bear the Planet Hollywood logo. If you really need to have one of their tee shirts, you can pick it up here without journeying out to their restaurant in Downtown Disney. With Disney's new philosophy of selling out to corporate sponsors, we knew it wouldn't be long before stores and restaurants started slithering their way into the parks, but is this really necessary?

The Scary Apothecary   The place to pick out that Halloween costume you'll need once October comes around, or whenever you want to dress up.

Sunset Club Couture   If you're looking for a hand-drawn watch featuring your favorite Disney character, then this is the place to go, however, since the pictures are hand-drawn, the watches are fairly expensive, and certainly not within a cheapskate's budget. There is also a nice collection of better-quality jewelry (all with Disney characters, of course), but some of these might also be out of the range of us cheapskates. Hey, it doesn't cost a thing to look!

Sweet Spells   Another candy store—and remember, hard candies will survive in the hot, Florida sun a lot better than chocolate!

Villains in Vogue   Walt Disney knew that in every movie you needed a villain so that people would really root for the heroine and become elated when good finally conquered evil. However, lately there has been a renewed interest, not only in the heroines of the early animated classics, but also with the villains. This store is devoted to those villains who gave us the scares and thrills in the early movies: like Maleficent, the Evil Queen from *Snow White,* and even Captain Hook. So if you're looking to reveal that little bit of bad boy or bad girl that dwells in each of us, stop in here for a little something sporting your favorite villain's likeness.

Winnie the Pooh's Gala Premiere   This is *the* place to be for all those Pooh-aholics who simply must have every item ever created with Winnie the Pooh's image on it.

HOLLYWOOD HILLS

This is the newest area developed in the Studios, and it is home to two of their biggest attractions and their nighttime extravaganza.

What You'll See

Fantasmic! Disneyland's spectacular show now in Florida! See "Free at Disney-MGM Studios" at the end of this chapter.

Rock 'n' Roller Coaster This is, by far, Disney's most thrilling ride and certainly not for the faint at heart.

The story behind this attraction is that you have stepped into a recording studio where the rock group Aerosmith is rehearsing. The band is late for an awards show, and although their harried manager tries to get them into their limo, the band refuses to go unless their loyal fans go along with them. Here's where the fun begins: your limo (i.e., your coaster) is propelled at high speeds on its course to the concert venue (going from 0 to 60 MPH in 2.8 seconds), and along the way makes three 360° rotations, until you arrive safely at the event.

This is the first inverted roller coaster on Disney property, and it sure is a hair-raiser. The track is 3,400 feet long (more than half a mile), and along the way you pull 4-5 Gs (more than an astronaut feels at takeoff). Kids must be forty-eight inches tall to ride. *Don't Miss This! FASTPASS!*

The Twilight Zone Tower of Terror At this, Disney World's tallest attraction, the scene is an abandoned, dilapidated hotel where you'll see a video of Rod Serling recounting as only he could (actually, it's clips of him interspersed with a voice imitator—after all, he's been dead a number of years) the story of guests who mysteriously disappeared on a night long ago when lightning hit the building. As you embark on your own elevator ride to investigate the mystery for yourself, will you face a similar fate? Anything can happen. This is, after all, the Twilight Zone!

Look for small details while waiting on line—see the lobby, library, and boiler room just as they were the night the lightning struck. You might be waiting on line a *long* time. Your elevator drops thirteen stories, which would be bad enough if it were just free-falling. But thanks to a "helper" car, the elevator is pulled down faster than the force of gravity. Drops are controlled by computer, so your ride can change from visit to visit.

People have complained that this ride was too short—that after an hour's wait in line, they expected a ride that lasted more than a few minutes. Disney struck back by adding some new drops—twice the falls means twice the terror. You asked for it! Kids must be forty inches tall to ride. *Don't Miss This!*

The Tower of Terror is one of those rides that people race to first thing upon entering the park. It is not for the faint of heart, and health restrictions are posted. Fortunately, you can chicken out right before the big drop and take a slow elevator back down. The ride also offers you an unparalleled view of the park—but look quick!

Secret Tip—How to Get Onto the Elevator First

In the room with the TV playing, stand in back, near the painting. When it's time to go, you'll be among the first to exit the basement and enter the elevators.

Where You'll Eat

Snacks/Drinks

Fingas Coffee, espresso, cappucino, and coffee coolers. Pastries and cookies. Up to $4. This coffee wagon is located at the exit to Tower of Terror, which is Disney's subtle way of warning you not to eat *before* going on this ride. Actually, if you do plan on doing Tower of Terror first thing in the morning, this is a nice place to grab a quick breakfast bite after you take the plunge.

Where You'll Shop

Tower Hotel Gifts At the exit of Tower of Terror, this shop, of course, features all sorts of souvenirs from the thrilling attraction. This is where you'll find those oft-coveted I-survived-Tower-of-Terror tee shirts, hats, and buttons. The store also has a large selection of videos from the *Twilight Zone* television program, submitted for your approval, and your wallet.

ANIMATION COURTYARD

Discover how animated movies are made, and enjoy one of the Studio's most entertaining stage shows (indoors, thankfully!).

What You'll See

Bear in the Big Blue House—Live on Stage!   For families with very young children (who subscribe to the cable Disney Channel), we don't need to tell you who the Bear in the Big Blue House might be. Your children are probably glued to the TV screen whenever this show is on. If you are one of these families, then you don't want to miss this stage show where you can watch Bear, Ojo, Tutter, Treelo, Pip and Pop perform live on stage. If you don't have young children, by all means, skip this show and proceed to the next attraction!

The Magic of Disney Animation   After passing through a waiting area that exhibits animation art from Disney's classic and most recent features, you'll see how Disney animated movies are created. Watch cartoon artists at work (provided you're there during working hours). See a funny, informative movie about the animation process, starring Robin Williams and Walter Cronkite, then take a short tour through the animation production facility.

Try to tour this building during the day, on a weekday, so you can see the Disney animators in action on an upcoming animation feature. (Can you imagine what it must be like to work in a fishbowl and have someone in a Goofy-eared hat staring at you?) Like most of the real working world, the animators go home at 5:00 P.M.

Voyage of the Little Mermaid   Special effects, puppets, animation, live performers, music, and lights combine to create one of the Studios' most popular attractions. It goes without saying that kids will love this *Reader's Digest* version of the Little Mermaid cartoon feature—maybe it's because it's a timeless tale with some of Disney's most delightful music and strongest characters. In this specially equipped theater, you'll literally feel like you're "under the sea," as lights twinkle and water mists down upon you.

There are several "voyages" daily. Stop and check the line continually throughout the day, and if you time it just right, you won't have to wait too long for the next show to start and the line will be manageable. *Don't Miss This! FASTPASS!*

Where You'll Eat

Sorry, there are no restaurants in the Animation Courtyard.

Where You'll Shop

Animation Gallery   For all of the real Disney nuts in the world. This is our favorite store. It offers a fantastic collection of Disney animation art, figurines, and art books. But a word of warning: Almost everything in this store is *expensive!*

The Studio Store   Gifts with the theme of Disney's latest cartoon feature. Clothing and accessories for fans, big and small. Stuffed animals and toys.

Under the Sea   At the entrance to Voyage of the Little Mermaid, this shop features character merchandise with Ariel, Snow White, Belle, Cinderella, and Sleeping Beauty—Disney's princess collection.

MICKEY AVENUE

Discover how feature films are made, and how special effects are added to make the films more spectacular.

What You'll See

Backstage Pass   This is a walking tour through the soundstage area of the Studios. First, venture into a studio where you'll understand how filming in front of a blue screen allows a different background to be added later (did you ever wonder how Mary Poppins "flew" over London?). Then, the tour takes you past some soundstages, and you may actually get a glimpse of shows currently in production at the Studios.

Please bear in mind that this is a *walking* tour and offers no seating at any point on the tour. Although you'll spend most of the time standing (not walking), make sure your feet are up to it before embarking on this 25-minute tour.

Studios Backlot Tour   Yes, this is a real working studio. Take a tram ride through parts of the backstage area where scenes from movies and television shows are filmed. Then, it's on to the costume and lighting departments and past some props from popular movies and TV shows. The highlight of the tour is an ill-advised (or so they want you to think) pass through Catastrophe Canyon, where you're in the middle of a real special-effects show demonstrating the use of explosives, fire, and a flash flood. (Tip: You have a better chance of getting wet on the left side of the tram.) *Don't Miss This!*

Bear in mind that the tram tour takes about a half hour (not including time waiting for the tram to arrive) so plan accordingly. And rumor has it that the Catastrophe Canyon segment may change somewhat in the near future. Stay tuned.

Who Wants to be a Millionaire—Play It!   If you're a fan of the hit television show, then you'll love this newest attraction at the Disney-MGM Studios. Seated in a 650-seat soundstage, you'll face a 4-button control pad (A, B, C, D) which is next to your seat number. A fastest finger question will be asked, and the member of the audience who has the fastest finger gets called onto the stage, which is an exact replica of the show, complete with the familiar lighting and music—unfortunately, though, Regis couldn't make it. While in the hot seat, the contestant will be asked a series of questions, and he or she will be able to use three lifelines—50/50, Ask the Audience, or Phone a *Complete Stranger*. Yes, you read that right—there is a phone set up outside of the studio, and guests strolling along the street will randomly be picked to take part in the show. All members of the audience play along with the contestant, and the audience member who has the highest score is the next person called into the hot seat.

The show is quite fun at times and is definitely a must-see. And we'd like to say that it's a chance to win some real money, but you'll be playing for points, not dollars. But the contestants will get to cash the points in for some merchandise, pins, hats, and shirts, depending on what level they reach. And anyone lucky enough to reach the million dollar level wins a trip to New York to watch the taping of the real television show. *Don't Miss This! FASTPASS!*

Where You'll Eat

Fast-Food/Counter Service

Studio Catering Co.   Stacked sandwiches made with roast beef and cheese, Italian meats, and turkey, along with a club sandwich (that means there's three slices of bread on each). Most under $7.

Snacks/Drinks

Studio Catering Co. Ice Cream Fountain   If you have any room left after eating your stacked sandwich, here's a good place to enjoy some gourmet ice cream, sundaes, and apple pie. Up to $4.

Where You'll Shop

Ooops, looks like Disney actually designed a section of a park without a store in it! Maybe they decided to give your wallet a well-deserved rest! Periodically, however they wheel out some carts with merchandise from *101 Dalmations*, along with other animated films.

NEW YORK STREET

When the Studios first opened, you would just take a tram ride along this lifelike set. Now you can walk around the façades and cardboard skyline, and enjoy a fun, family Muppets movie and outdoor stage shows.

What You'll See

Backlot Theater   Enjoy periodically changing live productions based on popular Disney films in this outdoor theater.

The most recent production is a variation on Disney's 1996 animated film *The Hunchback of Notre Dame*, using live performers, puppetry, singing effects, and the theater itself.

The theater is outside, so if you plan on sitting for one of these distractions from the attractions, it's best not to go while the Florida sun is at its hottest.

Honey, I Shrunk the Kids Movie Set Adventure   We recommend that they should rename this attraction, Honey, the Exhibit Ate Up the Kids.

The backyard from the popular movie has been recreated as an oversize playground, with 30-inch-tall blades of grass, huge Lego toys, a giant leaky garden hose, a lawn sprinkler, and more to climb on, around, and through. This distraction is great for the kids (we've never seen an adult running around on this "set"), but it's a real time waster, and your time is precious when visiting Disney World. If your kids just won't let you say no, give them a time limit.

Jim Henson's Muppet*Vision ~~3-D~~ 4D   This multimedia attraction, incorporating dramatic 3-D cinematic effects, live puppets, and even a specially designed interactive theater, will delight children of all ages, especially those little ones familiar with the Muppet characters. You really feel like you're part of the show, especially when Waldo, the 3-D character, floats seemingly inches from your nose. You'll find yourself reaching out to the screen. *Don't Miss This!*

Where You'll Eat

Sit-Down

Mama Melrose's Ristorante Italiano   Brick oven, thin-crust pizza, lasagna, beef, chicken, espresso, cappuccino, and more, offered in the tackiest, most delightful setting, with decor straight out of Little Italy. (Many items under $20.) And everyday seems like Christmas!

Fast-Food/Counter Service

Toy Story Pizza Planet   Pizza, salads, espresso, and cappuccino, most under $8. A word of warning: As with the Pizza

Planet restaurant in the movie *Toy Story*, this restaurant includes a video arcade. So if you don't want to hear your kids hound you for roll after roll of quarters—and you'd rather spend time seeing the rest of the studio's attractions—find another restaurant.

Snacks/Drinks

The Writer's Stop   It didn't take Disney long to open up one of those increasingly trendy combination bookstore/coffee shops. Of course, all of the books in this store are published by Disney (who else?). Cappucino, espresso, and a nice selection of cookies and sweets. Up to $3.

Where You'll Shop

It's a Wonderful Store   Another Christmas store, but this one primarily features ornaments and decorations starring the Disney gang. Check out a "snow"-covered Mickey, Goofy, and Donald outside!

Stage One Company Store   Close to the exit of Muppet*Vision. A small collection of Disney Babies clothing for the tots, but this store mainly features the characters from Jim Henson's Muppet*Vision 3-D 4D. Dolls, tee shirts, and toys with Kermit, Miss Piggy, and Fozzy Bear.

COMMISSARY LANE/ECHO LAKE

Commissary Lane/Echo Lake is home to several audience participation/how'd-they-do-that? shows, as well as a stunt show and the ever-popular Star Tours.

What You'll See

Disney's Doug Live!   Once again, for those of you with young children (elementary school age), you'll know who Doug is, and your kids will not let you bypass this show. Doug, the star of the One Saturday Morning cartoon show with the same name, performs live on stage with his friends, Patti and

Roger, and also his dog, Porkchop. If you don't have children, or you are lucky enough that you successfully distract your kids and they've missed the sign for the show, skip this attraction and proceed on to the next.

Indiana Jones Epic Stunt Spectacular The work of stunt performers is on display here at this live-action show that re-enacts scenes from *Raiders of the Lost Ark*. Viewers learn how stunts are performed and how special effects (like fires, explosions, gunfire, and car wrecks) are created. With any luck, you may even be chosen as an extra to participate in the show—don't worry, you won't do anything unsafe, and the whole show is well-planned and choreographed. The best views are from the seats in the upper center of the outdoor (i.e., hot, yet out of the direct sun) theater.

The line to get in may seem long upon your arrival, but the theater is large—it's been known to gobble up as many as 2,000 people—so don't be discouraged if the line winds around out front. Check the schedule for the next show times. *FAST-PASS!*

Sounds Dangerous Starring Drew Carey Drew stars as a bumbling undercover detective, attempting to crack the case of the mysterious snowglobe smugglers. This attraction plays on your sense of hearing, as most of the action takes place in total darkness. Wearing headsets, incredible audio effects surround you as Drew Carey tries to solve the mystery.

We don't want to give away too much of the plot, which is quite funny at times. Although this is not one of the most popular attractions at the Studios, it is amusing, so if time permits, *Don't Miss This!*

Don't miss *SoundWorks* as you leave the theater—most people walk right past the hands-on sound-effects fun. In particular, we recommend that you fiddle with the Soundsations exhibit, the row of soundproof booths that line the walls. (If you just want to play with the hands-on exhibits, or if the crowd is too large when you're there, come back later. Enter directly through the Drew Carey show's exit doors.)

Star Tours This is the first ride visitors used to race to upon entering the park—at least until the Tower of Terror on Sunset Boulevard opened. But many still go on this ride early because the line (due to the attraction's popularity) can be very long at times.

Star Tours is a flight simulator—a little more subdued than the Body Wars ride in EPCOT's FutureWorld, but it's rough nonetheless. It's based on the hugely popular *Star Wars* trilogy and stars those lovable robots R2D2 and C-3PO. The premise of the ride is that you are about to embark on an intergalactic vacation to tour the Moon of Endor. But it's not all smooth space sailing, and, along the way, you'll have to contend with meteors, attacking enemy ships, and more. Pay attention to the pre-ride show. At the very least, it gives you something to do while you're waiting on the long line.

If you like a rougher ride, try sitting in the back of the simulator. We recommend you go on Star Tours early in the morning, but not right after you've eaten breakfast, for all the obvious reasons. *Don't Miss This! FASTPASS!*

TV Academy Hall of Fame Plaza   This outdoor exhibit, located outside of SuperStar Television, is affiliated with the Academy of Television Arts and Sciences and features statues honoring the academy's Hall of Fame inductees.

Where You'll Eat

Sit-Down

Echo Lake Café   This 32-seat restaurant features sandwiches and salads and is open for lunch and dinner. Lunches to $15, most dinners under $20.

50s Prime Time Café   You'll feel as if you've joined the cast of *The Donna Reed Show!* Each table is set in an authentic 1950s-style kitchen—complete with Formica-topped kitchen and dinette tables, checkerboard-tiled floor, and black and white TVs playing vintage sitcoms. You'll enjoy typical "homemade" fare, served by a waitress who calls herself "Mom," and who even reprimands you if you don't clear your plate. Enjoy macaroni and cheese, burgers, tuna sandwiches, chicken pot pie, pot roast, roast lamb, meatloaf, fish, alphabet soup, ice cream sodas, shakes . . . even s'mores!

Best to make your reservations ahead of time—it's difficult to get a same-day table in this popular restaurant. Lunches to $17, many dinners $15 and up.

Sci-Fi Dine-In Theater   In our opinion, this is the Studio's best restaurant—maybe not for the food, but for atmosphere. Sit in an authentic 1950s convertible, retrofitted to accommodate a table, chairs, and you! You feel as if you are parked at a drive-in theater (but it's indoors), and the waitresses (many on roller skates) serve burgers, pasta, steaks, fresh fish, salads, and, of course, popcorn, while trailers for hokey sci-fi films play on the restaurant's oversized drive-in movie screen. This is also one of Disney's quietest restaurants, since just about everybody gazes, zombie-like, at the drive-in screen instead of talking. Lunches to $17, dinners up to $20.

Cafeterias/Food Courts

Hollywood and Vine   This restaurant showcases the glamour of Hollywood during its heyday. Minnie Mouse is the hostess here, and some of her friends join in to make you feel right at home. This restaurant is open for breakfast and lunch daily, and serves buffet-style only. If you are planning on having a character meal while at Disney, it might be best to luncheon here with the characters, and that way you won't have to give up viewing the prime attractions in the early morning. Prices up to $20.

Fast-Food/Counter Service

ABC Commissary   Dine in a replica of an old studio commissary from the 1940s. The food is actually pretty good, and there is a nice variety to please everybody's tastes. Grilled chicken sandwiches, hamburgers, sandwich wraps, and a hefty chef salad. Up to $8. Before 10:30 A.M., this restaurant serves breakfast.

Backlot Express   Chicken, burgers, hot dogs, sandwiches, and salads, most under $8.

Min and Bill's Dockside Diner Delicious taco salads, tacos, and nachos. To cool down your palate, a selection of ice creams, ice cream sundaes, and floats. Up to $7.

Snacks/Drinks

Dinosaur Gertie's Ice Cream of Extinction This interesting ice cream stand is located *inside* the big green Brontosaurus, which resides in the pond to the left, as you face the Chinese Theater. It offers ice cream novelties, cappucino, espresso, and cold drinks. Up to $3.

Echo Park Produce A variety of fresh fruit is available at this fruit stand, along with cold drinks. Prices to $3.

Tune In Lounge Located next to the 50s Prime Time Café, this bar offers what you'd expect a bar to offer, but in an unexpected, authentic, 1950s setting—formica end tables, naugahyde couches, and fuzzy, black and white TVs. Prices under $6.

Where You'll Shop

Golden Age Souvenirs Hats and tee shirts bearing the Disney-acquired ABC-TV sports and ESPN cable sports channel logos.

Indiana Jones Adventure Outpost This shop features clothing and accessories for your everyday adventurer, but with the Indiana Jones insignia on them. (That would be the movie Indiana Jones, not the attraction at the Disney-MGM Studios.)

Tattooine Traders This is the store you enter upon exiting Star Tours—what a coincidence! It's the place to go for Star Tours tee shirts and souvenirs, but mostly this store sells *Star Wars* collectibles and toys.

FREE AT DISNEY-MGM STUDIOS
Check the park's daily Entertainment Schedule for more details.

Fantasmic! Witness the classic battle of good versus evil when you enter the imagination of Mickey Mouse as he battles a slew of Disney villains. Through the use of lasers, lights, fountains, music, and dazzling special effects, you'll remain spellbound as Mickey conquers a host of Disney baddies in this spectacular 25-minute show representing Disney at its best.

This is the first time in Disney history that an arena was built specifically for a nighttime show, and this 6,900-seat amphitheater is a welcome change from their other outdoor shows (plus, there is standing room available for 3,000 latecomers.

Fantasmic! features scenes from some of the modern Disney classics—*Pocahontas, Beauty and the Beast,* and *The Little Mermaid*—along with plenty of the original Disney standards. But to enjoy it to the fullest, you'll want to be seated in a section that is dead-on to one of the three water screens. If you don't directly face one of the screens, the images displayed on them will be blurred and you'll lose some of the show. You'll want to arrive at least 60–90 minutes before show time to get the best seat available. But don't sit too close to the action, because you will get wet once the water screens are turned on if the wind is blowing in your direction. (The pre-show performers will help the wait to seem a little shorter!)

So now that you've taken our advice and you have a great seat for one of the greatest shows on Disney property, we're going to give you the best tip you'll ever hear: how to get out after the show. Remember, there are 6,900 seats filled with people and only one exit. Everyone makes their way from the bleacher seats to the closest aisle and stands, packed like sardines, waiting with everyone else for the exit to clear. What you smart cheapskates should do is continue walking down the row of your seat, cutting through the aisles, until you reach the sign for the "Sebastian" section (you know, the cute crab from *The Little Mermaid*). Then, duck up that aisle and straight out of the exit, leaving about 6,000 people to eat your dust.

And if the thought of waiting over an hour for a good seat just isn't your idea of fun, there is another option. Disney is offering Fantasmic! dinner packages, which include priority seating at one of the Disney-MGM Studios sit-down restaurants, and a ticket that gets you into a special reserved section of the theater. Bear in mind that the "special reserved section" may not be the best section to see the show, but at least you're guaranteed a seat (although the seats in the section are also on a first-come, first-served basis so you still need to arrive 45 minutes before show time). As of this writing, The Brown Derby, Mama Melrose's, and Hollywood and Vine are the only restaurants that offer the package (double check at Guest Relations). And one other benefit to partaking of the package: the section you sit in is the closest to the exit, so you will be one of the first to leave once the show is over.

There is no charge for the dinner package other than the cost of your dinner. You order off of the restaurant's normal menu, and the only requirement is that every adult must order an entrée. Reservations may be made 7 days in advance, either in person at the Studios, or by contacting Guest Relations at any of the parks or resorts. You will not be able to reserve the package by calling the normal Disney dinner reservation line.

Feature Parade   Held once or twice daily (depending on the season; check the schedule), these entertaining parades change periodically. The most recent parade extravaganza celebrates the animated features with a motorcade of specially designed cars filled with your favorite Disney stars.

The best viewing spots are along Hollywood Boulevard, but a warning to those who line up early with a prime spot at the curb: Stand firm. Those who arrive late often try to sneak a spot right in front of you. Bear in mind that there is very little shade along this parade route.

And remember, if you're not someone who gives a hoot about parades, parade time is your time to see all the most popular attractions, which are sure to be less crowded.

7

Animal Kingdom

Animal Kingdom is Disney's newest and largest theme park—and it is also Disney's most controversial, at least at its outset. With the incredible amount of "bad press" that surrounded the opening of the park (including somewhat exaggerated news about a number of accidental animal deaths), many people have asked us if it was really worth adding a fourth theme park to their already hectic Disney vacation. Our answer is an exuberant, "Yes!"

It has taken over 10 years to complete the park, from the initial planning stages to opening day on April 22, 1998. At an estimated cost of over $800 million, it's pretty obvious that Disney hasn't skimped on much. More thought (and money) has gone into creating the whole atmosphere of this park than any park before it. Here's an example: Simply landscaping with the native plants of Florida just wouldn't do, so Disney transplanted over 3 million plants from around the world to create their authentic African savanna in the middle of Central Florida.

Even though Disney boasts that this is their largest park, they are speaking purely about acreage (this one is just over 500 acres). It's true that each of the other three parks could easily fit within its borders, but that's only because the safari attraction alone encompasses over 100 acres. At this early stage, there are nowhere near the amount of attractions at Animal Kingdom as there are in the other parks, so don't plan on spending a lot of time there. Visiting Animal Kingdom is reminiscent of attending any of Disney World's other theme parks during its first year: With major expansion coming in the next several years, right now you can easily see it all in about a day. Bear in mind that everybody else will be coming into the park first thing in the morning and rushing to the safari. So if you would rather see herds of animals instead of herds of fellow tourists, plan on seeing at least the safari late in the afternoon!

How to Get There

Disney World buses reach the Animal Kingdom from all the theme parks and Disney resorts. Visitors arriving by car park in the adjacent lot; the lot is free to Disney hotel guests (others: $5).

Key Animal Kingdom Landmarks

- Baby Needs/Changing Station—In Safari Village, behind Creature Comforts.

- Banking Services—An ATM machine is located to the right of the park Entrance Plaza, next to Garden Gate Gifts.

- First Aid—In Safari Village, behind Creature Comforts.

- Information—Guest Relations, at the left of the park Entrance Plaza.

- Lockers—To the left of the park entrance.

- Lost and Found, Lost Persons—Safari Village, behind Creature Comforts.

- Stroller Rentals—Strollers are available for $5 per day (plus $1 deposit) at the right side of the park's Entrance Plaza, next to Garden Gate Gifts. The rental is valid in all four Disney theme parks. Save money (and time waiting on the rental and returns line) and bring your own.

- Wheelchair Rentals—Wheelchairs are also available for rental next to Garden Gate Gifts. Rental fee $5, plus $1 refundable deposit.

ENTRANCE PLAZA AND THE OASIS

You'll know you've left the outside world in the dust when you step through the main entrance of Animal Kingdom and into the tropical paradise known as "The Oasis." This is the home to a variety of exotic animals and birds, from an anteater to a two-toed sloth. The lush landscaping sets the theme for what you're about to see, but don't spend too much time here looking at plants—the *really* good stuff is yet to come! (We've actually seen people stand around for 30 minutes waiting for the sloth to move, and guess what! It rarely does. There's a reason why they call lazy people sloths.)

Where You'll Eat

Sit-Down

Rainforest Café   Dine in the middle of a tropical rainforest under a larger than life banyan tree, surrounded by Audio-Animatronic jungle animals who periodically come to life. The café is one of the new breed of chain restaurants (not operated by Disney) that are cropping up inside of Walt Disney World (somewhat disturbing to us purists). This one offers a mix of healthy items on its menu. Because it is located at the Entrance Plaza, you will need to exit the park to enter the restaurant (be sure to have your hand stamped!). There are actually two entrances to the restaurant, one is on your right before you exit the park. This exit actually is used the most, and therefore, tends to have a long line of people waiting to leave their names (oh, did we forget to mention that they do not take advance reservations?). You will be better off if you exit Animal Kingdom and enter the restaurant through their main entrance. Come early and leave your name: they will give you a time to come back. Then reenter the park and enjoy the sights around The Oasis while waiting for your table to be ready.

The Rainforest Café offers a very extensive menu, from sandwiches to burgers, pasta to Amazon flatbread (their word for pizza). We recommend the Mojo Bones (barbecue spare ribs), close to the best we've ever had! They also offer an assortment of healthier choices. Prices up to $18; open 6:00 A.M. until park closing.

Where You'll Shop

As is true with the rest of Disney's parks, the most important thing to do first is to see the attractions. Resist temptation: Save your shopping until later in the day, just before you are ready to leave, but if you do buy some things during the day and you don't want to carry packages onto the rides, Disney will hold them for you. Just tell the cashier you want to arrange for the packages to be held for later pickup, and if you're staying on-site, you can arrange to have the items shipped directly to your room!

Garden Gate Gifts   Animal Kingdom souvenirs, buttons, coffee mugs, keychains, etc. If you do decide to have any of the purchases that you make during the day held for you, this is the place where you would pick up your packages.

The Outpost Shop   Animal Kingdom souvenirs, tee shirts, and hats. Located outside the park's entrance, this is your last chance to buy that all-important souvenir before leaving the area.

DISCOVERY ISLAND

Walk through a grotto and enter into the "Main Street" of Animal Kingdom. It is here that you will get your first real glimpse of the Tree of Life, the centerpiece of the park. It serves the same purpose as Cinderella Castle does in the Magic Kingdom: it is the focal point, the central hub. All other themed lands radiate from it like the spokes on a wheel. As long as you can see the Tree of Life, you'll always be able to find your way through the lush, tropical jungle that is Animal Kingdom.

Another interesting point is that Discovery Island is encircled by (what else!) the Discovery River. You will need to cross over a bridge before entering each of the other themed lands. Each bridge fits architecturally with the land that it leads to. If you look carefully at the bridge, you'll be able to figure out which land you are entering without looking at your guide map. Amaze your friends and family with your navigational skills. (You don't have to tell them that you read it here!)

What You'll See

Discovery Island Trails   Explore this exotic trail that ventures through the vast root system of the Tree of Life. Every twist and turn gives you a different view of the Tree of Life, and a different view of the creatures sculpted into it. But real animals also inhabit the garden. Don't be surprised if you have an encounter with an otter, flamingo, stork, lemur, or tortoise along the way.

The Tree of Life   This is the icon of Disney's Animal Kingdom. Towering over 14 stories tall—with an oil derrick at its core—this "tree" is quite unlike any other you would find in the wild. Measuring 50 feet wide at its base, it has a canopy over 170 feet wide. We don't know who bothered to count, but the tree reportedly has 103,000 leaves on it, each and every one having been attached by hand (not by the hand of God, but by Disney's Imagineers). The tree, however, is best known for the 325 animal forms that have been sculpted into its gnarled roots, trunk, and branches (20 artists labored over the sculptures, all made from that unique natural resource, Disney cement). Walk around the tree and you will be amazed at the beauty and the intricacies of the carvings, but don't spend too much time looking for your favorite type of animal—there are still plenty of attractions to see.

It's Tough to Be a Bug!   Enter into this 430-seat theater located inside the base of the Tree of Life and be prepared to be "bugged" out of your mind. Put on your "bug-eyes" (otherwise known as 3-D glasses) and get set to view life through the eyes of a bug. This show has state-of-the-art effects the likes of which have never before been seen at any of the Disney parks.

Inspired by characters from Disney/Pixar's film release, *A Bug's Life*, this show's stars include the Termite-ator, Chilly the tarantula, and a truly lovable stink bug (can you imagine the effect they used for the stink bug?). We don't want to tell you too much about the movie because we don't want to spoil the surprises!

As cute as this show is, we would not recommend it for families with small children who do not like bugs. The effects can seem very realistic at times, and there's no sense in torturing your more sensitive loved ones! For everybody else, this is a definite must-see, one of our favorite attractions of the park. *Don't Miss This! FASTPASS!*

Where You'll Eat

Fast-Food/Counter Service

Flame Tree Barbecue   Smoked meat sandwiches, spare ribs, steak fry baskets, vegetarian wraps, and sodas and coffee. Prices up to $8.

Pizzafari   Personal-sized pizzas, Italian hoagie sandwiches, Caesar salads, calzones, and sodas and coffee. Prices for lunch up to $6.

Safari Barbecue Hut   Barbecue sandwiches, soda, and coffee. Prices up to $7.

Snacks/Drinks

Safari Pretzel   As the name implies, get your hot pretzels here! Also serves soda. Prices up to $4.

Where You'll Shop

Beastly Bazaar   Reasonably priced souvenirs, jewelry, coffee mugs, tee shirts, stuffed toys, candy, and film.

Creature Comforts Gifts for all those little ones that you were fortunate enough to leave at home, including children's clothing and stuffed toys.

Island Mercantile Tee shirts, hats, Animal Kingdom souvenirs, stuffed animals, candy, and film.

Wonders of the Wild Collectibles (another name for "higherpriced souvenirs"), nice quality clothing (not just tee shirts!), jewelry, watches, and film.

CAMP MINNIE-MICKEY

Have you ever wondered where Mickey and Minnie Mouse—who, as we all know, live at the world's number 1 tourist destination—go when they take a vacation? Well, we've been told that they like to frequent Camp Minnie-Mickey. Styled after the rustic camps found in the Adirondack Mountains of upstate New York, the whole Disney gang has been known to gather here.

Not unlike Mickey's Toontown Fair in the Magic Kingdom, this area's basically for the little ones. Not a heck of a lot to interest the adults, except for the "Festival of the Lion King" show, but if you do have children, it will be their only opportunity while at Animal Kingdom to see the traditional Disney characters—they are not seen anywhere else in the park.

What You'll See

Character Greeting Pavilions Meet your favorite Disney characters up close and personal. It's a good chance for picture and autograph opportunities throughout the day with Mickey, Minnie, and the rest of the gang, but don't stand around waitin' for 'em!

"Festival of the Lion King" This musical salute to the Disney favorite is full of dancing, tumbling, circus-style acrobatics, stilt-walking, and even boasts a hula fire dancer! They encourage audience participation, and the performers and stage props roll out from the four corners of the theater, surrounding you and yours in the festivities. This show is 30 min-

utes long, so keep that in mind if you have any dining reservations, or need to be somewhere quickly. *Don't Miss This!*

Pocahontas and Forest Friends   Join Pocahontas and Grandmother Willow for a short stage show on the importance of ecology. This show is purely for the kids, and the smaller they are, the more they will enjoy it. There is nothing here to hold the attention of anyone over the age of 10—just some singing and a few visits from Pocahontas's wild animal friends (in other words, a raccoon and some mice walk across the stage). Watch out because this show's seating is entirely in the sun. So, unless you have a daughter who is truly in love with Pocahontas, you can definitely skip this.

Snacks/Drinks

Chip 'n' Dale's Cookie Cabin   Sugar cookies, chocolate chip cookies, ice cream cookie sandwiches, soda, and coffee. Prices up to $3.

Forest Trail Funnel Cakes   Funnel cakes, corn dogs, fruit, soda, and coffee. Prices up to $4.

AFRICA

Enter into modern-day Africa through the fictional village of Harambe, a worn little hamlet built on the edge of a wildlife reserve. Harambe (which means "coming together") is a sleepy little marketplace whose existence is based solely on tourism from its safari park.

When Disney's Imagineers designed this place, they did everything in their power to literally transport you to another place and time. The whitewashed buildings are built of coral stone and look as though they have been standing there, untouched, for the last 100 years. The cracks in the pavement also look as though they've been there forever. Why, the Disney folks even brought real Zulu tribesmen over from Africa to thatch the roofs of the huts so that they would look completely authentic.

What You'll See

Kilimanjaro Safaris Step aboard Simba One, an authentic-looking open-sided safari vehicle (which seats 32 people), and get set for quite an adventure! Here's your chance to come face-to-face with over 1,000 exotic animals representing 200 different species, roaming free on 110 acres of savanna and forest. Zebras, giraffes, Thompson gazelles, elephants, rhinos, hippos, ostriches, and lions inhabit this representation of the Serengeti grassland system. Your safari really gets exciting once poachers appear and your driver chases them away amidst a hail of gunfire.

As you cross flooded brooks and navigate over the bumpy roads, you'll notice that, unlike any other Disney attraction, this ride is different every time you ride on it. Even Disney can't control how wild animals react (you just *know* they tried to train them!).

And the one thing that the animals have learned is that they do not like the hot, Florida sun. They try to control their body heat in the middle of the day the same way that we would like to: they chill out! So, if you want to see the animals while they are active and moving about, go early in the morning (this attraction usually opens at 7:30 A.M.) or go at dusk when it begins to cool off. Of course, everyone will be in line first thing in the morning, so our recommendation would be to avoid the herd mentality, and take this adventure in the afternoon or at dusk. Without having to wait an hour in line, you'll be able to take this 20-minute ride two or three times and get to see more of the animals than those who rode just once in the morning.

One word of caution: Be aware of the number of pictures you shoot while on the safari. The animals are so close and the scenery is so authentic that you'll be tempted to keep snapping away. So, sit back, enjoy the ride, and limit your pictures to just a few of each species. Besides, how many pictures of a giraffe do you really need? *Don't Miss This! FASTPASS!*

Pangani Forest Exploration Trail Get up-close and personal with two troops of African lowland gorillas. This self-guided walking tour (which starts where the safari ends) allows you to see the gorillas in a re-creation of their natural habitat, although sometimes the viewing is better at the glass-in observation room located halfway through the trail.

Along the trail you will have the opportunity to view other animal species in their natural setting. We particularly enjoyed watching the hippopotamus from the underwater viewing area and the exhibit of meerkats (although Timon from *The Lion King* was nowhere to be found). *Don't Miss This!*

Wildlife Express to Conservation Station Train   Board this wacky-looking train for a one-way excursion to Conservation Station. The train ride itself is not much to write home about, but it is your only way of getting to Conservation Station. As you travel along the rails, you will pass the sleeping quarters of the animals you've just seen at Kilimanjaro Safaris (yes, they do bring all the animals in at night).

Make sure that you do not board this train until you are ready to see Conservation Station. It is a one-way trip, and you will not be allowed to stay on the train to return to Africa. You will need to get off and stand in the back of the line to wait for the next returning train.

Where You'll Eat

Fast-Food/Counter Service

Tusker House Restaurant   Rotisserie roasted meats, chicken, prime ribs, fried chicken, chicken breasts with portabello mushrooms, lasagna, grilled chicken salads, and roasted vegetable sandwiches. A kid's combo is also available. All meals are served with garlic mashed potatoes and a vegetable. In our opinion, this is the best restaurant in the park—excellent food at a moderate price.

They also serve breakfast breads in the morning. If the line is too long to grab a bite at Kusafiri Coffee Shop, come inside to the Tusker House where there's rarely a line. Prices up to $8.

Snacks/Drinks

African Lounge   Listen to live, contemporary African musicians while sipping your favorite cocktail. (We remember when there was no alcohol allowed in the Disney parks!)

Harambe Fruit Market   Fresh fruit stand, also offers juices and drinks. Prices up to $4.

Kusafiri Coffee Shop and Bakery   Muffins, Danish, and cinnamon buns. Coffee, cappuccino, latte, hot chocolate, and juice. A good place to grab a quick breakfast and be on your way. Prices up to $4.

Tamu Tamu Refreshments   Frozen yogurt, soft ice cream, cones, sundaes, ice cream sodas, and drinks. Prices up to $3.

Where You'll Shop

Mombasa Marketplace / Ziwani Traders   Souvenirs and collectibles, tee shirts, and stuffed animals. Unlike most of the other stores, not all of the items here will be just the typical Animal Kingdom souvenirs. There is a variety of goods actually imported from Africa, and a large selection of books on Africa. Not all of the tee shirts have Mickey Mouse on them; there are some cool ones with lions, and tigers, and bears (oh, my!).

Duka La Filimu   Yes, you guess it—it's a film kiosk, and your last chance to buy that extra roll of film before going on Kilimanjaro Safaris.

RAFIKI'S PLANET WATCH
(Conservation Station)

Board the Wildlife Express train in Africa (it's the only way to get here), and take a trip backstage to see how Disney cares for all of the critters living at its park. Ecology is the rule here as Disney stresses the important role conservation plays in their operation of Animal Kingdom. You will also be able to learn how you, too, can help preserve the Earth while trying out the hands-on activities and interactive exhibits.

There are no real attractions at Conservation Station, and, quite honestly, not much to keep an adult amused, but the kids will have fun with the exhibits, and it does send a universal message that we can all do something to help our planet survive.

What You'll See

The Affection Section   Just your typical petting farm, basically not much more than a bunch of goats; but, for some reason, little kids love to chase after goats. If you don't watch out, you could spend a lot more time here than is necessary, so make sure you have a scheme for luring the kids away (something like, "Let's go back to Africa and get some ice cream!").

Animal Cam   Lets you watch the antics of the animals in their backstage homes through the use of closed-circuit television.

Animal Health and Care   Windows allow you to look into a nursery of baby animals where you can "ooh" and "aah" over the cute little creatures. Windows also allow you to watch veterinarians as they care for sick or injured animals. Warning—sometimes this can be a little too graphic for the little ones. (We were there when they amputated the toe of a crane—it didn't do much for *our* stomachs!)

Eco Web   Links you to worldwide conservation organizations via a computer.

Habitat Habit!   Get up close and personal with some cottontail tamarins while you learn how to make your backyard a haven for our fury friends.

Rafiki's Planet Watch and Eco Heroes   Through the use of interactive videos, connects you with world-renowned conservationists to learn more about what you can do to help the environment.

Song of the Rainforest   Very reminiscent of the Soundsations sound booths at Disney-MGM Studios. Sit back and relax in your private sound booth, and get prepared to experience three-dimensional sound. While listening to the sounds of the rainforest, you'll understand the crucial role these endangered resources play in the overall ecology of our planet Earth.

Where You'll Eat

Fast-Food/Counter Service

Munch Wagon   Hot dogs, chips, drinks. Not much to choose from, and this is the only place to find food in Conservation Station. Our suggestion would be to eat in Africa before boarding the train. Prices up to $4.

Where You'll Shop

Out of the Wild   One of the few stores in Animal Kingdom that doesn't just sell park souvenirs. Conservation-themed clothing and decorations. Good collection of books for the ecology-minded.

ASIA

This is the newest land at Disney's Animal Kingdom. It's also one of the smallest. There are really only two attractions in Asia, and one of those is a walk-through. But if you get the chance, look to your right as you enter Asia—sometimes there is a family of chimpanzees swinging from the trees above you. But don't look too long, you need to find the line for Kali River Rapids.

What You'll See

"Flights of Wonder" at Caravan Stage   What self-respecting animal park could call itself an animal park without having a bird show? Although the storyline for this 30-minute show is rather lame, they do break from the ordinary at times and feature an interesting selection of trained birds, including hawks, vultures, barn owls, hornbills, storks, and a grape-eating toucan.

Originally, this show was completely outdoors with no shade in sight. They have recently added some screening over the seats, but it still can get pretty hot during the middle of the day. If you insist on seeing this show, do it during the cooler times of the day.

Kali River Rapids   On a hot Florida afternoon, why not take this whitewater rafting trip down the Chakrandi River. You'll float down the river and experience the destruction of the rainforests firsthand. There will be drops and falls along the way, and we'll guarantee you: you will get wet! Actually, *soaked* is more like it, but what could be more refreshing after a long day of walking in the sun (we would think twice about going on this attraction on a cool day in the winter, though).

The best time to do this ride is right before you leave the park (you can go back to your room and dry yourself off in private). Another option would be to take your ponchos out of your backpack and wear them (we did—it might look stupid but it works!). Also, before you leave your hotel, you might want to pack a towel in your backpack. But please, make use of the watertight compartment in the middle of the raft to hold your valuables. (Our traveler's checks turned to mush when we didn't take our own advice.) And make sure that you put your feet up onto the bar surrounding the bottom of the compartment. It's not much fun to walk through the rest of the park with soaking wet sneakers!

Don't let all of this talk about water disturb you. It's a fun ride (although it is a bit too short) so *Don't Miss This!* Kids must be forty-two inches tall to ride. *FASTPASS!*

Maharajah Jungle Trek   This is a walk-through adventure into the world of the mythical Anandapur Royal Forest. Explore the surroundings inhabited by tamirs and komodo dragons. Get up-close and personal with a beautiful family of tigers. And you'll get even closer to some giant fruit bats when you enter the bat house. We'll bet you won't even notice that there's no glass in the windows of the bat house, and there is nothing to stop the bats from flying into your room. But don't worry, it's the middle of the day and bats are only active at night (we hope!).

> **Sshhhh!**
>
> The least crowded restroom in Animal Kingdom is to the left of the "Flights of Wonder" bird show, especially while the show is in progress.

Where You'll Eat

Fast-Food/Counter Service

Chakranadi Chicken Shop   Asian specialties, including chicken satay, along with roasted corn on the cob. Prices up to $7.

Mr. Kamil's Burger Grill   Burgers, cheeseburgers, and soda served in an Animal Kingdom souvenir cup. Prices up to $7.

Snacks/Drinks

Anandapur Ice Cream   Ice cream cones and floats. Prices up to $3.

Drinkwallah   Cold drinks (brought to you by Coca-Cola). Prices up to $3.

Where You'll Shop

Mandala Gifts   A small shop featuring Asian-themed gifts. There are also carts nearby that sell Kali River Rapids souvenirs and towels to dry yourself off (for those of you who forgot to bring in your own!)

DINOLAND, U.S.A.

Pass under the "Oldengate Bridge," a 40-foot-tall replica of a Brachiosaurus skeleton, and enter into a world like you've never seen before—unless, of course, you're a product of the 1950s and 1960s, and your parents brought you to those mom-and-pop-operated amusement parks of the time (whoops, now we're showing our age).

After spending all that time with the real animals at the rest of the park, here's your chance to spend some with the extinct. Play the part of a paleontologist in one of the quirkiest dig sites on Earth, but be careful when you do dig: All the bones here have been created, again, from that curious substance, Disney cement.

What You'll See

The Boneyard   Here's the place to bring your kids to let them release some of their pent-up energy. Send them on a dinosaur dig where they can pretend to dig up the bones of a *T. rex* in a huge sandbox. Plenty of places to run, jump, and just act like a kid, but a word of warning: Once you set your kids loose in this larger-than-life-sized playground, you may not be able to get them out! Don't let the dinosaurs eat up your time—you still have plenty to see!

Cretaceous Trail   If you have ever wondered what the Earth looked like during the time of the dinosaur, take a stroll through the winding paths of the Cretaceous Trail. Along the way you'll view a vast collection of plants that have faced the test of time, surviving from prehistoric times to the present. The plants look so different than those we often see that you will be tempted to reach out and touch each one, and we can tell you from experience, some feel pretty weird. Don't be surprised if you stumble on some dinosaur dig sites along the way.

Dinosaur   Hop aboard your Time Rover and get ready to be whisked back in time 65 million years. Prepare for the adventure of your lifetime as you attempt to bring back the last remaining dinosaur. But will you be able to grab the creature in time and make it back to the present before a giant meteor slams into the Earth, sending all remaining dinosaurs into extinction?

This attraction is a technological marvel, just like the Indiana Jones ride at Disneyland in California! Imagine being in a flight simulator (similar to the ones used in Star Tours and Body Wars), only this one's on wheels and actually moves through the attraction! The show itself, however, lacks the adventure and thrills of the Indiana Jones ride. This whole ride's basically just a bunch of dinosaurs in a very dark chamber (the dinos in EPCOT's Universe of Energy are much cooler), but the vehicles themselves are incredible!

Please note that the ride is very rough, so think twice about it if you suffer from severe motion sickness. Also, if you have small children, ask a cast member about doing a baby swap. Kids must be forty inches tall to ride. *Don't Miss This! FASTPASS!*

Dinosaur Jubilee   Here's where you get to view a collection of dinosaur remains that could fill a small warehouse. If you're wondering where they got all those bones, we'll let you in on a little secret: These are not the real things, they are just castings taken from the originals. It's still worth going on a quick walk-through, though, because it gives you a perspective on the different sizes and types of dinosaurs that once roamed the Earth.

Fossil Preparation Lab   This small, walk-through exhibit teaches you how castings are made from fossils, and then formed into replicas of dinosaur bones.

Tarzan Rocks!   This is one of the swingingest shows at the Animal Kingdom! This live-stage show features Tarzan and his friends from the jungle in a performance full of extreme stunts and gymnastic moves that will keep the whole family on the edge of their seats. The action takes place all around you as you are entertained by a live performance of the movie's soundtrack.

This high-energy show is a must-see, but remember, as with all outside shows, this stadium gets very hot during the middle of the day. It's better to put off seeing this show until late in the afternoon or, better yet, you could catch the first performance in the morning. *Don't Miss This!*

Where You'll Eat

Cafeterias/Food Courts

Restaurantosaurus   Cheeseburgers (thankfully, not McDonald's), hot dogs, grilled chicken salad, vegetarian platters.

Also has McDonald's Chicken McNuggets and Happy Meals available for the kids. Prices up to $6.

In the morning (until 10:00 A.M.), join Donald Duck and his friends here at Donald's Prehistoric Breakfastosaurus. You'll be able to meet the Disney gang up-close and get plenty of photos with the kids, while enjoying an all-you-can-eat buffet breakfast.

Fast-Food/Counter Service

DinoLand Snacks   Serves McDonald's French fries and drinks. (McDonald's is the corporate sponsor for DinoLand, U.S.A. As part of their "deal," they have become the first restaurant chain to sell their goods inside a Disney theme park—something that we're not very happy to see. Even though you would never call Disney's food world-class, at least you still felt as though you were dining at a Disney resort, not at your local McDonald's.) Prices up to $3.

Snacks/Drinks

Dino Diner   Traditional breakfast breads served in the morning. Later in the day it serves the ever-popular smoked turkey legs and drinks. Prices up to $5.

Where You'll Shop

Chester and Hester's Dinosaur Treasures   Here's where you can pick up all those souvenirs you crave from Dinosaur (you know, the "I survived the Dinosaur ride" tee shirts that you just have to have after experiencing the ride!). Good selection of kids clothes (with a dino theme), adult tee shirts, and large soft rubber dinosaurs.

Kudos to the Disney Imagineers for this store. The atmosphere is so tacky that you'll get quite a kick out of it. So spend a few minutes looking around and soaking it all in.

FREE AT ANIMAL KINGDOM

**Check the park's daily Entertainment
Schedule for more details.**

Animal Encounters   Periodically, Animal Kingdom keepers appear throughout the park with some of their smaller animal friends, answering questions and allowing you to get up-close and personal with some interesting animal breeds.

March of the Artimals Parade   This is, without a doubt, the worst parade Disney has ever staged! It is just a bunch of cast members dressed in some pretty strange-looking animal costumes. No wonder it's free. Take our advice and don't bother with it, but if you won't be satisfied until you see it for yourself, show times are at 11:00 A.M. and 2:00 P.M. daily.

8

The "Lesser" Attractions

Designed to distract you from the
four major theme parks.

DOWNTOWN DISNEY

The Disney Village Marketplace certainly has grown up. Once it only consisted of a half-dozen or so less-than-spectacular stores. In 1989, Pleasure Island, Disney's first-ever adult-oriented entertainment complex, was added. Now with the opening of the vast new West Side, as well as extensive renovation and refurbishing of existing stores and attractions, the newly named 120-acre Downtown Disney is like a theme park in itself. Between all the shops, clubs, movies, and restaurants, you could spend hours here (but best not make it your *only* destination in Disney World!).

To make your time here most productive, we've broken Downtown Disney down into three sections (as Disney does): Downtown Disney Westside, Downtown Disney Marketplace, and Downtown Disney Pleasure Island. Remember, however, even though Downtown Disney is calling itself "The heart of a city on a corner of our World," it remains a "lesser attraction." You should not spend valuable vacation time here, unless you've already seen all you need to see in the Magic Kingdom, EPCOT, Disney-MGM Studios, and the Animal Kingdom.

NOTE: If you're staying in a Walt Disney World hotel, you can arrange to have larger packages purchased at Downtown Disney delivered right to your room, free of charge.

How to Get There

Disney World buses make several stops in Downtown Disney from all Disney World hotels, and from the TTC. Boats also service the area from the two Port Orleans hotels and the Old Key West Resort. Visitors arriving by car park in the large Downtown Disney lot; parking is free to all. Valet parking is available for $6 after 5:30 P.M. All guests can take complimentary boat launches between the West Side and Marketplace from 6:00 P.M. to midnight.

DOWNTOWN DISNEY WESTSIDE

The newest addition to the Downtown Disney complex plays host to several world class restaurants and state of the art attractions and exhibits.

Key West Side Landmarks

- Baby Changing Station—In all restrooms.
- Banking Services—There is an ATM machine to the left of the House of Blues, and near the Forty Thirst Street shop.
- Information—Guest Services, in the AMC movie complex.
- Lost and Found—Guest Services.

What You'll See

AMC 24 Theatres Complex More than 6,000 seats to choose from make this the largest, most comfortable complex of its type in the Southeast—plus 16 of the 24 theaters feature stadium seating (i.e., seats are arranged in tiers, so you're not looking at the back of someone's head all night). If you must spend two hours of your precious vacation time in a movie theater, at least you've chosen one with a state-of-the-art sound system. Money-saving matinees are available, and guests staying at Disney resorts receive a 30 percent discount after 6 P.M.—just show your resort ID card at the box office. To avoid lines, you can charge tickets up to three days before the show (call 407-827-1311). For show times, call 407-827-1300.

Cirque du Soleil The special Disney World version of the renowned avant-garde stage extravaganza combines circus acts, acrobatics, music, costumes, humor, special effects, and dance. Shows are staged twice daily, five days a week in the 1,650-seat, 73,800-square-foot theater which resembles a circus tent. But at $67 for an adult ticket ($39 for a child 3–9 years of age) this show goes way beyond a cheapskate's budget.

DisneyQuest A glorified high-tech arcade, reminiscent of Innoventions in EPCOT, featuring all the latest cutting edge games, including interactive games and virtual reality. Your adventures in the massive five-story, 100,000-square-foot building include piloting an armed vehicle through rocky alien terrain; a virtual sword fight against comic book villains; a ride on a raft down a prehistoric virtual river; careening down a roller coaster track of your own design; a magic carpet ride through Aladdin's hometown; a spin at the wheel of Buzz Lightyear's Astro Blast futuristic bumper car; and much more. Many other Disney characters pop up from time to time. BEWARE: this place tends to swallow your children whole, so set some time limits, although it's easy for Dad to get in the spirit of things and spend way too much time here. Open 10:30 A.M. to midnight. (This is the first of what will probably be 20 to 30 DisneyQuests worldwide.)

House of Blues Top-rated musicians playing all kinds of music perform nightly in this Hard Rock Café-inspired blues hall/restaurant, owned by Blues Brother/actor Dan Aykroyd, Jim Belushi, John Goodman, and the rock band Aerosmith. Featured performances take place nightly, and reservations are recommended, especially for live shows. Check the entertainment schedule for show times, or call their hotline at 407-934-2222. Food available (read on).

Where You'll Eat

Sit-Down

Bongos Cuban Café Just what you'd expect from a restaurant owned by Latin superstar Gloria Estefan and her husband, Emilio. A taste of Miami's vibrant South Beach, Bongos serves authentic Cuban cuisine in a festive, art-deco setting, complete with a giant three-story pineapple rising through the middle of the place. Strolling Latin guitarists set the Caribbean mood, serenading you while you eat. Two dance floors, naturally, in case you just gotta do that conga! Serving lunch and dinner, from 11:00 A.M. to 2:00 A.M., and reservations cannot be made. Most items under $20.

House of Blues Tasty Cajun food from the Mississippi Delta region, from whence the Blues came (like jambalaya, etouffee, and po'boys), as well as pasta, burgers, seafood, and more. The restaurant/concert hall resembles a home from the Old South adorned with photos and art celebrating the great "Bluesmen." The gospel brunch, at $26, is probably not in the budget of most cheapskates. Serving lunch and dinner, from 11:00 A.M. to 2:00 A.M., with many entrees under $20.

Planet Hollywood This huge sphere-shaped 26,000-square-foot restaurant is Disney's version of the restaurant chain run by partners Sylvester Stallone, Arnold Schwarzenegger, and Bruce Willis, and, like the others in the chain, it is packed with interesting movie memorabilia and props, including Gene Kelly's *Singin' in the Rain* duds and the bus from *Speed*. The food is considered New American cuisine (burgers, fish, steak, pasta), but let's face it: It's nothing to write home about, and calling it that won't be going here for the food anyway. We recommend you just walk through the place and check out the museum-like artifacts, maybe even buy a tee shirt (that should make 'em happy). Serving lunch and dinner, from 11:00 A.M. to 1:00 A.M.

Wolfgang Puck Café That world-renowned chef brings his unusual taste sensations, from pizzas to pastas, to Disney World and this exotic, postmodern setting. Serving lunch and dinner—including gourmet pizzas, grilled fish, salads, sushi, and more—from 11:00 A.M. to midnight. Up to $20.

Snacks/Drinks

Disney's Candy Cauldron   Hand-spun cotton candy and more sweet sensations in this fairy-tale dungeon.

Forty Thirst Street   Warm up with coffee or cappuccino, or cool off with fresh-squeezed juices, smoothies, and much more.

Virgin Café   Typical coffeehouse fare.

Where You'll Shop

All Star Gear   Logo merchandise from the All Star Café (the new sports-themed restaurant chain, owned by today's professional athletes, including Shaquille O'Neal, Joe Montana, and Wayne Gretzky, with Disney's version appearing at the Wide World of Sports). Tee shirts, sweatshirts, jackets, and more.

Celebrity Eyeworks Studio   Designer shades and prescription eyewear—even replicas of glasses worn in recent popular movies.

Guitar Gallery by George's Music   You can buy a guitar from anywhere from $200 to $25,000, from such leading guitar makers as Gender, Guild, Ibanez, and Washburn, as well as accessories, books, and sheet music. Why not go in and browse around?

Hoypoloi   A unique gallery of art glass, ceramics, and sculptures made of metal, wood, and stone.

Magnetron   More than 20,000 refrigerator magnets of just about every ilk, including some that talk, sing, and even glow in the dark.

Sosa Family Cigars   Handrolled stogies from the finest tobaccos (probably not for the White Owl/Cheapskate's crowd, but maybe you can find a decent "cheap" cigar if you look hard enough).

Starabilias   Celebrity autographs, memorabilia, and collectibles offered in a nostalgic showroom. No matter who you idolize, you're sure to find something here to spend money on.

Virgin Megastore   Almost an attraction in itself, this massive 49,000-square-foot, three-story store sells everything from music to books to videos to software. It's fun just to sample the goods at the hundreds of listening stations, viewing stands, and computer terminals. You might even check out a live performance on the elevated outdoor stage. Opens 10:00 A.M.

Wildhorse Store   Pick up your Nashville music souvenirs, as well as contemporary country and western apparel.

DOWNTOWN DISNEY PLEASURE ISLAND

During the day, visitors can browse through its friendly shops free-of-charge; at night (from 7:00 P.M. to 2:00 A.M.), the klieg lights and neon click on and Pleasure Island is transformed. There's a New Year's Eve party every night in the street, and partygoers walk from club to club, sampling the music, dancing, and fun.

Admission to Pleasure Island is often included in multiday package deals to Disney. If you don't buy a package, and you're not much of a party animal, you might want to think twice about going. It costs about $20 to get in (not including drinks, souvenirs, and the like), and after a full day of touring one of the resorts, you may be too tired to fully enjoy the place.

After 7:00 P.M., no one under 18 is admitted onto Pleasure Island without an accompanying parent or guardian. When you arrive, check an entertainment schedule for possible shows at the Waterfront and West End Stages. And before you go, check on the starting time of the New Year's Eve show (407) 934-7781.

Key Pleasure Island Landmarks

- Baby Changing Station—In all restrooms.
- Banking Services—There is an ATM and change machine

located under the stairs leading up to the Rock N Roll Beach Club.

- Lockers—The BET SoundStage, 8Trax, Mannequins, the Rock N Roll Beach Club, and across from the Wildhorse Saloon.

What You'll See

Adventurers Club   You'll feel as if you walked right into a 1930s explorer's club, replete with veddy British, eccentric folks (actually performers, as if we had to tell you) who recall their supposed travels and expeditions to anyone who might be eavesdropping (that means you). They'll argue amongst themselves and mingle with you—if you like it or not—while you check out the Victorian style decor, photos, and memorabilia from exotic places. There's even a haunted organ. This place—and its denizens—are definitely, shall we say, different. It's worth a few minutes as an interesting diversion, but if you stay too long, you might become as nutty as the people who work here. The doors open at 7:00 P.M.; check the entertainment schedule for special show times.

BET SoundStage Club   This is the home of the best in R&B, jazz, soul, and hip-hop, presented by Black Entertainment Television in an atmosphere of flashing lights, blasting sound, a large dance floor, and dozens of video monitors that show the programming of BET. Regular live performances by known and unknown performers of diverse musical styles. Must be 21 years old to enter. Formerly the Neon Armadillo. Opens 8:00 P.M. Food available (read on).

The Comedy Warehouse   This popular multileveled club, decorated with movie props, is the scene of several family-style comedy shows a night (we've never heard a bad word uttered there, but then again, we've never heard one of the "name" comedians perform there). The 35-minute show, performed by the Who What and Warehouse Players, is high on improvisation and audience participation. Opens at 7:30 P.M.; check the entertainment schedule for show times.

8Trax This club's urban-industrial atmosphere (exposed pipes, chain-link fences) make it a favorite among the young crowd. The exceptional sound system blasts out disco sounds of the 1970s (songs you remember hearing on your old 8-Track players). Opens at 8:00 P.M. Food available (read on).

Hub Video Stage The scene of live bands and hot music, for those seeking to avoid the crowds at the West End Stage, but not wanting to miss any of the action (catch it all on a wall of 25 video monitors). Check the entertainment schedule for all the details, or call Pleasure Island information.

Mannequin's Dance Palace Pulsating light, lasers, and high-tech sound; special effects; live on-stage performances; a giant turntable-shaped revolving dance floor; and mannequins (as per the name of the club) comprise this hot and hip nightclub, which guests name among their Pleasure Island favorites. Opens at 8:00 P.M.; check the entertainment schedule for times when a special show will take place. Must be 21 years old to enter.

Midway Games Games of chance, skill, and fun: distractions you'd see (and drop money at) at almost any carnival.

Pleasure Island Jazz Company In a circular room accented by the wares of traveling musicians, you'll enjoy live jazz and blues music, performed by known and soon-to-be-known musicians and vocalists. Opens at 8:00 P.M. Check the entertainment schedule for show times. Food available (read on).

Rock N Roll Beach Club Follow the surfboards that line the three flights of stairs to this bar featuring, on different levels, pool tables, video games, a stage, and a dance floor. Live musicians perform 1960s to 1990s rock, with deejays filling the breaks in between. Opens 7:00 P.M., with live shows starting around 8:00 P.M. Check the entertainment schedule for show times. Food available (read on).

Waterfront Stage Live bands and deejays kick things off around 7:30 P.M. to get you in the celebratory spirit. Check the entertainment schedule for all the details, or call Pleasure Island information.

West End Stage Top-name music artists appear regularly at this outdoor venue. Check the entertainment schedule for all the details, or call Pleasure Island information.

Wildhorse Saloon One of the new brand of today's trendy comedy-western clubs where urban cowboys (and gals) do the Texas two-step and all that. This place has the ambiance you would expect from Disney, plus live performances that take place every night, often by name performers, and free dance lessons (yee ha!) on a huge dance floor. The club, formerly the Fireworks Factory, opens at 7:00 P.M.; check the entertainment schedule for show times and dance class availability. Food available (read on).

Where You'll Eat

Sit-Down

Fulton's Crab House This replica of a nineteenth-century paddle-wheeled boat used to be called *The Empress Lily*. It was named after Walt's wife, and was a rather elegant restaurant, where jackets and ties were de rigeur. Now, with nary a thought for tradition, it's been converted to a seafood restaurant. We think it's a sin that the name and whole dignified aura of the place has been changed, and we hope Walt's ghost comes to haunt the Disney brass. Open 8:00 A.M. to midnight, serving breakfast, lunch, and dinner; daily character breakfast available (see chapter 9). Crab, lobster, seafood, and pastas. Prices up to $35.

Portobello Yacht Club Italian food, including thin-crusted pizza, seafood, homemade pastas, espresso, cappuccino, and delicious desserts, served amidst a collection of boating trophies and momentos that fill this elegant dining hall. Serving lunch and dinner; 11:30 A.M. to midnight. Prices up to $35.

Wildhorse Saloon Tasty, downhome American barbecue, grilled meats, seafood, pasta, snacks, salads, appetizers, and home-baked desserts. Dinner served until 2:00 A.M., entrees under $20.

Snacks/Drinks

BET SoundStage Club   Enjoy some barbecue items and Caribbean-style appetizers as you listen to the contemporary music in this waterfront club. Love that jerk chicken! Many items under $10.

8Trax   This retro club offers a selection of snacks and appetizers.

D-Zertz   Pastries, candy, ice cream, coffee, cappuccino. Open until 2:00 A.M.

Fulton's Stone Crab Lounge   Light entrees available, including fish and salads, and views of Lake Buena Vista.

Missing Link   Snacks, sodas. Open until 2 A.M.

Pleasure Island Jazz Company   Hot and cold snacks, appetizers, and desserts.

Portobello Yacht Club Bar   Italian appetizers, espresso, and cappuccino.

Rock N Roll Beach Club   Pizza is served, whole or by the slice, in this beach-style nightclub.

Where You'll Shop

Avigators Supply   Clothing and accessories for the wannabe adventurer: merchandise befitting the gang inhabiting the Adventurers Club and anyone who enjoys the great outdoors. Hiking boots, backpacks, and other outdoor gear.

Changing Attitudes   Hip duds for the well-dressed and trendy young man and woman. Up-to-the-minute fashions and accessories.

DTV   Pleasure Island's requisite Disney character shop, which stocks the usual assortment of character merchandise, like tee shirts, watches, jewelry, and other apparel. Why shop here when you're so close to the far superior World of Disney store in the Marketplace?

Island Depot   Duds for the surfer dude, including tee shirts, baggies, and other surfwear, both trendy and retro, as well as Rock N Roll Beach Club logo merchandise.

Mouse House   Another chance to buy Disney character merchandise.

Music Legends   Collectibles and memorabilia from the legends of the music industry. CDs, tee shirts, autographed photos, and posters of your favorite rock stars. Located below the Pleasure Island deejay booth (of course!).

Superstar Studios   Karaoke fans can make their own music video or audio recording in a professional studio setting. It's just as much fun to walk by and listen to the people who think they have a really great voice attempting to sing.

Suspended Animation   Another shop featuring the art of Disney as depicted in animation cells, prints, and other collectibles. Lithographs are available for most of the Disney classics, and are available framed or unframed. Most items in this store are too expensive for us, but the unframed posters are of a very good quality and only sell for about $15.

> Beware: The busiest night on Pleasure Island is Thursday. That's the night employees (oh, we mean "cast members") head to the Isle in record numbers because they receive special discounts on is food and attractions.

FREE AT DOWNTOWN DISNEY PLEASURE ISLAND

New Year's Eve Street Party   Fireworks, lasers, confetti, dancers, and music set the stage for Pleasure Island's nightly New Year's Eve Party. The countdown to "midnight" begins at the West End Stage at 10:45 P.M. (11:45 P.M. on Fridays and Saturdays), and you'll soon find yourself singing, dancing, and drinking—maybe even joining the conga line!

DOWNTOWN DISNEY MARKETPLACE

There's really only one reason to head to the Downtown Disney Marketplace—to shop!

Key Marketplace Landmarks

- Information—Guest Services, next to Europsain.

- Baby Changing Station—In all restrooms.

- Lost and Found—Guest Services.

What You'll See

Not much to see here, besides, of course, the shops. The Marketplace is open from 9:30 A.M. until 11:00 P.M., so on those nights when the parks close early, it's a good place to go to kill some time. Remember, if you're staying at an on-site Disney resort, your purchases can be delivered straight to your room.

Where You'll Eat

There's nothing spectacular here. If you're looking for a quick bite while shopping, you may want to walk next door to one of the places in Pleasure Island—provided admission is free at the time! Or, hop a boat to the West Side.

Sit-Down

Cap'n Jack's Oyster Bar   Open from 11:30 A.M. until 10:30 P.M. for lunch and dinner. Fresh seafood, shellfish, chowder, and pastas, served in a nautical setting. Views from this restaurant at the end of a pier are beautiful since you actually dine over the lake, looking out at the marina. Prices up to $20.

Rainforest Café   You really feel as though you are in a lush rainforest when you dine in this restaurant! You are surrounded by lush tropical plants and exotic animals (some live, many animated), and you may actually experience a thunderstorm or two. Serves seafood, pastas, salads, chicken, steaks, pizza, and sandwiches—many exotic and most of the kind of overpriced fare you can get at any Planet Hollywood–type themed restaurant. Open 10:30 A.M. to 11:00 P.M. for lunch and dinner. Since they do not take reservations in advance, be prepared to wait. Prices up to $20.

Fast-Food/Counter Service

The Gourmet Pantry   Fresh baked pastries and cookies, homemade salads and sandwiches sold by the inch, plus gourmet coffees—even iced cappuccino. Opens at 9:00 A.M. to 11:00 P.M., many items under $10.

McDonald's   (or is it "Mickey D's"?!) If you've read this book to this point, you know how we feel about McDonald's: decent food, but they don't belong in Disney World. You know what they serve and you know what it costs. Okay, at least the kids' play area is kind of neat. Open Sunday to Wednesday 8:00 A.M. to 1:00 A.M., Thursday to Saturday until 2 A.M.

Wolfgang Puck Express   That master chef redefines fast-food. Watch as your meal is prepared right in front of you, as the chefs whip up an eclectic assortment of appetizers, pizzas, soups, sandwiches, salads, and more. Hours: Sunday to Thursday 11:00 A.M. to 11:00 00 P.M.; Friday and Saturday until midnight. Prices up to $20.

Snacks/Drinks

Ghirardelli Soda Fountain and Chocolate Shop   San Francisco's world famous old-time chocolate marker invades the Marketplace. Have a treat any time of day: ice cream, shakes, sundaes, chocolates, and other delicious delectables. Sweet gifts also available. Open 10:00 A.M. to 11:00 P.M. weekdays, until midnight on weekends. Many items under $10.

Rainforest Café Magic Mushroom Juice and Coffee Bar   Exotic and traditional drinks, plus coffees, served in the lush Rainforest setting.

Sunset Cove   Sip a refreshing drink by the water.

2 R's Coffee Bar Walk right up and order your favorite cappuccino and espresso.

Where You'll Shop

The Marketplace boasts more than a dozen unique shops, but most of them aren't worth mentioning. The important thing to remember is that, if you are a Magic Kingdom Club member, the Marketplace is the one place where you receive 10 percent off your purchases (as long as they are over $10), if you show them your card. (Shops are open from 9:30 A.M. to 11:00 P.M. Sunday through Thursday, 9:30 A.M. to 11:30 P.M. Friday and Saturday.) So before making your souvenir purchases in the park, check out the World of Disney shop at the Marketplace.

The World of Disney The largest Disney character store anywhere in the world, with over 50,000 square feet of space in 12 huge rooms. Chances are that anything you could possibly want to buy at one of the parks will be in the World of Disney—from infant wear to intimate apparel. And if you wait to buy it there, you can save 10 percent with your Magic Kingdom Club card. (See "Sources for Additional Savings" for all the details.)

Additional Stores

The Art of Disney Nice quality (and expensive!) selection of Disney animation art and collectibles. When there are commas in the price, we tend to steer clear: too rich for us cheapskates!

Disney's Days of Christmas The place to go for that Snow White tree topper you've always wanted—it's Christmas 365 days a year in this beautifully decorated shop! Good selection of affordable ornaments, which can be personalized so you can remember your special vacation better.

Disney at Home Imaginative and useful items for your bedroom and bath.

EUROSPAIN   Presented by Arribas Brothers: glass-blown and etched decorative items, crystal, jewelry, gifts, and glassware. Custom engraving/etching available.

Gourmet Pantry   Kitchen accessories, gadgets, and cookbooks—some may even feature your favorite Disney character! Check out the decorative copper molds for your kitchen walls shaped like—who else—Mickey and Minnie. Large selection of cookie jars, salt and pepper shakers, even fine wines.

Harrington Bay Clothiers   Casual resort wear and dress fashions and accessories for men—from such designers as Polo, Nautica, and Tommy Hilfiger, among others.

LEGO Imagination Center   Kids can literally build to their heart's content in this one-of-a-kind interactive, hands-on superstore using Lego, Duplo, and other colorful building blocks. There's even an interactive outdoor playground for the littlest shoppers. Look for the "life-size" dinosaur and sea monster made entirely of Legos.

Pooh Corner   The Hundred Acre Wood Superstore featuring thousands of items featuring Winnie the Pooh and his friends.

Resortwear Unlimited   Women's casual resort and swimwear from a variety of designers and in a variety of styles. Lancôme skin care and beauty products.

Studio M   Using the wonders of modern technology, you can picture yourself (literally!) with Mickey and his friends at this one-stop photo shop.

Summer Sands   Pick up that gift that will remind you most of Florida. Clothing, jewelry, straw hats, and bags—all with a tropical look. Also carries a supply of sun-care products.

Team Mickey's Athletic Club   Sports-related clothing and accessories with the Team Disney logo emblazoned thereon. Also has a good selection of professional and college sports team logo clothing, accessories, and memorabilia.

Toys Fantastic   Brought to you by Mattel: good selection of Hot Wheels toys, Barbie dolls, and any conceivable Disney character item manufactured by Mattel.

2R's Reading and Riting   Quaint little bookstore stocked with Disney-related books and merchandise, as well as today's bestsellers. Story books for the kids, videos, magazines, Disney software, and a large selection of greeting cards and stationery.

THE WATER PARKS

Back in the eighties Disney took a look at the flood (pardon the pun) of Florida's water parks—Wet 'n' Wild, Watermania, and others—and realized that their quaint little River Country just did not cut it. So, since 1989 they've opened two new water parks, Typhoon Lagoon and Blizzard Beach, leaving you one less reason to venture out of the Disney gates. We recommend at least one day of relative relaxation at one of these parks during your Disney stay (especially if admission is included in the ticket plan you purchase, because a single day admission at one of the water parks ranges from $16 to $30 if purchased separately).

When you're thinking about which park to visit, keep in mind that some call for more advanced swimmers than others. Blizzard Beach is the newest and also the most challenging. Typhoon Lagoon is still pretty intense, but definitely milder than Blizzard Beach. River Country is the oldest and tamest. It doesn't have the thrilling speed slides that Blizzard Beach has, but if you have small kids who don't swim particularly well, River Country has more to offer them (although there are kiddie areas in the other two parks).

Each of the parks offers towel and locker rentals, showers, and changing areas. Life jackets are available free of charge if you leave a refundable deposit. And please note that you will not be able to ride any of the slides or attractions if your swimsuit has any buckles, rivets, or other exposed metal surfaces on it (you could damage the equipment, or, even worse, yourself). Fortunately for the cheapskate, you are allowed to bring coolers into the water parks, but you cannot bring any glass containers or alcoholic beverages. So make a sandwich and bring it along—the food here is nothing special, so you won't be missing a culinary delight.

And whichever park you visit, bring sunscreen, sunglasses, and some kind of water shoes, as the sand and walkways tend to get scorching hot!

Now Read This!

Florida often bears the brunt of brief tropical downpours, especially during summer months. If it rains, you will be chased from the water for your safety's sake. You might even be asked to leave the park, especially in the afternoon. If you're there first thing in the morning, as we suggest, and it does rain, by all means, don't leave! Because when all the other discouraged bathers go back to their rooms, you'll be waiting on the sidelines, and when the clouds break, you'll be able to enjoy the crowd-free attractions.

The water parks can get very busy later in the day. If the parking lots fill up, the only people allowed in are those who use the Disney World transportation system (in other words, you must be a Disney World resort guest). All the more reason to get there early.

Before You Go: Call ahead for operating hours. The park

Note Regarding Cheap Eats in the Water Parks

No one goes to the water parks expressly to eat. But if hunger pangs strike, each has its share of vittles (although the food in River Country is much better than the burger joint variety of Typhoon Lagoon and Blizzard Beach. Read on.).

And This One's for the Ladies

Take our advice: Wear a one-piece bathing suit to the water parks, unless you're an exhibitionist. The rushing water on many of the water attractions has a tendency to make a suit ride up or off, if you know what we mean.

you have in mind may be closed for maintenance, especially during off-peak times or in colder months.

And if you enjoy marinating in the Florida sun on a beach chair, please realize that everyone entering the park runs right to the first beach chair they lay eyes on. If you want the best selection, start at the back of the park. And while you're there, do some of the more popular rides and slides before everybody else catches up to you.

BLIZZARD BEACH

This is Disney's newest water park. It opened in 1995 with more water slides than Typhoon Lagoon and River Country combined.

The story goes that once upon a time, a freak snowstorm hit Florida. Somebody came up with the brilliant idea to build a ski resort, but unfortunately, the snow began to melt rapidly once the temperature started to rise back to its tropical norm. Water began to cascade down the snow-covered mountains, and then everything was frozen in time, sort of in a half-frozen, half-melted state. And when someone spied an alligator frolicking in the slush, the idea for the Blizzard Beach water park was born.

Well, dare we say that all of that sounds quite farcical. But one thing is for sure: Blizzard Beach is the wettest ski resort you'll ever see—and probably the wildest! The slides and rides here are the most thrilling we've experienced.

How to Get There

Disney World buses reach Blizzard Beach from most hotels, parks, Downtown Disney, and from the Transportation and Ticket Center.

Key Blizzard Beach Landmarks

- First Aid—Near Lottawatta Lodge, by the main entrance.

- Life Vests—Available free (with deposit) at Snowless Joe's

Tube and Towel Rentals. You can bring your own flotation equipment to the park, but no masks or fins.

- Lockers—Lock up your stuff near the restrooms at Ava-lunch, or at the park's dressing rooms. Pick up keys at Snowless Joe's Tube and Towel Rentals.

- Towels—Rent them at Snowless Joe's Tube and Towel Rentals, or save a few bucks and bring one with you.

- Showers and Changing Area—Dressing rooms are located near the park entrance.

- Wheelchair Rentals—Just inside the entrance gate. Most of the paths around the park are wheelchair accessible, and the chair lift to the top of Mt. Gushmore can even accommodate wheelchairs!

What You'll See

Blizzard Beach Ski Patrol Training Camp   A section of the park designed with preteens in mind. Its diversions, somewhat scaled-down adventures for those less daring, include:

- Mogul Mania—Descend in an inner tube over knobby terrain while being misted by "snowmaking" machines.

- Ski Patrol Shelter—Hang on a suspended T-Bar and drop out into an icy cold pool, or take the fast slide route into the same cool water.

- Thin Ice Training Course—Walk across a pool on bobbing chucks of fake ice while holding the overhead cargo net.

Chair Lift   Most slides and rides start from the top of Mt. Gushmore. The chair lift is one of two ways to get to the summit of this ninety-foot mountain (the other way is to walk)—and one way down is the Summit Plummet. The ride up is relatively slow, and you have to get off the lift quickly, but after climbing up the mountain five times, we suggest the chair lift! And make sure you enjoy the view on the way to the top.

Cross Country Creek Now this is more our speed after a long week at Disney World: Lounge around on an inner tube and let the current move you along this meandering creek that circles the park. The whole circuitous route takes about thirty relaxing minutes, and there are some diversions along the way—interesting scenery, a spooky ice cave (watch out for the melting ice that drips from the ceiling), and more. You can get in at six different points along the creek—enter without a tube, or grab one that floats by (one that doesn't already have someone in it!).

Downhill Double Dipper Travel at speeds of up to 25 MPH on your bathing-suited butt, racing against your opponent on this, the world's only side-by-side speed slide. *Don't Miss This!*

Melt Away Bay At the base of Mt. Gushmore lies this tranquil, one-acre lagoon allegedly created by the mountains' snow runoff. While away the hours on the white sand beach or float in the gentle manmade waves. Your only protection from the sun is found at the limited in number, covered picnic tables, so grab your spot early.

Mt. Gushmore Enjoy a bird's-eye view of the park from the observation tower at the top of this mountain, the park's focal point.

Runoff Rapids Three different, bumpy inner tube rides, designed for single riders, doubles, or threesomes, twist and turn their way down the slope of the mountain. Try the middle flume—it's fully enclosed (and dark inside) so you never know when to expect the next drop.

Slush Gusher This water slide is a smaller version of *Summit Plummet,* and you will still reach speeds approaching 50 MPH on your descent. Hold onto your swimming trunks!

Snow Stormers Bring a raft up from the bottom and ride one of the three individual slalom courses that twist down the mountain. Like a real ski slalom course, your mission (should you choose to accept it) is to zigzag around the flags and gates you encounter on the way down.

Summit Plummet   Supposedly the fastest waterslide around (according to Disney). You'll cruise down this 120-foot high, 500-foot long water slide at 60 MPH, and it's all over in about a minute. It's the closest you can come to jumping off a 12-story building (and surviving!). Not for the ill of health or the faint of heart. Kids must be 48 inches tall to ride. *Don't Miss This!*

Teamboat Springs   Finally, a waterslide for the whole family! Up to five people can laugh and shriek their way down this twisting quarter-mile flume ride. By the way, you'll need to hold on tight as you careen down the ride. One of our favorites! *Don't Miss This!*

Tike's Peak   And finally, a special area for the kids where parents can rest assured that their little ones are safe. Here kids can enjoy kid-sized versions of some of the wilder slides and rides in the park. It also has a play area with a snow-castle fountain and water jets.

Toboggan Racer   As its name implies, you'll lie face down, head first, on a toboggan-like mat traveling down one of eight side-by-side waterslides descending Mt. Gushmore. You can control the ride experience somewhat—pull up on the front handles to go faster, push them down to slow down. Watch out for the dips and valleys! *Don't Miss This!*

Where You'll Eat

Fast-Food/Counter Service

Avalunch   Hot dogs, snacks, snow cones, ice cream, and cold drinks, most under $6.

Lottawatta Lodge   The largest refreshment stand in the park, fashioned in the style of a ski lodge. It has walk-up windows offering burgers, hot dogs, pizza salads, sandwiches, drinks, and ice cream—and definitely the best onion rings to be found on Disney property! The lodge also offers a nice, shaded view of the pool. Most items under $7.

Picnic Areas Grab a hard-to-find picnic table along the shores of Meltaway Bay, first thing upon your entering Blizzard Beach.

Snacks/Drinks

The Warming Hut Sausages, snacks, popcorn, ice cream, cold drinks—and some welcome shade. Most items under $6.

Where You'll Shop

Beach Haus Blizzard Beach logo items, tee shirts, and souvenirs. Beachwear, film, and sunscreen products. Hats, towels, and thong sandals are also available here.

TYPHOON LAGOON

There's a legend behind this 56-acre water park, too. Those Disney folks are just so dang creative. . . . The tale is that one day there was a tremendous storm. After it was over, what was once a quiet, peaceful resort village was destroyed. Wreckage was strewn everywhere. Why, a fishing boat was even impaled on the top of a mountain! You can still hear *Miss Tilly's* foghorn from atop Mt. Mayday as she spouts water from her smokestack every thirty minutes.

Typhoon Lagoon opened in 1989.

How to Get There

Disney World buses reach Typhoon Lagoon from most hotels, parks, Downtown Disney, and from the Transportation and Ticket Center.

Key Typhoon Lagoon Landmarks

- First Aid Station—Located to the left of the Leaning Palms store.

- Life Vests—Available free (with deposit) at High and Dry Towels. Tubes for bobbing in Typhoon Lagoon's waves can be rented at Castaway Creek Raft Rentals; you cannot bring your own floatation equipment to this park.

- Lockers—Lock up your stuff near the dressing rooms, or at Typhoon Tilly's. Pick up keys at High and Dry Towels.

- Towels—Rent them at High and Dry Towels, by the front entrance, or save a few bucks and bring your own.

- Showers and Changing Area—Dressing rooms are located near the park entrance.

- Wheelchair Rentals—Just inside the entrance gate. Most of the paths around the park are wheelchair accessible, and many of the attractions accommodate disabled visitors.

What You'll See

Castaway Creek   Relax in an inner tube while floating in this meandering water trail that encircles the park. This 2,100-foot-long stream floats you through an obstacle course left by the mighty typhoon that destroyed the island. Grab a tube at one of five entry spots, or float without one. Make your way around floating debris, broken pipes that shower unsuspecting swimmers as they pass by, and the remnants of a rain forest (complete with rain).

Humunga Kowabunga   This 214-foot-long pair of speed slides takes a 51-foot drop in less than thirty seconds. You're propelled along at 30 miles per hour as you pass through a cave that supposedly was created by an ancient earthquake. Caution: Once you reach the end of the slide, check your bathing suit before standing up. The slide's been known to reposition swimsuits, and usually not in the most flattering way. You'll hit the water pretty hard at the bottom, so be careful. Kids must be 48 inches tall to ride.

Ketchakiddie Creek   As you can imagine from the name, this is the children's section of the park. In fact, you must be 40 inches or *under* to go on these rides (you won't hear that often around Disney!). Ketchakiddie Creek offers scaled-down versions of the adult rides so the half-pints can have the same thrills as their parents and older siblings.

Raft Rides   Mayday Falls, Gangplank Falls, and Keelhaul Falls all offer an exciting raft ride through caves, around rock formations and through waterfalls, but the ride and scenery are different on each. You'll journey on oversized inner tubes for each of these rides. Some of the rafts seat as many as four people.

Shark Reef   If you've ever wanted to swim with the sharks, and live to tell the tale, this is the place for you. Shark Reef is a simulated Caribbean reef that's stocked with lots of tropical fish—a few real—and live bonnethead and leopard sharks (both look fierce, but are pretty tame and passive, and they'll go out of their way to avoid you). Disney provides you with a snorkel, mask, and life vest, and even gives you a brief how-to lesson (comes in pretty handy for your next trip to the islands!). However, you must shower before entering this pool (it's for the health of the fish, folks!), and you must make a beeline through the pool—no stopping too long to look around. You must be at least ten years old to participate.

Shark Reef is typically kept colder than the rest of the water in the park, so this is a good place to cool off. And don't forget to check out the underwater viewing station—it's an upside-down vintage submarine.

Storm Slides   Stern Burner, Jib Jammer, and Rudder Buster are three body slides that twist and turn their way down Mt. Mayhem. You'll reach speeds up to twenty miles per hour on these slides, far less than Humunga Kowabunga. They are actually pretty enjoyable, since you won't be scared out of your wits!

Typhoon Lagoon   This main swimming area encompasses two-and-a-half acres and is actually the world's largest wave pool. Manmade waves are created every 90 seconds and can reach a height of over four feet—pretty rough, so don't venture out too far unless you're a good swimmer! And if all that surf is too much for you, there are two tidal pools, Blustery Bay and Whitecap Cove, where you can chill out with some gently rolling waves.

Where You'll Eat

Fast-Food/Counter Service

Leaning Palms This largest-on-the-lagoon refreshment stand offers burgers, pizza, sandwiches, salads, ice cream, and beverages (even beer!). Most items under $7.

Typhoon Tilly's Galley and Grog Hot dogs, sandwiches, and hot and cold beverages, most under $6. Closes during off-peak seasons.

Snacks/Drinks

Low Tide Lou's Snacks and beverages, most under $6, served amid all the noise of nearby Ketchakiddie Creek.

Slurp's Up Snacks, frozen fruit drinks, and alcoholic refreshments, most under $7.

Where You'll Shop

Singapore Sal's Typhoon Lagoon logo items, tee shirts, and souvenirs, as well as beachwear, film, and sunscreen products. Hats, towels, and thong sandals are also available here.

RIVER COUNTRY

This good ol'fashioned swimmin' hole captures the feel of Tom Sawyer adventures. River Country is the oldest and mildest of the three water parks on Disney grounds. So you really should consider going here if you have young kids who may not swim too well. Unfortunately, you'll miss the thrills and chills of the other parks, since this one really doesn't have much to offer. But if your kids are older, and you're all comfortable in the water, definitely skip River Country and go straight to Blizzard Beach!

How to Get There

River Country is located in Disney's Fort Wilderness Campgrounds, along the shores of Bay Lake. Disney World buses reach Fort Wilderness from all the resorts, and from the Transportation and Ticket Center. Boats also service the area from the Contemporary Resort, Discovery Island, and the Magic Kingdom. Parking in the Fort Wilderness lot is free to all guests staying at Walt Disney World hotels.

Key River Country Landmarks

First Aid Station, Lockers, Towels, Showers and Changing Area, Wheelchair Rentals; all of these services are offered in a building near Pop's Place restaurant, just past River Country's main entrance.

What You'll See

Bay Cove This inlet of Bay Lake is bordered on one side by a large sandy beach and on the other by the park's waterslides. A section of Bay Cove is a sort of aquatic playground, complete with a rope swing, T-bar, tire swing, and boom swing. Two rickety bridges span the cove—you just may fall in! Great for the preteen crowd. A children's playground area is also included.

Cypress Point Nature Trail This short, often-overlooked trail weaves you through the wetlands near Bay Lake. Keep your eyes peeled, and you may be able to spot an egret fishing among the reeds.

Upstream Plunge Pool and Slippery Slides This is a crystal-clear, 330,000-gallon swimming pool that's heated in the winter. It offers a pair of slides that plummet you straight down into the water from a height of about seven feet. Some people actually think that's fun. If you prefer, relax on one of the surrounding lounge chairs.

White Water Rapids This takes you (via an oversized inner tube) for a white-knuckle ride from the crest of Raft

Rider Ridge to the depths of Bay Cove. Honestly, this is a very mild raft ride and is also good for the less adventurous swimmer. The ride was designed with little pockets of whirlpools that catch and hold you until another unsuspecting rafter comes along and bumps you out of the way. That starts you on your way again, but usually traps the unsuspecting soul in the same whirlpool. It's sort of like bumper cars in water! If you're in no rush, choose these not-so-rapids.

Whoop-'N'-Holler Hollow   The home of two flume body slides. The longest is 260 feet and both twist and turn you around Whoop-'N'-Holler Hollow, until you plunge into Bay Cove with a whoosh! Unlike the other water parks, the water here is only about four feet deep where you land, so even poor swimmers can walk away from the exits of these body slides.

Where You'll Eat

Fast-Food/Counter Service

Pop's Place   Burgers, hot dogs, chicken sandwiches, nachos, caramel apple wedges, pretzels, and beverages. Most items under $7.

Where You'll Shop

Thankfully, there's nowhere to shop in River Country. Give your wallet a much-needed rest!

9

Other On-site Attractions, Distractions, and Diversions

BOARDWALK RESORT

This waterfront village, which opened in 1996, has architecture and an attitude that evoke a Jersey beach town circa 1930. The resort-entertainment complex is located on 45 acres along the southern shore of Crescent Lake, between EPCOT and Disney-MGM Studios, across from the Yacht Club and Beach Club hotels. It offers 378 hotel rooms and 383 time-share accommodations, and is too costly for the average cheapskate. We include it here because its shops and attractions can offer a pleasant nighttime diversion, no matter what your budget.

How to Get There

The BoardWalk Resort is within walking distance to the Yacht Club and Beach Club, the Dolphin, and Swan resorts, and the International Gateway of EPCOT's World Showcase. Disney World buses reach the BoardWalk from most hotels, parks, and from the Transportation and Ticket Center. Boats also service the area from Disney-MGM Studios. Visitors arriving by car park in the large BoardWalk guests' parking lot. Valet parking is free for Disney World Resort guests.

What You'll See

Atlantic Dance Hall   This re-creation of a 1930s-era supper club features a huge dance floor that would surely be a home away from home for Fred Astaire. A live band performs nightly—everything from rock to big band to Motown music, and a sweeping staircase leads to a second-floor balcony. Open until 2:00 A.M., $3.00 cover charge. Food available (see Where You'll Eat). Guests must be 21 or over.

The Boardwalk   This idealized re-creation of the East Coast's romantic past offers free entertainment all night, including carnival games, caricaturists, clowns, fire-eaters, jugglers, and stilt walkers. All that's missing is the crashing surf!

ESPN Club   Sports lovers will think they're in heaven as soon as they enter this 13,000-square-foot restaurant-sports club. The main features of the place are the TVs—more than seventy of them. In the main dining room, a 108-square-foot wall of video monitors shows all the action of the day's most popular sporting events. Four forty-inch monitors giving up-to-the-minute scores and highlights hang 20 feet above the floor. In a second dining room there is a sound box at your table so that you can switch audio back and forth between the different games shown. Even in the bathroom you can watch the game on TV. Adjacent to the dining area is the Yard, an arcade full of virtual reality and interactive sports games. Being at the ESPN Club is the next best thing to being at the game. And since it's that loud, you and your kids can make all the noise you want and you'll fit right in. Food available (see Where You'll Eat).

Jellyrolls   This rowdy piano bar offers no dance floor, but bartenders get up on the stage—and even the bar—to engage the crowd in spirited singalongs. The club resembles an old warehouse, with bric-a-brac (a.k.a. junk) cluttering the floor, walls, even the ceiling. There is a $3 cover charge Sunday through Thursday evenings; $5 cover charge on Friday and Saturday. Guests must be 21 or over.

Where You'll Eat

Sit-Down

Atlantic Dance   Light appetizers—like sushi, pizza, and smoked salmon—served in a beautifully rendered deco-style supper club. Most food items under $10. Open till 2:00 A.M., $3 cover charge.

Big River Grille and Brewing Works   A pub serving lunch, dinner, and late-night snacks, with three beers brewed right on the premises. Menu items include basic pub fare, like lobster pot pie, pot roast, meatloaf, sandwiches, and chicken breast sauteed with mushrooms and red ale sauce; all meals under $20.

BoardWalk Baker   Pastries and specialty coffees served from a walk-up counter. Most items under $6.

ESPN Club   Hearty appetizers, build-your-own burgers, a kids menu and more, served in a mega-sports-bar environment. You can even pick up your favorite foods from the ballparks, including Fenway Franks and Dodger Dogs. Many items under $10. Open daily at 11:30 A.M.

Flying Fish Cafe   Seafood, vegetarian, and meat dishes; imaginative desserts; cappuccino and espresso; entrees between $20 and $40. Open for dinner only, 5:00 P.M. until 11:00 P.M.

Snacks/Drinks

Seashore Sweets   Choose from Italian gelato, specialty coffees, salt water taffy, and more goodies that you can enjoy inside or out on the boardwalk. Most items under $10, open 11:00 A.M. to midnight.

Spoodles   Mediterranean dishes including Moroccan beef kabobs, toasted almond couscous, lamb, artichoke ravioli, grilled vegetables, and more, served in a small dining area or outside "on the boards" for people-watching. Most entrees under $15. Kids can make their own pizzas—an uncooked pizza dough round and toppings are brought to the table and they do the rest. Those who simply can't wait can order pizza slices from the takeout window. Open 7:00 A.M. to 10:00 P.M.

Where You'll Shop

Disney's Character Carnival   Disney character merchandise, including a large assortment of dinnerware items (pasta bowls, mugs, pitchers, plates) featuring our favorite mouse and the gang. Also children's and adult's character clothing and accessories, including a vast selection of embroidered shirts and hats.

Screen Door General Store   Located on the boards, this store will remind you of an old-time general store. This one sells an assortment of groceries, snacks, and beverages.

Thimbles and Threads   Resort wear for men and women —only here you won't see any Disney characters on the clothes (who needs 'em, then?). Swimwear and accessories are also available.

Wyland Galleries   Distinctive depictions of marine animals as contemporary art. Costs nothing to look!

MINIATURE GOLF

If you're growing a little tired of the parks and you're still looking for something fun to do, why not try one of Disney's newest on-site diversions: miniature golf, Disney style, of course!

Fantasia Gardens   Located near the Swan and Dolphin hotels, this was the first miniature golf course built at Disney in 1996. Themed after Disney's original *Fantasia* animated classic, you'll putt your way through five musical sequences from the movie, complete with animated dancing hippos, ostriches, and Mickey as the Sorcerer's Apprentice. This 18-hole course was designed with skill in mind, and some of the holes are extremely challenging.

Also located at Fantasia Gardens is *Fantasia Fairways*—a pitch and putt course that combines par-three and par-four holes that range in length from 40–75 feet. This course is truly a "miniature" golf course, full of sand traps, tricky putting greens, and water traps.

Winter Summerland After the success of Fantasia Gardens, Disney built their second miniature golf course in 1999 in the parking lot of Blizzard Beach. Winter Summerland includes two 18-hole courses where Christmas is the theme. In fact, the story goes that while flying his sleigh one Christmas Eve, Santa spied this little piece of land and decided to build an off-season resort for his elves. But his elves were divided as to what they would enjoy—some wanted the Florida sun, and some wanted the snow and cold of the North Pole. So they built two courses. On the winter course, you find Santa and the elves in their more traditional, snow-clad surroundings. The summer course is more reminiscent of a tropical Christmas, with ornaments hanging from palm trees. Both courses are just as cute as could be with plenty of interactive obstacles to get in your way. However, neither course is terribly challenging, and most of the holes are so slanted that the golf ball rolls right into the cup, making it easy for even the youngest of players to compete. But if you're looking for a little bit of a challenge, play the summer course, which is a little trickier than the winter.

Unfortunately, neither Fantasia Gardens nor Winter Summerland is cheap to play. At a cost of $9.25 for an adult and $7.50 for a child aged 3 to 9, this may not be in a cheapskate's budget. But both courses offer lots of discounts, including Disney Club and annual passholder specials, and they usually let you come back and play again on the same day for 50% off, although you must keep your original receipt. One slight problem is that both courses are out in the full sun (Fantasia is worse than Winter Summerland), so try not to play in the middle of the day.

Fantasia Gardens is open from 10:00 A.M. until midnight, and for more information you may call 407-560-8760. Winter Summerland is open from 10:00 A.M. until 11:00 P.M. and their information line is 407-939-7639.

WIDE WORLD OF SPORTS

Who'd thunk that an entertainment resort, hosted by a mouse, would become a virtual Mecca for the sports enthusiast. With Disney's acquisitions of ABC-TV sports and the ESPN cable sports network, however, it was only natural that they would build a haven for all you sports nuts out there.

This one-of-a-kind 200-acre sports complex includes a 7,500-seat baseball stadium that has become the spring training facility for the Atlanta Braves, and a 30,000-square-foot Fieldhouse used by the Harlem Globetrotters. More than 30 Amateur Athletic Union (AAU) gymnastics, wrestling, and weightlifting events are also held at the Fieldhouse. A state-of-the-art track and field complex, an 11-court tennis complex, and several football soccer, and softball fields round out this haven for sports lovers. While you're here, enjoy a meal in the Official All Star Café theme restaurant.

So if you are really into sports, and you're willing to give up precious time at the theme parks, you might want to take a side trip over to the Wide World of Sports complex. Just bear in mind that events are not held daily—call 407-363-6600 in advance of your trip for a weekly update on scheduled sporting events. And please remember that even if your admission ticket to the parks includes admission to the sports complex, there may be an additional charge for some premium sports events.

Off-site Attractions

If you're looking for some excitement off-site, don't bother—unless places like Gatorland, Monkey Jungle, Sunken Gardens, and Boggy Creek Airboat Rides sound exciting to you. With its four major parks, three water parks, Downtown Disney, and more, there's so much to do in Disney World, you won't want to go anywhere else. Besides, if you follow our itinerary, your days will be spent on-site, with little time to venture outside of the World.

Pick up a general book on Florida travel if you really must know about off-site attractions.

WHERE TO MEET THE CHARACTERS

If you're traveling with children, your kids probably will not be happy until they get to see their favorite Disney character in person. Disney characters appear daily in each of the four parks and they're easy to find, if you know where to look.

Most Worthwhile Off-site Destination

Character Warehouse   If you plan on buying lots of souvenirs to bring back to all your loved ones at home, then a trip to the Character Warehouse is a definite must!

Have you ever wondered what happens to all the souvenirs that don't sell in the Disney parks. Well, believe it or not, Disney sells them through a retail store in an outlet center called Belz Factory Outlet World. Although you will not see the Disney name anywhere on this store, it is in fact owned by Disney, and carries authentic Disney World souvenirs at *drastically* reduced prices. So, if you have use of a rental car during your trip, take a ride over to the outlet before buying your souvenirs at the parks, and save yourself a bunch of money.

From Disney World, take Interstate 4 East to exit 30A. Turn left at the traffic light at the end of the exit onto International Drive. Follow the road until it dead ends. Mall 2 of the Belz Factory Outlet World will be to your left. The Character Warehouse is located at outlets #109 and #110. Call 407-345-5285.

Magic Kingdom

The characters make surprise appearance s throughout the park. But to improve your odds of seeing your favorites, it is best to get a copy of the Character Greeting Location Guide at City Hall on Main Street when you enter the park. The guide will give you details of character appearance s scheduled for the day. Daily appearances are made by:

- Mickey Mouse—Watch for Mickey to appear at the Judge's tent in Mickey's Toontown Fair from parking opening until park closing.

- Minnie Mouse—The Tour Garden, adjacent to City Hall on Main Street, is Minnie's (and various other Disney characters') favorite spot to be seen.

- Jungle Book, Lion King, and Aladdin—The gang hangs out at Congoasis (the little character greeting area near the exit to the Enchanted Tiki Room).

- The Whole Disney Gang—(i.e., Mickey, Goofy, Donald, etc.) appear periodically at the Fantasyland Character Festival (across from the Winnie the Pooh ride).

- Ariel—The Little Mermaid and her prince, Eric, can be found at Ariel's Grotto in Fantasyland.

- Alice in Wonderland—Look for Alice and her friends near the Mad Tea Party in Fantasyland.

- Brer Fox and Brer Bear—Brer Rabbit's nemeses hang around Splash Mountain's exit.

EPCOT

When the park originally opened, it was rare to see a Disney costumed character at EPCOT—maybe the Disney powers-that-be thought this gave some kind of mixed message or something. Nowadays, it's easy.

Stop by Guest Relations and pick up a copy of the daily entertainment schedule to ensure character spotting. Look for characters to appear daily at the American Adventure Rose Garden and at the Showcase Plaza. They also tend to appear in the countries where their characters originated: Pinocchio appears in Italy, Snow White frequents Germany, Beauty and the Beast hang out in France, and Peter Pan and Alice in Wonderland can be found in the United Kingdom.

Disney-MGM Studios

Be sure to get the latest Character Greeting Location Guide at Crossroads of the World upon entering the park.

- Mickey Mouse—Catch Mickey throughout the day at the Animation Courtyard.

- The Whole Disney Gang—Can be spotted along Mickey Avenue.

- Toy Story—Buzz and Woody hang out periodically at Al's Toy Barn across from the entrance to the Backlot Tour.

Animal Kingdom

Perhaps in an effort to separate the real mice and lions from the Disney-style mice and lions, it's next to impossible to see Mickey and his friends roaming around the park. If you're spending the day at the Animal Kingdom and your kids have got a character spotting itch they've just got to scratch, head for the character greeting pavilions in Camp Minnie-Mickey.

Character Dining

If the success or failure of your vacation depends upon your children getting to see a particular character, you might not want to rely on a chance meeting in one of the parks. It might be worth the extra expense of dining with the characters to guarantee that your kids meet the Disney character of their choice. Although certainly not a bargain at $13–$20 for an adult and $8–$10 for each child (ages three to 11), you are guaranteed that the characters will spend a good deal of quality time with each child (and adult) during the meal, allowing for countless photo opportunities. (Note: There is no Disney Club discount given for any of the character dining experiences.) Be sure to bring an autograph book along. (And here's a tip: leave every other page blank so you have room to insert photos of your kids and the character.)

You can dine with the characters for either breakfast or dinner at a number of Disney resort hotels. Children of all ages love to eat overcooked scrambled eggs, dry sausages, and cardboard-flavored French toast with their favorite Disney characters (truthfully, the meals aren't all *that* bad). Choose the meal with the character(s) you find most interesting. We list the "host" character below, but other characters will join the festivities at each meal:

Goofy	Yacht Club and Beach Club Resort Cape May Café—7:30–11:00 A.M. Buffet breakfast with Admiral Goofy and his crew
Mary Poppins	Grand Floridian Beach Resort 1900 Park Fare—7:30–11:30 A.M. Breakfast buffet with Mary Poppins and friends

Mickey Mouse	Contemporary Resort
	Chef Mickey's Buffet—7:30–11:30
	  A.M.; 5:00–9:30 P.M.
	Breakfast or dinner with Mickey and
	  the gang

Minnie Mouse	Polynesian Resort 'Ohana—7:30–11:00 A.M. Family style breakfast with Minnie Mouse and friends
Winnie the Pooh	Wilderness Lodge Artist Point—7:30–11:30 A.M. Breakfast with Pooh, Eeyore, and Tigger

Pooh and Tigger	Old Key West Resort
	Olivia's—On Monday, Wednesday, and
	  Sunday only—7:30–10:15 A.M.
	Breakfast with Christopher Robin's
	  friends

Villains	Grand Floridian Beach Resort 1900 Park Fare—5:30–9:30 P.M. Dinner buffet with the villains

Many off-site and hotel plaza hotels (as well as the Dolphin and Swan) also offer kid-friendly character dining. Ask at your hotel.

Each of the theme parks also offers character dining; however, park admission is required.

Magic Kingdom	Cinderella's Royal Table—8:30–10:00 A.M. Sit down breakfast with Cinderella and friends Liberty Tree Tavern—from 4:00 P.M. Family style dinner with Colonial Mickey and Goofy Crystal Palace—hours vary Breakfast, lunch, and dinner with Pooh, Tigger, and Eeyore
EPCOT	Garden Grill Restaurant—hours vary Family style breakfast, lunch, and dinner with Farmer Mickey and friends
Disney-MGM Studios	Hollywood & Vine Breakfast—8:30–11:15 A.M. Lunch—11:30 A.M.–3:30 P.M. Buffet meals with Minnie Mouse and Friends
Animal Kingdom	Restaurantosaurus Park opening until 10:00 A.M. Breakfastosaurus with Donald Duck and his friends

Character dining is very popular, and your spot can be difficult to guarantee unless reservations are made in advance. Priority seating is available for all locations and can be arranged by calling 407-WDW-DINE up to 60 days before your visit.

Please remember that the morning hours in the theme parks are the best hours for seeing the attractions. Dining with the characters for breakfast means you will lose one morning of prime time in the parks. If you're only in the parks for a few days, it might be a better idea to eat lunch or dinner with the characters.

There are many dinner shows offered throughout the park, some featuring Disney characters, but many that do not. At prices of up to $40 a head, we won't even waste the cheapskate's time mentioning them here.

Important Note No. 1: If you book a package deal that includes a breakfast with the characters, you often have to go to the breakfast for which you're booked. When you make your vacation reservations, ask them where your breakfast will be. If you would like a breakfast somewhere with a different theme, ask if you can select your breakfast location.

Important Note No. 2: If your child is afraid to sit on Santa's lap, then he or she might be petrified at the sight of a big guy approaching in a Goofy suit. Use your best judgment— you know your kid better than anyone else—and don't ruin your own, and someone else's meal, if you even suspect your child is going to freak out.

Baby-sitting Services

Baby-sitting services are available through an outside agency, KinderCare. In-room baby-sitting is available for Disney resort hotel guests and for guests staying at the larger hotels near the Disney World property. Rates are $12 an hour for one child, $13 an hour for two children, and $14 an hour for three kids. There is a four-hour minimum, and one-half-hour travel time is included for the caregivers, who are bonded and are ages 18 and up. Reservations can be made one to thirty days in advance by phoning 407-827-5444.

If you need a whole day off from the kids, drop-off service is available for all Disney park visitors at KinderCare's daycare center (which is conveniently located near the Disney Village Marketplace). Rates for drop-off service are $8 an hour per child, or $36 per child for a 10-hour day. The center offers a playground, computers, and organized activities. Hours of operation are from 6:00 A.M. to 9:00 P.M., Monday through Friday; and 6:00 A.M. to 6:00 P.M. on Saturdays and Sundays. Reservations can be made in advance by calling 407-827-5437 for Saturdays and Sundays, but Monday through Friday is done on a space-available basis.

There are numerous baby-sitting facilities sponsored by the Disney resort hotels, but they are restricted to on-site hotel guests only. Cub's Den at the Wilderness Lodge offers supervised activities from 5:00 P.M. to midnight at a rate of $7 an hour per child, with a one-hour minimum. The Never Land Club at Disney's Polynesian Resort is also open from 5:00 P.M. to midnight, but it charges $8 an hour per child, with a three-hour minimum. The Harbor Club at the BoardWalk is open from 4:30 P.M. to 11:45 P.M. at a rate of $5 an hour per child. The Sandcastle Club at the Yacht Club and Beach Club resorts offers supervised activities from 4:30 P.M. to midnight and charges only $4 an hour per child. Children can range in age from four to 12 years, and must be potty-trained. The Grand Floridian and the Contemporary resorts also have in-house baby-sitting facilities, but they are available only to guests of the respective hotels. Reservations are required and can be made up to 60 days in advance by calling 407-WDW-DINE, but same-day reservations will be taken if space is available.

10

Exclusive Cheapskate Itineraries

About the Itineraries

Realizing that different cheapskates have different needs, we've devised two different itineraries to help you get more Disney bang for your buck. The first is the Ambitious Cheapskate's Itinerary, and the second is the Cheapskate Family Itinerary.

The first itinerary is designed for the energetic, fit cheapskate, and those cheapskate families without young (i.e., under age eight) cheapskate kids in tow. You'll be doing much more running around with the first itinerary—you've got more ground to cover, more attractions to see, and since you won't be weighed down by strollers, diaper bags, and all the other baby accoutrements—this shouldn't be a problem. By moving fast, you're virtually guaranteed to see everything. In the Cheapskate Family Itinerary, we've cut out the rides with height restrictions, on which your kids couldn't ride anyway, and have also noted which rides might be uninteresting to children or too scary. (We still list these at the end, however, in case one adult wants to ride and one wants to watch the kids.) We've allowed time to meet some of the roving Disney characters and see a live stage show—we've even built in some nap times, which you may or may not want to take advantage of (if you don't, just continue with the itinerary; you'll finish earlier and can then put the kids to bed earlier).

Read both itineraries first, while your trip is still in the planning stages. And please note that these tour plans are not set in stone. If your family is interested in a ride we've left out, hop on as you pass. You can even go on a favorite ride more than once, if you want, but don't spend time on a long time twice if you can help it.

Both model itineraries are based on six-night stays in one of Disney's All-Star Resorts, and you've bought the All-In-One Hopper Pass. In our opinion, this is the optimum time frame and accommodation for a cheapskate to thoroughly enjoy a Walt Disney World vacation. Your situation, however, may not be optimum:

Maybe you can't afford to stay six nights . . .

Maybe you think the money you can save off-site far outweighs the benefits of staying at the All-Star . . .

. . . So do your homework! Read this book from cover to cover before you leave, and then bring it with you on your trip. If you have less vacation time than we recommend, choose to visit only the parks and attractions that interest you most. Then, if you have time, go back to see the ones you missed, or reride your faves.

Don't worry if you think you look like a geek with your nose in the book while you're walking around World Showcase Lagoon. Those who look at you funny will be eating your dust as you tear up the parks with nary an attraction missed. Jut watch where you're going. We wouldn't want you to get in the way of one of Main Street's firetrucks!

Always pick up an entertainment schedule immediately upon entering whatever park you're visiting. This will help you plan your day, because it shows what events they've got planned, the delayed opening times of some attractions, what attractions are closed for renovation, etc. These are factors that may alter your plans somewhat. And as we've stated throughout the book, if you're the type who couldn't care less about parades or fireworks, visit the more popular attractions during those times, since most people will be at the event.

Miscellaneous Tips

- Make the not-so-supreme sacrifice and get up early! The time you spend walking around the parks while everyone else is snoozing will be well worth the loss of sleep. Early arrival at the parks is crucial to seeing it all.

- Wear comfortable, worked-in walking shoes. You're going to give your feet a good workout, so pick a durable shoe!

- Supplies to bring along:
  1. Poncho—Let it rain! Most attractions are indoors, so while other vacationers may be discouraged by a few raindrops and go home, you'll be dodging the drops in your rain poncho. If you don't bring a poncho, you can buy one throughout the parks, but why spend the extra money?
  2. Light jacket—The air conditioning can get pretty cold at times; and, depending on what time of the year you go, it can get a little nippy in Florida at night.
  3. Sunscreen
  4. Backpack (to hold it all)
  5. Sunglasses
  6. Wide-brim hat
  7. Casual, lightweight attire is the norm at Disney—The people who work at the Canada pavilion *have* to wear those flannel shirts and lumberjack work boots, but you sure don't!
  8. Food—Disney has a rule against your bringing your own food into the parks, but we've never seen anyone having their bags searched by Mickey's security guards. So we say, feel free to bring snacks, baby formula, etc. in with you. (Okay, if you're paranoid, pick up your baby needs at the appropriate areas in the park, but don't be surprised if they cost more.) Just don't do anything obvious, like stuffing an Igloo cooler down your shirt. If you don't do anything dumb or conspicuous, you'll be fine. (A neat little trick is to freeze some juice boxes and put them in your backpack. They'll keep the food cold, and the juice should be melted just enough to be icy cold in time for lunch.)

9. Squeeze water bottle—Fill it up at a water fountain for a quick, cold pick-me-up.

10. Refillable mugs—Here's another way that staying at a Disney resort can save you some time and hassle. At your hotel's food court, buy a refillable mug and hold onto it. It can cost you a little at first (at some places upwards of $10) but refills (soda, coffee, whatever) are then free. So after the initial purchase, you'll drink free the rest of your trip. Plus you'll have a souvenir mug when you get home!

11. Gum—Oddly enough, there's nowhere to buy gum in Walt Disney World, so if you want to flap your gums, bring those Chiclets with you. (While we're at it—there's no booze to be found in the Magic Kingdom, either. But don't bring *that* with you!)

- Always call ahead for park hours. And now, with Disney's automated phone line—407-824-4321—it's easier than ever to get information months in advance. Operating hours at the Disney parks change seasonally. The phone service will also tell you the times for the evening entertainment for the duration of your stay, such as the Fantasy in the Sky and IllumiNations fireworks. We urge you to call this line at least once before you leave and have that list of questions ready!

- No matter which park you're visiting, get there at least one hour before its scheduled opening time. They will always open at least one section of the park before its scheduled opening time, and if you're already at the gate when it opens, you'll have a head start on everybody else. But be ready for the morning sprint, in which the early birds make a mad dash for the ride that most interests them. You should join the fun, too. Pick the ride that most interests you and head for it first thing (read on for our suggestions).

- Group attractions into your own Must See, Second Choice, and Ones We Can Live Without lists. See our descriptions and evaluations throughout the book.

- Stay on foot whenever possible. Unless someone in your group just has to experience the romantic thrill of riding the boat over to Tom Sawyer Island or Cousin Ida has just got a thing for the Friendships in EPCOT, you'll find you can move faster by hoofing it, especially when you factor in the time you'll be wasting waiting on line for the ride!

- As you approach an attraction, look before you leap. Notice what's going on. For example, if the ride next door has just let out ahead of you, a huge influx of people may have just headed right for the attraction line you're about to enter. In those cases, wait: In just a few moments, the line will die down.

- If an attraction has two lines, choose the line on the left. For some reason, it will always move faster than the one on the right. Perhaps it has something to do with the fact that most law-abiding people drive on the right (in the United States, anyway!) and most of us stick to this mindset and tend to gravitate to lines on the right side. As you know, we're advising that you do things a little bit differently than the norm. so, if there are two lines into a show or attraction, always choose the line on the left. It will move faster because there are usually fewer people on it (and most of them are left handed? Just a theory). Whatever the reason, trust us—9 times out of 10, this simple technique works. And it feels great when you get to walk past a long line on the right. Make sure you wave when you go by!

- To make the best use of your time, it is highly recommended that you eat during "off hours," i.e., lunch at 11:00 or 11:30 A.M., dinner at 4:30 P.M. Eat on the run, i.e., eat as few sit-down meals as possible—you'll be seeing the best attractions while everybody else is sitting down! Read our earlier recommendations on where to eat throughout the World.

- Pay attention to small details throughout the park you're visiting—be it the simulated smoke on chimneys in EPCOT's United Kingdom, the way Disney gardeners prune the shrubs and trees into interesting shapes, the cast members' (that's Disneyese for "employees") costumes that reflect the area where they're employed, etc. Disney takes a lot of time—and spends a lot of money—on the little things in order to make it a better vacation experience for you. But don't be overwhelmed or overly awestruck by the place. Think rationally, follow our itinerary, and heed our advice, or many of the rides and attractions will just not fit into your schedule and you may have to add them to your "next time" list.

A Word of Caution About Early Admission

Typically, the park that offers early admission to Walt Disney World hotel guests is also the most crowded park the rest of the day. It makes sense: Guests staying in a Disney hotel go to, say, the Magic Kingdom, early; then they say to themselves, Selves, we're here, let's stay here until we've seen our fill. So while visitors enjoy the park and its relatively uncrowded attractions first thing in the morning, they'll pay the price later in the day, when the park fills up almost to unbearable. What's more, they'll be exhausted from having to get up so early! You may either want to go to a different park each day other than the one opening early (which would change the day order of the itinerary), or go to a park early, then park-hop around lunchtime to a less-crowded park.

If you go to a park that has early admission, let's say, at 8:00 A.M., get there at 7:30 so you'll be among the first of the firsts to enter the park. And, check other lands to see if you can ride some of their rides early. For example, sometimes when Fantasyland is open early, you can run over to Tomorrowland and ride Space Mountain. Most people don't attempt this, so it's smooth sailing for you.

- Bear in mind: A park's closing time is optional (meaning, subject to the whim of the management). Technically, this means that closing time is the last time a guest is allowed to join a line at an attraction, as well as the time they begin herding you out of the park. Generally the park is empty and doors securely locked one hour after official closing time. So if you're about to get on line at Splash Mountain five minutes before Mickey's quittin' time, go for it. Don't feel like you have to go running for the exit.

- Least crowded days at Walt Disney World: Fridays and Sundays (most families visit the parks Monday through Thursday).

- Least crowded times of the day in most any park: First thing in the morning or in the evening, an hour before closing.

- Plan where you will be each day of your trip and if at all possible, make dining reservations before you arrive in Florida. Call 407-WDW-DINE for the details.

Lost Children

If you lose a child, with Disney's ubiquitous, attentive security force on patrol, rest assured the child won't be lost for long. Lost children logbooks are located at Baby Services or City Hall in the Magic Kingdom, at Guest Relations or Baby Services in EPCOT, Guest Relations in the Disney-MGM Studios, and Discovery Island in Animal Kingdom. You can check the nearest log if your child is lost. *Even more effective:* Although there are no obvious loud speakers or pagers in the parks—that would ruin the effect—in case of an emergency, what amounts to a Disney all-points bulletin can be broadcast to all employees. Each member of the security force is equipped with remote microphones and ear pieces. They look kind of like Mickey's very own Secret Service, but you'll be glad they're there if it's *your* child that is lost.

Strollers

- Bring your own. If not, keep reading.

- If you've rented one, and you're headed out of the park (any park) for a little R and R, but you plan on coming back, mark the stroller somehow (with a name tag, colored bandana, something so you can recognize it), and leave it near the park's entrance. When you come back, it will make it easier to find.

- If you're in EPCOT, rent your stroller at the International Gateway entrance—less crowded than the rental place by the main gate.

- If you are park-hopping and you've rented a stroller, keep the receipt. When you get to the new park, you'll get a free stroller.

- If you lose your rented stroller, bring your receipt to the nearest stroller rental window and get a new one.

THE AMBITIOUS CHEAPSKATE'S ITINERARY

Day 1: EPCOT

Following your arrival at your hotel, your goal today is to see as much of EPCOT's FutureWorld as you can before heading off to Downtown. (Trust us: If you plan on going to Downtown Disney, you should go your first night in Disney. You'll be too tired on subsequent nights.)

Obviously it's to your advantage to have your flight arrive early in the day on your first day at Disney! This gives you more time to enjoy EPCOT. Hotel check-in time is 3:00 P.M. in most Disney hotels (1:00 P.M. at the Fort Wilderness Campsites)—no earlier—so if you get to the hotel early, have them hold your bags and officially check in when you come back.

Miscellaneous EPCOT Tips

- See map for bathrooms

- Check the tip board near Innoventions for news on the day's events, rides that may be closed for renovations, fireworks schedule, etc.

Eat a quick lunch at your hotel. Arrange for the storage of your bags, or check into your room, then get the bus to EPCOT as soon as you can. Pick up an entertainment schedule at Guest Relations in Innoventions East. While you're in Innoventions East, pick which restaurant you'd like to eat dinner at and make your reservations for 6:30 P.M. (or, if you'd prefer to get a quick bite around the same time at a less expensive, fast-food place, you obviously won't need a reservation).

After deciding on your dinner plans, go to Body Wars first. Then visit Universe of Energy and Test Track (skip the exhibits for now). These attractions should take about an hour. Eat dinner at 6:30 P.M. as planned. Or, if you have time, continue with the itinerary.

Next, go to Honey, I shrunk the Audience and the Journey Into Imagination ride (which both take at least one and a half hours). Then go to either Living Seas (visiting the Coral Reef Ride, Seabase Alpha, and Seabase Concourse will take about one hour) or The Land (Listen to the Land, Food Rocks, and Symbiosis will take you about one and a half hours). Keep checking the line at Body Wars if you haven't gone already. Check the line at Spaceship Earth on your way out—if the wait is less than a half hour, and you have time, go on the ride. If there's still some time, ride some rides you might have missed.

Note 1: Go to FutureWorld's shops, Innoventions, and the Test Track exhibits when the park is most congested.

Note 2: If you haven't seen everything in FutureWorld in the few hours you just spent in the park, don't panic: You'll be returning to EPCOT on day 5 of your trip. If you *have* seen everything, you can go back and ride your favorites on day 5.

Take a bus to Downtown Disney to arrive by 9:00 P.M. (give yourself about a half hour to get there). Grab an entertainment schedule as you enter Pleasure Island.

Bearing left from the admission windows, proceed to the Comedy Warehouse. (If a show is scheduled to being within a half hour, browse the shops until 10 minutes to showtime. *Then* go to the Comedy Warehouse.)

After the comedy show, cross the street to Adventurers Club and see the unscheduled comedy show in the club's private library. (Ask the attendant about it. If it's more than 20 minutes until the next show, stop at the BET Soundstage now, if you haven't already done so.) After the Adventurers Club go to BET Soundstage, then proceed clockwise toward the West End Stage, stopping in at the Rock N Roll Beach Club, the Pleasure Island Jazz Company, Mannequin's, and 8Trax. Shop at the shops along the way. Go in and at least look around at the Fireworks Factory and Portobello Yacht Club. Grab a snack at D-Zertz.

Check out Planet Hollywood, the House of Blues, and the rest of the West End restaurants and shops. Stay in the park for fireworks and the New Year's Eve celebration, but don't stay out too late—you've got to get up early!

Day 2: Magic Kingdom

On your first full day arrive at 8:00 A.M. (assuming the park opens at 9:00). Upon entering the park, check City Hall and the tip board at the lower end of Main Street for news on the day's events, rides that may be closed for renovations, fireworks and parades schedule, live entertainment, etc. (Characters show up next to City Hall often, so keep your eyes peeled. Plus, you can buy stamps there if you need them—how's that for a non sequitur?)

Grab a light breakfast at the Main Street Bake Shop or at one of the Main Street wagons (if you haven't eaten already—actually, you might be better off eating before you get to the Kingdom because the early morning crowd at the bake shop is rather large). Then make your way up Main Street and be at the Central Plaza end by the time the park officially opens.

Miscellaneous Magic Kingdom Tips

- See map for bathrooms.

- Decide which rides are most important to you (the most popular rides that cause the most bottlenecks are Splash Mountain, Space Mountain, Big Thunder Mountain Railroad, Pirates of the Caribbean, and the Fantasyland rides) and enjoy as many of these rides as possible early, before the park gets too filled up.

Once the park opens, the rope divider between Main Street and the rest of the park drops. Make a beeline for Frontierland. See Splash Mountain.

(An arguably faster way to reach Splash Mountain before most of the crowds: Go up the Main Street platform of the Walt Disney World Railroad as soon as you enter the park. That way you'll be one of the first on the train. The first stop is Frontierland, very close to Splash Mountain. If your timing is perfect, you'll beat the people who are running over!)

After Splash Mountain, head to that other famous Frontierland mountain, Big Thunder Mountain Railroad (least crowded before 11:00 A.M. or after 5:30 P.M.), then to the Country Bear Jamboree (before noon or during the last two hours before closing time). On your way past the Diamond Horse-shoe, ask how you might get a spot at the 12:00 P.M. lunchtime show.

Then go to Fantasyland: See Dumbo, Cinderella's Golden Carousel, Snow White's Adventures (before 11:30 A.M. or after 5:00 P.M.), Legend of the Lion King, Peter Pans' Flight (before 11:30 A.M. or after 5:00 P.M.), and the Many Adventures of Winnie the Pooh. Ride Small World now if there's time (between 11:00 A.M. and 5:00 P.M.), or head to Frontierland's Diamond Horseshoe for lunch and the 11:20 show.

> Remember: If you're not one for live shows or parades, those are the times to try the most popular rides.

After lunch: Stop in at a few Main Street shops if they're not too crowded, then proceed to Liberty Square to see the Hall of Presidents (before noon or after 4:00 P.M.) and the Haunted Mansion; then on to Adventureland: Pirates of the Caribbean (between 11:30 A.M. and 4:30 P.M.), the Enchanted Tiki Room (almost never crowded), the Jungle Cruise (the two hours before closing), the Magic Carpets of Aladdin and the Swiss Family Treehouse (late afternoon or early evening); then on to Fantasyland and Small World (if you missed it earlier); next it's Tomorrowland: Buzz Lightyear Spin, Alien Encounter (after 4:00 P.M.), Timekeeper (between 11:30 A.M. and 4:00 P.M.), Tomorrowland Speedway, Astro Orbiter, Tomorrowland Transit Authority, and Space Mountain (during the hour before closing, or between 6:00 and 7:00 P.M.).

Slip in a fast-food dinner somewhere in the schedule—how about some Tex-Mex at Pecos Bill's Café in Frontierland?

To escape the crowds and the midday heat, try a boatride on Rivers of America; head to Tom Sawyer Island and relax with a lemonade on Aunt Polly's porch; or go back to your hotel (if you're staying on-site), enjoy a swim and maybe a nap and come back later (if your admission ticket permits).

If you have time, ride the railroad from Frontierland to Mickey's Toontown Fair (if you've got kids in tow, you'd *better* go here sometime during the day—preferably early, since the

Toontown Fair closes before the rest of the park—or you may never hear the end of it!) This area may be less crowded during the day's early parade—all the kids will be at the parade, get it?

One Hour Before SpectroMagic

Head over to Main Street and get a good spot for the parade. (Best seats: at the very center of the platform of the Walt Disney Railroad's Main Street Station where not obstructed by trees. Next best: on the curb. Or to see the parade and escape the crowds, go to Pecos Bill's in Frontierland and sit on a stool by the parade route.)

Important parade notes: The earlier parade, when there's more than one, is typically more crowded—check when it's scheduled. And it's always a good idea to ask a Disney cast member the direction the parade will be approaching from.

After the parade, see the Fantasy in the Sky fireworks—if you're not interested in the parade, go to Bill Thunder Mountain (even if you rode it already, it's especially neat at night). Then leave the park and see the Electrical Water Pageant on Seven Seas Lagoon (take the monorail to Contemporary or Polynesian and sit at the waterfront).

Or, if you've seen everything and you have no interest in the parades, the pageant, or the fireworks, take a bus to Downtown Disney (usually open until 11:00 P.M.).

Alternatives to Magic Kingdom itinerary: You may want to change the order in which you visit the most popular rides, depending on your interests. Discuss which rides seem most interesting and go on those immediately when the park opens. But the main thing is to be at the rope barrier when it drops and spring to one of the following, rather than Splash Mountain:

- Space Mountain, then Alien Encounter, and the rest of Tomorrowland

- Fantasyland, especially Dumbo, which is a major time consumer

See the most popular attractions/lands early and then fill in the others, according to our suggestions.

Note: If you're leaving the park at closing time—along with the rest of the mob—avoid the monorail out of the Magic Kingdom. Take the ferry to the Transportation and Ticket Center, or get on the "local" monorail train that stops at the monorail hotels before arriving at the Transportation and Ticket Center.

Day 3: Disney-MGM Studios

Grab breakfast at your hotel. Arrive by 8:00 A.M. (provided the park is officially opening at 9:00). Pick up an entertainment schedule at Guest Services, and stop at the Production Information window at the entrance to see if they're filming anything in the park during your visit. Dining reservations can be made at the end of Hollywood and Vine at information booths; make your 11:30 A.M. lunch reservations early to avoid disappointment if you haven't already made them.

Make a beeline down Sunset Boulevard to the Tower of Terror and the Rock 'n' Roller Coaster. Skip the stores along the way—go back and shop there when the park gets crowded. Check out the timing for the Voyage of the Little Mermaid (if it's within 20 minutes, stay and see show, otherwise go to the Great Movie Ride); then, on to Star Tours (choose the left line). Check out the line for Muppet*Vision and go on it if it's not too crowded. If you have not yet been on the Voyage of the Little Mermaid and the Great Movie Ride, do so now.

You now should have seen the most popular attractions and the ones with the potential for the longest lines—if not, go back and see the ones above you may have missed. Now you have time to leisurely go on the Studio Tour (Catastrophe Canyon, etc.—this line may seem long, but each tram swallows up a lot of people at once); Bear in the Big Blue House show; Animation Tour; Sounds Dangerous starring Drew Carey; Backstage Pass; Doug; the Indiana Jones Epic Stunt Show; and whatever else you may have missed.

One of the least-known attractions at Disney-MGM Studios (and one we enjoy best) is Soundworks. At the exit of the Drew

Carey show, there is a room with hands-on sound effects. Along the walls are doors with red and green lights next to them. Find a room with a green light, enter, put on your earphones, relax and enjoy the show. It's a great respite from a hectic Disney day. Then, lunch by 11:30 A.M. and you can shop the stores in the afternoon.

If you finish the park early, this would be a good opportunity to go back to the hotel to pursue resort activities like boating, tennis, beach sitting, swimming, biking, or horseback riding.

Miscellaneous Studios Tips

- See first thing or in the last hour before closing: Rock 'n' Roller Coaster, Star Tours, Tower of Terror, Muppet*Vision, Great Movie Ride, Disney Animation, Indiana Jones, Backstage Tour, and Voyage of the Little Mermaid.

- Good midday breaks: the Doug and Drew Carey shows

Another alternative when you're done in the Studios is to take a boat launch to the BoardWalk Resort for some dining and entertainment options.

But if you're one of the diehards waiting for that fat lady to sing, stay in the park for Fantasmic! (You'll be glad you did.) Check at Guest Services for times.

Day 4: Animal Kingdom

This will be a much less hectic day for you for two reasons: First, there are currently less attractions at Animal Kingdom than there are in the other three theme parks, so you will need less time to see everything. Second, most people head for the Animal Kingdom very early because that's when they've heard that the animals are most active. The critters, however, are also active as it cools down in the early evening. So, while everyone's gone home, you'll enjoy a less crowded park and see active animals.

Sleep in, or enjoy the recreational activities of your hotel. Get on a bus and head to Animal Kingdom in time for lunch—it shouldn't take very long, since it's the closest theme park to the All-Stars. Pick up an entertainment schedule at Guest Services—since we've advised you to forego the parade, you might be able to take in the most popular attractions during those times.

Proceed with determination to Africa and eat at Tusker House, or stop off for a bite in Pizzafari in Safari Village. Then, head over to Asia and enjoy the rides (if they're too crowded, try going during the hour or two before the park closes).

Head to Camp Minnie-Mickey to see the Festival of the Lion King show (unless you have kids in tow, don't spend a lot of time at the character greeting pavilions, and don't bother with the Colors of the Wind show, right now or at all).

After Lion King, head to DinoLand and the Dinosaur ride. On your way, spend a few minutes looking through the shops of DinoLand. After Dinosaur, you should probably see the Tarzan Rocks! show. From DinoLand browse through the shops of Discovery Island on your way to the Tree of Life. Walk around the Tree of Life, checking out its myriad of sculptures and surrounding gardens, then go inside the Tree to the It's Tough to Be a Bug! show.

At around 5:30 P.M. take the Kilimanjaro Safari ride (if it's not yet 5:30 or so, browse around the shops of Harambe). After the Safari, walk the Pangani Forest Exploration Trail. Then, take the Wildlife Express to Conservation Station and see its exhibits. At this point, you have seen all of Animal Kingdom's main attractions and are free to see the ones you might have missed, go back and reride your favorites, or browse in the shops.

Day 5: EPCOT

Arrive at 8:15 A.M. and wait at the gate. FutureWorld opens at 9:00 A.M., with World Showcase opening at 11:00 A.M. That gives you plenty of time to see the FutureWorld attractions you may have missed on day 1, or to revisit those you've already enjoyed. Be one of the first people on Spaceship Earth before the lines develop. After the ride, make lunch reservations for 11:30 A.M. at any of the World Showcase restaurants (unless you've made them in advance). Then walk to Journey Into Imagination. Do the ride, play at the Imageworks, and don't miss Honey, I shrunk the Audience.

Talk to people in World Showcase—they're from the country of the pavilion where they work and they're usually very friendly, funny, and informative about their country and their culture.
Reminder: World Showcase opens at 11:00!

If you finish shrinking early enough, go to The Land. At about 10:45 A.M., line up at the rope barrier and when it drops, walk briskly to World Showcase. Most people will stay behind at FutureWorld, so you will be able to breeze through World Showcase. Start at the American Adventure, then go back to Canada and double back counterclockwise around the World Showcase Lagoon (most people go clockwise starting from Mexico; maybe it's hereditary).

As an alternative to the restaurants at EPCOT: a short walk to the Yacht Club and Beach Club might be appreciated. Enjoy the old-time soda shoppe called Beaches and Cream, which is located where the Yacht Club and Beach Club meet. You get there by exiting EPCOT via the International Gateway—be sure to get your hand stamped so you can return later.

After lunch, head back to FutureWorld—most of the crowd will have begun heading to World Showcase at this point. You should have plenty of time before dinner to see Test Track, Universe of Energy, Body Wars, Cranium Command, and the Innoventions buildings—basically, whatever you may have missed your first time in EPCOT, or maybe want to see again.

Thirty minutes before dinner, begin heading back to World Showcase. Grab a quick bite somewhere on the fly for dinner. After dinner, don't miss the American Adventure show if you haven't seen it, or if you want to catch it again. It lasts 35 minutes, so make sure you leave enough time before the beginning of IllumiNations (the fireworks and laser show). Line

> ### IllumiNations Tip:
> Always check the wind direction when choosing a spot for Illumi-Nations. There are many ground-level fireworks which create a lot of smoke. If you stand downwind, not only will you not be able to see the second half of the show, but it will be very uncomfortable standing in the fallout of the fireworks.

up a half-hour early at the fence surrounding the World Show-case Lagoon to insure a good spot.

Day 6: Choose a Disney Water Park

Have breakfast in your hotel and plan on arriving at the park of your choice—Blizzard Beach, Typhoon Lagoon, or River Country—at least one-half hour before opening. (Note: Call 407-824-4321 to make sure the water park you've chosen will be open at the time of your visit.)

If You Choose Blizzard Beach

When the park opens, walk straight to Snowless Joe's and rent towels and a locker. Find a shady spot on the far side of Meltaway Bay. Go to Cross Country Creek, grab a tube, and float around awhile. Head to Runoff Rapids. Then grab a raft and head for Snow Stormers and Toboggan Racers.

After that, ride the chair lift to the top of Mt. Gushmore (if it's busy, it might be faster to climb the steps). Head down Teamboat Springs. Head back up the mountain for the other slides, then up again if you're ready to graduate to the Summit Plummet. Finally, rest in Meltaway Bay or on your sunny lounge chair.

If You Chose Typhoon Lagoon

When the park opens, walk straight ahead to Castaway Creek, turn left, and head to the raft rental shack and rent a raft. Lockers and bathrooms are to the right of the entrance. Stake out a sunny spot for the day—the breeze is best along the beach's surf pool. Stow your raft for future use and walk around the right side of the lagoon to Shark Reef (obtain snorkel and fins at the wooden building flanking the diving pool).

After snorkeling, go counterclockwise around the surfing lagoon in the direction of Mount Mayday to the body slides on the right side of mountain—ride three storm slides once first, then speed slide. Continue counterclockwise, passing via the tunnel through Mount Mayday, to the three raft rides. Now's the time to try repeating any of the above if the park is still not crowded. Go to the surf pool and Castaway Creek whenever you want—you usually can find a spot.

If You Choose River Country

When the park opens, rent a towel and a locker if you need them. Stake out a nice spot on the beach. Then ride the waterslides of Whoop-'N'-Holler Hollow, then the White Water Rapids. Play in the Upstream Plunge Pool at your leisure and splash in and out of Bay Cove and its distractions. It's all pretty relaxed and casual at River Country!

After your day at the water park, head back to your hotel for a shower and a quick change of clothes, then:

- Go to the shops in the Downtown Disney Marketplace and eat in one of its restaurants; or

- Head back to your favorite park to reride your favorites; or

- Check out one of the other Disney World hotels, maybe grabbing a bite to eat there; or

- Visit the BoardWalk Resort, which has attractions that will keep you entertained for a few hours; or

- Stay in your own hotel, eat there, and unwind from your fun Disney World vacation.

Variations to the Itinerary

- If you've got kids in your party, you might want to go to the Magic Kingdom for two days, rather than going to EPCOT a second time. Discuss the attractions with your family be-

The Ambitious Cheapskate's Itinerary at a Glance

Day 1 (the afternoon you arrive)—Go to EPCOT's FutureWorld. Eat an early dinner in a World Showcase restaurant. Go to Downtown Disney.

Day 2—Visit the Magic Kingdom.

Day 3—Visit Disney-MGM Studios; perhaps go to the BoardWalk Resort in the evening.

Day 4—Visit Animal Kingdom.

Day 5—Go to EPCOT World Showcase (lunch in a World Showcase restaurant and have a fast-food dinner). Stay in park for IllumiNations.

Day 6—Choose a water park. Shop in the Disney Village Marketplace (or take one of our other suggestions in the evening).

fore you leave and see where your interests lie. Of course, if you substitute one park for another, that can leave you with more time in one park and no time in the other. So plan your day accordingly, visiting only those attractions that interest you in the park you're seeing once (you might have to literally run to get it all done!). If you've got very young kids, you may choose to follow the Cheapskate Family Itinerary, or some hybrid of the two.

- In many instances, we tell you to forego ridiculously busy lines and come back later or better yet, grab a FASTPASS! Let's be reasonable: you can only do that so often. Face facts: You're gonna have to wait on lines in Disney World, so pick and choose which ones you can handle or you won't get to see anything.

- If the water parks don't interest you, on day 6, revisit a park you've already seen and enjoyed. Nothing wrong with Splash Mountain, Round Two! Or hang back at your hotel pool; or visit one of those hokey tourist traps outside of Walt Disney World (. . . well, on second thought . . .).

- If your list of favorite attractions doesn't match ours, then see your favorites first thing and go to ours later in the day if you have the time.

- If your energy level doesn't match ours, you can proceed at a slower pace, but you may miss some rides in the process, especially during the busiest seasons. At least try to stick with the basic order we've suggested.

- You can change the order of the days you see each park, but keep in mind things like early entry days, the weather, what you might want to see again, etc.

THE CHEAPSKATE FAMILY ITINERARY

Day 1: Magic Kingdom

As noted elsewhere, it's to your advantage to have your flight arrive early in the day on your first day at Disney! This gives you more time to enjoy the Magic Kingdom. Hotel check-in time is usually 3:00 P.M. (1:00 P.M. at the Fort Wilderness Campsites)—no earlier—so if you get to the hotel early, have them hold your bags and officially check in when you come back.

Miscellaneous Magic Kingdom Tips:

- See map for bathrooms.

- Decide which rides are most important to you and enjoy as many of these rides as possible early, before the park gets too filled up.

- Pace yourself: The distance from the Magic Kingdom to your hotel makes it virtually impossible to run back to the room for a midday break. So rest often, if necessary, in an air-conditioned or shady spot.

After your arrival, eat a quick lunch at your hotel. Arrange for the storage of your bags, or check into your room, then get the bus to the Magic Kingdom ASAP. Pick up an entertainment schedule at City Hall on Main Street and look at the tip board at the lower end of Main Street for news on the day's events, rides that may be closed for renovations, the fireworks and parades schedule, live entertainment, etc. (City Hall is also the place where there's a good chance you'll run into some Disney characters, but don't spend hours trying to pose your kids for a photo. Being the place where people first set foot on Magic Kingdom soil, it tends to get a little crowded here. We promise you'll run into some characters throughout the day, especially in Fantasyland.)

Then walk briskly up Main Street (you'll have time to shop when you return to the Magic Kingdom on day 5), through Cinderella Castle to Fantasyland. Hopefully, by the time you've arrived, the early-in-the-day Fantasyland crowds will have died down somewhat. Go on the following rides, seeing as many as you can, but avoiding those with forbidding lines (because, remember, you're coming back): Dumbo, Cinderella's Golden Carrousel, Snow White's Adventures (scary, see notes), Legend of the Lion King, Peter Pan's Flight, Winnie the Pooh. If you encounter a bottleneck anywhere in Fantasyland, that's usually a good time to ride It's a Small World, since its line (if any) moves pretty quickly. (You can always come back on day 4 to go on a ride that was crowded.) At some point, while you're on the go, pick up a fast-food-type dinner or snack and eat it while waiting on a line.

If you're interested in such things, be sure to catch a live stage show or a parade. The best parade viewing spot is in Frontierland, near the Diamond Horseshoe, or from the Main Street platform of the Walt Disney World Railroad.

If you have time, ride the railroad from Frontierland to Mickey's Toontown Fair. This "land" ranks right up there with Fantasyland on the kid fave-o-meter; only problem is, it closes earlier than the rest of the park. If necessary, you can visit the Toontown Fair on day 4; or, if you've foregone the parade, maybe you can run over to it while everyone else is watching the floats float by? Just a thought. But you'll definitely have another chance to see Mickey's Toontown Fair if you missed it today.

Try to leave the Magic Kingdom an hour before closing, or later; depending on how the kids are holding up. You'll be getting up early tomorrow and you'll want everyone to be fully rested.

If you're feeling up to it tonight, and the kids are being

safely watched by Disney's own baby-sitting service (see page 188 for details), you might want to go spend an hour or two at Downtown Disney. Read the end of day 1 of the Ambitious Cheapskate's Itinerary for suggestions.

Day 2: EPCOT

There's not a lot to keep a young child interested in EPCOT, so you might be able to see everything you need to see here in one full day, although it does take some extra, spirited walking. Hopefully the kids will hold up till the end of the night so you can all enjoy the spectacular IllumiNations fireworks show, which takes place at EPCOT's closing time.

Arrive at 8:15 A.M. and wait at the gate. FutureWorld usually opens at 9:00 A.M., with World Showcase opening at 11:00 A.M. Be one of the first people in the park to ride Spaceship Earth before the lines develop (scary, see notes). After the ride, make lunch reservations for 11:30 A.M. at any of the World Showcase restaurants—if your kids are finicky, you may want to fast-food it. Take a gander at the menus ahead of time (best World Showcase bets for sit-down meals with kids: Canada, China, Germany, Italy, Japan). See the Where You'll Eat in World Showcase section o pages 97–101 for more information.

As an alternative to lunch at EPCOT: a short walk to the Yacht Club and Beach Club might be enjoyable. Grab a bite in the old-time soda shoppe called Beaches and Cream, located where the Yacht Club and Beach Club meet. You get there by exiting EPCOT via the International Gateway—be sure to get your hand stamped so you can return later.

Give the kids time to fiddle around in both Innoventions East and West, but if it starts to get too crowded, come back later.

Then walk to the Journey Into Imagination building. Do the ride and play at the Imageworks (unless your kids are too young to understand or care). You may want to bypass Honey, I Shrunk the Audience, due to the fright factor (see notes).

If you finish shrinking early, go to The Land. Your kids

Miscellaneous EPCOT Tips:

- See map for bathrooms

- Check the tip board near Innoventions for news on the day's events, rides that may be closed for renovations, the fireworks schedule, etc.

- Talk to people in World Showcase—they're from the country of the pavilion where they work and are usually very friendly, funny, and informative about their homeland and their culture. Your kids—and you!—might even learn something.

- Even if your kids are getting a little too old for a stroller, you may want to rent one anyway. EPCOT is roughly twice the size of the Magic Kingdom and we're telling you to see it all in one day. Near the end of the day you—and your kids' sore tootsies—may be longing for that four-wheel power!

- Reminder! World Showcase opens at 11:00!

might tune out the Living With the Land ride (discuss it ahead of time), but chances are, they'll love Food Rocks.

At about 10:45 A.M., line up at the rope barrier between FutureWorld and World Showcase; and when it drops, walk briskly to World Showcase. Most people will stay behind at FutureWorld so you will be able to breeze through World Showcase. (There's not a lot here for young families, anyway. There are really only three attractions here for you: the American Adventure, Mexico's El Rio del Tiempo, and Norway's Maelstrom. The latter may be too scary for kids.) Start at the American Adventure (a bit long for younger kids), then go back to Canada (the movie may bore the kids), and double back counterclockwise around the World Showcase Lagoon (you may get them to catch a nap in one of the darkened movie theaters).

After lunch head back to FutureWorld, since most of the crowd will begin heading to World Showcase at this point. FutureWorld tends to close early (usually at 7:00 P.M.), but you should have plenty of time before dinner to see what you've missed: Universe of Energy (scary, see notes) and the Wonders of Life pavilion. Although Body Wars may scare the kids (see notes), they'll love Cranium Command, Goofy About Health, and maybe even The Making of Me (provided they're ready for Disney's version of sex ed). You can go to Test Track (check height restrictions), and Innoventions—basically, whatever you may have missed earlier in the day, or maybe want to see again. Hopefully, the crowds at this point in the day will be centered in World Showcase, affording you smooth sailing!

Thirty minutes before dinner, begin heading back to World Showcase. Grab a quick, fast-food bite for dinner. After dinner, don't miss the American Adventure show if you haven't seen it, or if you want to catch it again. Just leave enough time before the beginning of IllumiNations. Line up at the fence surrounding the World Showcase Lagoon at least 30 to 45 minutes before the show to insure a good spot.

IllumiNations Tip:

Always check the wind direction when choosing a spot for Illumi-Nations. There are many ground-level fireworks which create a lot of smoke. If you stand downwind, not only will you not be able to see the second half of the show, but it will be very uncomfortable standing in the fallout of the fireworks.

Note: Go to FutureWorld's shops, Innoventions, and Test Track's exhibits when the park is most congested.

Nap Time

EPCOT is fairly close to the All-Star resorts. If the kids seem to be getting cranky during the day, you may want to head there during the day for a much-needed nap (provided that's where you're staying, of course). Be sure to get your hand stamped as you leave.

Day 8: Disney-MGM Studios

Grab breakfast at your hotel. Arrive by 8:00 A.M. (provided the park is officially opening at 9:00). Pick up an entertainment schedule at Guest Services and stop at the Production

Information window at the entrance to see if they're filming anything in the park during your visit. Dining reservations can be made at the information booths at the end of Hollywood and Vine. Make your 11:30 A.M. lunch reservations early to avoid disappointment if you haven't made them in advance.

Miscellaneous Studios Tips:

- See first thing in the day or in last hour before closing: Star Tours, Tower of Terror, Rock 'n' Roller Coaster, Muppet*Vision, Great Movie Ride, Disney Animation, Indiana Jones, Backstage Tour, and Voyage of the Little Mermaid. (Note: Some of these may be scary, some have height restrictions. Read on.)

- Good midday breaks (i.e., least crowded): the Doug and Drew Carey shows.

Make a beeline up Hollywood Boulevard, skipping the stores along the way—go back and shop there later when the park becomes crowded. Check out the timing for the Voyage of the Little Mermaid (if it's within twenty minutes, stay and see the show, otherwise go to the Great Movie Ride); then check out the line for Muppet*Vision and go on it if it's not too crowded. If you have not yet been on the Voyage of the Little Mermaid and the Great Movie Ride, do so now.

You now should have seen the most popular attractions and the ones with the potential for the longest lines—if not, go back and see the ones above you have missed. If your kids are feeling particularly brave, maybe you'll want to attempt Star Tours, the Twilight Zone Tower of Terror, or Rock 'n' Roller Coaster.

Now you have time to leisurely go on the Studio Tour (Catastrophe Canyon, etc.—this line may seem long, but each tram swallows up a lot of people at once); Sounds Dangerous starring Drew Carey Show; Animation Tour; Doug; the Indiana Jones Epic Stunt Show; and whatever else you may want to see.

Then, lunch by 11:30 A.M. (we recommend the Sci-Fi Drive-In, or fast food) and shop the stores in the afternoon.

If you finish the park early, this would be a good opportunity to go back to your hotel to grab a nap, or to pursue resort activities like boating, tennis, sitting on the beach, swimming, biking, or horseback riding.

Another alternative: Take a boat launch to the BoardWalk Resort for some dining and entertainment options. The kids will not only enjoy the boat ride, they'll love the carnival-like atmosphere of the BoardWalk.

But if you're one of the diehards and can last until the park's closing, stay in the Studios for Fantasmic! (You'll be glad you did.) Check at Guest Services for times.

Nap Time

Disney-MGM Studios is fairly close to the All-Star resorts. If the kids seem to be getting cranky, you may want to head there during the day for a much-needed nap (provided that's your hotel, of course). Be sure to get your hand stamped as you leave. But, if you see you're nearing the end of the itinerary, you may instead want to stick it out, see the last few attractions, and head back early in the evening anyway.

Day 4: Animal Kingdom

This will be a much less hectic day for you for two reasons: First, there are currently less attractions at Animal Kingdom than there are in the other three theme parks, so you will need less time to see everything. Second, most people head for the Animal Kingdom very early because that's when they've heard that the animals are most active. The critters, however, are also active as it cools down in the early evening. So, while everyone's gone home, you'll enjoy a less crowded park and see active animals.

Sleep in, or enjoy the recreational activities of your hotel. Get on a bus and head to Animal Kingdom in time for lunch—it shouldn't take very long, since it's the closest theme park to the All-Stars. Pick up an entertainment schedule at Guest Services—since we've advised you to forego the parade, you might be able to take in the most popular attractions during those times.

Proceed with determination to Africa and eat at Tusker House, or stop off for a bite in Pizzafari in Discovery Island. Then, head over to Asia and enjoy the rides (if they're too crowded, try going during the hour or two before the park closes).

Head to Camp Minnie-Mickey to see the Festival of the Lion King show. If you have kids in tow, spend some time visiting Disney friends at the character greeting pavilions, and see the Colors of the Wind show. (If the lines at these kid-friendly attractions are exorbitant, promise the kids you'll come back later. And make sure you keep your promise!)

After Lion King, head to DinoLand and the Dinosaur ride (if height restrictions permit). On your way, spend a few minutes looking through the shops of DinoLand. After Dinosaur, check out the line at the Tarzan Rocks! show. If it seems doable, do it! From DinoLand, browse through the shops of Discovery Island on your way to the Tree of Life. Walk around the Tree of Life, checking out its myriad of sculptures and surrounding gardens, then go inside the Tree to the It's Tough to Be a Bug! show.

At around 5:30 P.M. take the Kilimanjaro Safari ride (if it's not yet 5:30 or so, browse around the shops of Harambe). After the Safari, walk the Pangani Forest Exploration Trail. Then, take the Wildlife Express to Conservation Station and see its exhibits. At this point, you have seen all of Animal Kingdom's main attractions and are free to see the ones you might have missed, go back and reride your favorites, or browse in the shops.

Day 5: Return to the Magic Kingdom

You'll spend a full day here—with no allotted nap times back at your hotel—so hopefully you'll all hold up to witness SpectroMagic.

Arrive at 8:00 A.M. (assuming the park opens at 9:00). Upon entering the park, check City Hall and the tip board at the lower end of Main Street for news on the day's events.

Grab a light breakfast at the Main Street Bake Shop or at one of the Main Street wagons (if you haven't eaten already—

you're better off eating before you get to the Kingdom because the crowd at the bake shop first thing is rather large). Then make your way up Main Street and be at the Central Plaza end by the time the park officially opens.

Once the park opens, the rope divider between Main Street and the rest of the park drops. Make a beeline to Fantasyland, through Cinderella Castle, and reride your kids' favorites. Then head to Frontierland and the Country Bear Jamboree (before noon or during the last two hours before closing time). Spend a few minutes taking potshots at the targets at the Frontierland Shooting Gallery (make sure to set limits with the kids). While in Frontierland, why not ride Big Thunder Mountain and Splash Mountain (read on for details on "switching off"). On your way past the Diamond Horseshoe, ask how you might get a spot at 12:00 P.M. lunchtime show.

Hopefully you'll have time to visit Mickey's Toontown Fair (provided you didn't go here on day 2). If not, eat lunch and be sure to come right back.

After lunch: Stop in at a few Main Street shops if they're not too crowded. Then proceed to Liberty Square to see the Hall of Presidents (it may bore the kids, or maybe they'll nap here) and the Haunted Mansion (if the kids won't be too scared); then on to Adventureland: Pirates of the Caribbean (scary, see notes), the Enchanted Tiki Room (almost never crowded), the Swiss Family Treehouse (late afternoon or early evening), the Magic Carpets of Aladdin and the Jungle Cruise. Tomorrowland: Buzz Lightyear, Timekeeper (scary, see notes), Tomorrowland Speedway, Astro Orbiter, and Tomorrowland Transit Authority. Alien Encounter is probably too scary for the kids, and they may be too short to ride Space Mountain. Why not ride the rides and switch off? Read on.

Slip in a fast-food dinner somewhere in the schedule—how about some Tex-Mex at Pecos Bill's Café in Frontierland?

To escape the crowds and the midday heat, try a boat ride on Rivers of America; head to Tom Sawyer Island and relax with a lemonade on Aunt Polly's porch; or go back to your hotel (if you're staying on-site, but it is a bit of a hike back to the All-Star), enjoy a swim and maybe a nap, and come back later (if your admission ticket permits).

Give the kids ample time to play on Tom Sawyer Island, but be sure to get here by early afternoon—the island closes at dusk.

> Remember: If you're not one for live shows or parades, those are the times to try the most popular rides.

One Hour Before SpectroMagic

Head over to Main Street and get a good spot for the parade. (Best seats: at the very center of the platform of the Walt Disney Railroad's Main Street Station where not obstructed by trees. Next best: on the curb.) Or to see the parade and escape the crowds, go to Pecos Bill's in Frontierland and sit on a stool by the parade route.

- Important parade notes: The earlier parade, when there's more than one, is typically more crowded—check when it's scheduled. And it's always a good idea to ask a Disney cast member the direction the parade will be approaching from.

Or, if you've seen everything and you have no interest in the parades or the fireworks, take a bus to Downtown Disney.

- Note: If you're leaving the park at closing time, along with the rest of the mob, avoid the monorail out of the Magic Kingdom. Take the ferry to the Transportation and Ticket Center, or get on the "local" monorail train that stops at the monorail hotels before arriving at the Transportation and Ticket Center.

Day 6: Choose a Disney Water Park

If you're feeling more daring, check out the other itinerary for one of the other water parks. For families with small children, we recommend River Country.

Have breakfast in the hotel and plan on arriving at River Country at least one-half hour before opening.

When the park opens, rent a towel and a locker if you need them rather than carry it all with you. Stake out a nice spot on the beach. Then ride the waterslides of Whoop-'N'-Holler Hollow, then the White Water Rapids. Play in the Upstream Plunge Pool at your leisure and splash in and out of Bay Cove and its distractions at your leisure. It's all pretty casual at River Country!

If you have time, why not check out some of the other sights in Fort Wilderness?

After your day t the water park, head back to your hotel for a shower and a quick change, then do one of the following:

- Go to the shops in the Downtown Disney Marketplace, and eat in one of its restaurants.

- Head back to your favorite park to reride your favorites.

- Check out one of the other Disney World hotels, maybe grabbing a bite to eat there.

- Visit the BoardWalk Resort, which has attractions that will keep you entertained for a few hours.

- Head over to Downtown Disney to check out the shops. Ask at your hotel's front desk when Pleasure Island opens—if you have to pay admission, don't go (unless it's included in your pass).

- Stay in your own hotel. Eat there and unwind from your fun Disney World vacation.

. . . But don't overdo it. Give your kids, and yourself, a much-needed rest.

Variations to the Itinerary

- In many instances, we tell you to forego ridiculously busy lines and come back later. Or better yet, grab a FASTPASS! Let's be reasonable: you can only do that so often. Face facts: You're gonna have to wait on lines in Disney World, so pick and choose which ones you can handle or you won't get to see anything.

- If water parks don't interest you, on day 6, revisit a park you've already seen and enjoyed. Nothing wrong with Splash Mountain, Round Two! Hang back at your hotel pool, or visit one of those hokey tourist traps outside of WDW (on second thought . . .).

- If your list of favorite attractions doesn't match ours, then see your favorites first thing and go to ours later in the day.

- If your energy level doesn't match ours, you can proceed at a slower pace, buy you may miss some rides in the process, especially during the busiest seasons. At least try to stick with the order we've suggested.

- You can change the order of the days you see each park, but keep in mind things like Early Entry days, the weather, what the kids want to see again, etc.

Rides That May Have Been Deleted From the Cheapskate Family Itinerary Due to Height Restrictions

(There is a minimum height requirement, and those under seven must ride with an adult):

Magic Kingdom

- Big Thunder Mountain Railroad (Frontierland)—40-inch minimum

- Tomorrowland Speedway (Tomorrowland)—52-inch minimum to ride alone, although many parents accompany their delighted preschoolers (kids steer, parents work the pedals).

- Space Mountain (Tomorrowland)—44-inch minimum

- Splash Mountain (Frontierland)—44-inch minimum

Disney-MGM Studios

- Rock 'n' Roller Coaster—48-inch minimum

- Twilight Zone Tower of Terror—40-inch minimum

EPCOT Center

- Test Track—40-inch minimum

Animal Kingdom

- Dinosaur—40-inch minimum

Obviously, if your children are tall enough and are interested in these rides, then get on their lines as you pass.

Rides That May Be Too Scary for Small Children

Magic Kingdom

- Alien Encounter (Tomorrowland)—Heck, this one may even be too scary for the adult cheapskate!

- The Haunted Mansion (Liberty Square)—Very dark, and things have a habit of jumping out at you on occasion.

- Pirates of the Caribbean (Adventureland)—Very lifelike robots in the dark.

- Snow White's Adventures (Fantasyland)—Dark, and that scary witch pops up on occasion.

- Space Mountain (Tomorrowland)—Roller coaster in the dark.

- Timekeeper (Tomorrowland)—Very realistic film presentation.

EPCOT

- Body Wars (FutureWorld)—Bumpy flight-simulator ride.

- Honey, I Shrunk the Audience (FutureWorld)—Intense, realistic 3-D effects; loud.

- Maelstrom (Norway)—Dark and a little frightening to the very timid. But, because it is one of Disney's shorter rides, kids will be free of that nasty three-headed troll before they know it.

- Spaceship Earth (FutureWorld)—Dark and realistic, but only frightens the very timid.

- Test Track (FutureWorld)—Fast, intense, and realistic.

- Universe of Energy (FutureWorld)—Dark, with realistic robot dinosaurs.

The Cheapskate Family Itinerary at a Glance

Day 1 (i.e., the afternoon you arrive)—Go to the Magic Kingdom. Eat a fast-food dinner and turn in relatively early.

Day 2—EPCOT (lunch in a World Showcase restaurant, fast-food dinner).

Day 3—Disney-MGM Studios; perhaps the BoardWalk Resort at night.

Day 4—Animal Kingdom

Day 5—The Magic Kingdom.

Day 6—River Country. Shop in the Downtown Disney Marketplace and/or go to Pleasure Island (or take one of our other suggestions for later in the day).

Disney-MGM Studios

- Rock 'n' Roller Coaster—Very fast coaster with multiple inversions.

- Star Tours—Bumpy flight-simulator ride.

- Twilight Zone Tower of Terror—Very fast freefall effect.

- Fantasmic!—Dark, and loud at times, with some scary Disney villains.

Animal Kingdom

- Dinosaur—Rough, dark ride with realistic robot dinosaurs.

We tried to give you a little idea of why your family might find the above rides scary. You know your kids better than anyone. The best bet is to tell the gang ahead of time what to expect, then let them decide. But don't advance-bill these rides too much—they're not *that* scary; after all, this is Disney World, not Friday the 13th: The Amusement Park.

If the kids decide to ride with you, but then chicken out at the last minute, that's okay. The ride operators are used to those things happening (many of the attractions have chicken-out escape passages, and if they don't, the attendants can show you how to get out without backtracking). But if you waited on the line the whole time and, doggone it, you're really determined to ride, we recommend the switching-off option, available at the following attractions: Alien Encounter, Body Wars, Big Thunder Mountain Railroad, Dinosaur, Rock 'n' Roller Coaster, Space Mountain, Splash Mountain, Star Tours, Test Track, and the Twilight Zone Tower of Terror.

What's switching off? Glad you asked. Here's how it works: You must have at least two adults in your party. Your entire party waits in line together. Once you reach your first Disney attendant, tell him or her that you want to switch off. Everyone will be allowed to enter the attraction, and when you reach the loading area, one adult stays with the too-small/too-scared kids, and the other adult(s) rides. When the ride is over, the adult who stayed can ride, and the one who just rode stays with the kiddies. (And, if you're the third adult, you can ride twice.)

Switching off is a neat option. Take advantage of it.

11

Sources of
Additional Savings

**Look up addresses and phone numbers in our
Disney Directory, pages 246–250.**

American Express   As the official charge card of Walt Disney World, Amex offers their own special, money-saving package deals, which include accommodations, admissions, discounted dinner shows, car rental savings, and more. Don't leave home without it—but if you don't already have it (an Amex Card that is), we wouldn't suggest getting one just for this reason.

AAA (American Automobile Association)   If you're not already a member of AAA, you should be. In addition to travel-planning services (free car route maps and tour books) and discounts at many hotels and attractions throughout the world, they also offer reliable road service and free towing. And as far as a trip to Disney World is concerned, they offer:

- 10 to 20 percent off accommodations at those hotels situated in Disney's Hotel Plaza

- Discounts on Walt Disney World vacation packages and at most car rental agencies

- Free parking if you buy your admissions media from AAA

For the location of your local AAA branch, check your phone book. At about $55 for the first year, and $40 thereafter, we can say that AAA is worth it.

Disney Club Membership A one-year membership is $39.95 (renewals are $29.95). As a member, you'll receive discounts throughout Walt Disney World, which include:

- Reduced prices on admission tickets to Disney theme parks worldwide

- Up to 20 percent savings at selected Disney hotels

- 10 to 20 percent discount at selected restaurants within Walt Disney World theme parks

- 10 percent discount at Disney Stores and at Disneystore. com

- 10 percent discount at selected shops at Disney Village Marketplace, Pleasure Island shops, and at the Crossroads shopping center ($25 minimum purchase)

- 10 percent discount on merchandise bought through the Disney Catalog

- Membership in "Travel America at HalfPrice," which offers a 50 percent savings at hundreds of hotels across North America

- Exclusive toll-free reservation and information service through the Disney Club Travel Centers (within the United States)

- A subscription to *Disney News* magazine

- Discounts on car rentals, airfare, and more.

We feel that being a Disney Club member is worth your while. Although it involves an initial investment, you're sure to recoup this amount in savings, especially if you take advantage of all the discounts the club has to offer. (Once upon a time, everybody who owned even one share of Disney stock was automatically a member. Alas, those days are over.)

ENCORE   Offers members 50 percent off room rates at several Hotel Plaza hotels and many area off-site hotels, discounts on packages through Walt Disney World, and savings at many car rental agencies. Membership in the club is $50.

Entertainment Publications   This company offers discount coupon books on attractions and restaurants throughout the world. Their book for the Walt Disney World area offers half-price lodging at several Hotel Plaza hotels and at many off-site hotels, savings on airfare, off-site attractions, and more.

Exit Information Guide   This is a book of discount coupons offering bargain rates at hotels throughout Florida. You can pick it up throughout Florida, which won't help you much in your pre-planning. You can also, however, send away for it in advance; call the number in the Disney Directory to see what they currently charge for postage and handling. Send away for it early.

Kissimmee-St. Cloud Fabulous Vacation Discounts   Big savings on off-site hotels and attractions throughout the area.

Orlando Magicard   Discounts on attractions, dinner shows, car rentals, outlet merchandise, and hotels throughout the Orlando area, and more:

- 10 to 20 percent off accommodations and package deals at those hotels situated in Disney's Hotel Plaza
- Discounts on multiday passes to the parks
- 20 percent off admission to Pleasure Island
- Discounts on the Polynesian Resort's luau dinner show
- 10 percent off car rentals at Alamo, Avis, or Hertz

. . . And best of all, it's FREE. Every cheapskate's motto should be, "If it's free, it's for me." So why not get it. It can only help you. But we suggest calling for one well before you leave to insure that it arrives in your mailbox on time.

12

The Future of
Walt Disney World

As you now realize after reading this book, the World is constantly changing, with renovations, updates, price increases, and even some major expansion on the way.

So what's next for Walt Disney World? What does the future hold?

- The ribbon was barely cut at the opening of Disney's fourth park, Animal Kingdom, when Disney chairman Michael Eisner began talking about plans for a fifth gated theme park at the Florida complex. Although Eisner admitted that preliminary plans were in the works on the park, he refused to discuss what the theme of the park would be. Rumors are running wild, but three possibilities are heard time and time again. One possibility is a villains' park. With the renewed interest in the Disney villains, it's not hard to imagine a park dedicated to scoundrels like the Big Bad Wolf, Jafar, Cruella De Vil, and Scar. It would give Disney the opportunity to create some "nasty" rides, with more thrills and chills than the "nice" type of attractions at the Magic Kingdom.

  Another possibility mentioned repeatedly is a park dedicated to roller coasters. Disney supposedly has expressed a desire to build a park with more roller coasters than any other park in the world. (To date, Cedar Point Amusement Park in Sandusky, Ohio, leads the world with 12 coasters within its fences.) The other possibility mentioned frequently is a park with a sports theme to be built near Disney's Wide World of Sports complex. No matter what theme Disney goes with, their fifth park is sure to be jam-packed with exciting new thrill rides.

- Lots of additions are in store for Animal Kingdom. Rumors of a new section called the Beastly Kingdom abound along with a possible area being devoted to mythical animals.

   Currently under construction at the park is Chester and Hester's Dino-Rama! Those crazy dinosaur nuts, Chester and Hester, are branching out from their dino-packed store and opening their own mini-theme park with their own "rides of extinction."

   This new mini-land is being designed with the younger crowd in mind. Two rides are currently planned for this kiddy carnival. The first is Triceratop Spin (due to open in 2001) which is reminiscent of the Flying Dumbo ride in Fantasyland, except your ride vehicle is a dinosaur. The other ride, Primeval Whirl, is a roller coaster, but instead of your car just following a track, you will be able to spin the car as you go. Primeval Whirl is expected to open sometime in 2002.

   We've heard rumors that a new inverted roller coaster is being considered for DinoLand USA. We'll wait and see.

- The largest attraction currently being constructed at EPCOT is Mission: Space, which replaces the old Horizons attraction. You will go where no man has gone before—at least not on Disney property—when you venture into outer space on this "astronaut-like experience. This simulated space adventure takes you from the launch pad to deep space, as you experience the sensation of weightlessness, sustained G forces, and other challenges normally faced in space flight. Mission: Space is scheduled for lift off in 2003, and is being developed jointly by Disney Imagineering, Compaq Computer Corp. and NASA consultants. This will definitely be a *FASTPASS* attraction and it sounds as though it will certainly be an improvement over the old Mission to Mars attraction.

The original building built for the Horizons ride was demolished in 2000 to make way for the new attraction. But don't be surprised if, in the future, you see familiar props from Horizons showing up in Mission: Space and other attractions. Many of the show elements are being recycled and will appear in attractions at other Disney parks worldwide and well as at Disney World.

- The rumor mill is always buzzing around what will become of the area that was once 20,000 Leagues Under the Sea. The recent buzz is something called Fire Mountain. Details are pretty sketchy, but it will supposedly be a high speed roller coaster. We'll believe it when we see it, as we can't see an attraction like that residing in Fantasyland. But, with the Imagineers at the drawing board, you never know!

- And finally, there's been talk of a fifth Florida theme park, with themes ranging from Coasters to Villains to Disney Seas (a la Tokyo Disney Seas). Don't expect anything for quite some time.

We're not entirely happy about the new interest in adding thrill rides at the parks. We can understand where Disney needs to compete with some of the spectacular rides at other area parks like Busch Gardens, but remember that not every child who goes to the parks is over 42 inches in height. Sure, new, exciting rides are great, but we hope they will recall that not everybody likes to flip upside down three times while traveling at 65 MPH on a roller coaster! Hey guys: let's not forget that Disney World stands for fun for the *entire* family.

So, you've seen what Disney World was, where it is now, and, hopefully, where it's going. It's hard to believe that on opening day, October 1, 1971, only 10,000 guests entered through the Magic Kingdom's turnstiles. Disney World now attracts hundreds of thousands of visitors on a single day (we'll never know exactly how many—Disney doesn't divulge attendance figures). If you look at the difference between what the park was then—one theme park and two hotels—and what it is today—a vast resort complex for every vacationer—you can see why Disney World has become one of *the* vacation destinations of the world!

The Cheapskate's
Disney Directory

Walt Disney World General Information
P.O. Box 10,040
Lake Buena Vista, FL 32830-0040   **407-824-4321**

AAA Emergency Road Service   800-222-4357

AIRLINES
Air Canada	800-776-3000
AirTran	800-247-8726
American	800-433-7300
American Trans Air	800-225-2995
America West	800-235-9292
Continental	800-525-0280
Delta	800-221-1212
Frontier	800-432-1359
Jet Blue	800-538-2583
Midway	800-446-4392
Midwest Express	800-452-2022
Northwest	800-225-2525
Southwest	800-435-9792
Spirit Airlines	800-772-7117
TWA	800-221-2000
United	800-241-6522
USAir	800-428-4322
Virgin Atlantic	800-862-8621

American Express Vacations   800-241-1700

Blizzard Beach Information   407-560-3400

Car Care Center   407-824-4813

CAR RENTALS

Alamo	800-327-9633
Avis	800-331-1212
Dollar	800-800-4000
Enterprise	800-325-8007
Hertz	800-654-3131
National	800-CAR-RENT
Rent-A-Wreck	800-535-1391

Central Lost and Found   407-824-4245

Character Warehouse   407-345-5285

COMPLAINTS AND COMMENTS
Walt Disney World Guest
Communications
P.O. Box 10,040
Lake Buena Vista, FL 32830-0040

DINING RESERVATIONS

At all Disney resorts	407-WDW-DINE
At Dolphin Hotel	407-934-4025
At Swan Hotel	407-934-1609

Disney Club   888-DISNEY-4-U
The Disney Credit Card   800-222-1262
P.O. Box 103000
Roswell, GA 30076-9864

Disney Cruise Line   800-951-3532

Disney News magazine
P.O. Box 3310
Anaheim, CA 92803

DISNEY ON-SITE RESORTS

All-Star Movies	407-939-7000
All-Star Music	407-939-6000
All-Star Sports	407-939-5000
Animal Kingdom Lodge	407-938-3000
Beach Club	407-934-8000

BoardWalk	407-939-5100
Caribbean Beach	407-934-3400
Contemporary	407-824-1000
Coronado Springs	407-939-1000
Dolphin	407-934-4000
Fort Wilderness	407-824-2900
Grand Floridian	407-824-3000
Old Key West	407-827-7700
Polynesian	407-824-2000
Port Orleans French Quarter	407-934-5000
Port Orleans Riverside	407-934-6000
Shades of Green	407-824-3600
Swan	407-934-3000
The Villas at the Disney Institute	407-827-1100
Wilderness Lodge Villas	407-938-4300
Yacht Club	407-934-7000

DisneyQuest   407-828-4600

Disney Switchboard   407-824-2222
(all Walt Disney World hotels)

Downtown Disney Marketplace   407-828-3058
   Information

Downtown Disney Tonight   407-WDW-2NITE

ENCORE Preferred Traveler Program   800-638-8976
4501 Forbes Boulevard
Lanham, MD 20706

Entertainment Publications   800-374-4464
P.O. Box 1068
Trumbull, CT 06611

Exit Information Guide   904-371-3948
4205 NW 6th Street
Gainesville, FL 32609

Fantasia Gardens Miniature Golf   407-560-8760

Harmony Barber Shop Appointments   407-824-6550
(Main Street, Magic Kingdom)

House of Blues Hotline	407-934-2222
Kennel	407-824-6568
KinderCare (Babysitting)	407-827-5444
Kissimmee/St. Cloud Convention and Visitors Bureau reservations P.O. Box 422007 Kissimmee, FL 34742-2007	800-33-KISS 800-327-9159 (information)
Local Weather	407-646-3131
Lost and Found (after visit)	407-824-4245
Mears Motor Shuttle Return Reservations	407-423-5566
Medical Care (in Walt Disney World)	407-648-9234
Merchandise Mail Order P.O. Box 10,070 Lake Buena Vista, FL 32830-0070	407-363-6200
Orlando Magicard Orlando/Orange County Convention and Visitors Bureau	800-643-9492
Pleasure Island Information	407-934-7781
Quick Transportation	888-784-2522
River Country Information	407-824-2760
Special Events (in Walt Disney World) P.O. Box 10,000 Lake Buena Vista, FL 32830	407-827-7600
Sun Bank of Lake Buena Vista	407-828-6100
Taxi Service at Walt Disney World	407-824-3360
Ticket Mail Order Department P.O. Box 10,030 Lake Buena Vista, FL 32830 (Buy your resort passes in advance)	407-W-DISNEY

Typhoon Lagoon Information	407-560-4141
Walt Disney Travel Company, Inc. P.O. Box 22,094 Lake Buena Vista, FL 32830	407-828-3255, 800-828-0228, or 800-327-2996
Walt Disney World Central Reservations P.O. Box 10,100 Lake Buena Vista, FL 32830-0100	407-W-DISNEY
Walt Disney World Gift Certificates P.O. Box 10,030 Lake Buena Vista, FL 32830-0030	407-824-4321
Walt Disney World Reservations	407-560-7277
Walt Disney World Switchboard	407-824-2222
Walt Disney World Tours	407-WDW-TOURS
Walt Disney World Transportation	407-824-4321
Weather (for Florida)	407-824-4104
Wide World of Sports	407-363-6600
Winter Summerland Miniature Golf	407-939-7639

Keep in Touch

What did you think of this book? Do you have any helpful hints for readers of future editions?

If you're Disney lovers like us, and you like saving time and money like we do, please write to us. Share your comments, suggestions, criticisms . . . whatever.

> Cheapskate's Guide to Disney
> Kensington Publishing
> 850 Third Ave.
> New York, NY 10022
> e-mail: SamsPop1@aol.com

We'd love to hear from you.

If you've got comments or criticisms regarding Walt Disney World and its attractions, send them to:

> Walt Disney World
> P.O. Box 10,000
> Lake Buena Vista, FL 32830

Hope you enjoyed reading this book as much as we did writing it. If we see you on a Disney trip, thumbing through this book, we'll be sure to say hello and thank you.

See you in the World!

Mike and Debbi

Attention Cheapskates

If you're headed to Disney, there's something you should know
... It's not such a small world after all, but *I Can Help You:*

- Maximize your vacation dollars and time
- Book air, hotel, rental car, transfers, and passes separately
- Disney Club discount bookings
- Request specific room locations at resorts
- Dine with priority seating
- Learn insider secrets and tips

Sue Pisaturo
Disney Specialist* / Travel Agent

... and a fellow cheapskate with firsthand knowledge of the
resorts and theme parks.
Small World Travel Adventures
888-704-4560 / 201-263-0363
e-mail WDWTravelAgent@aol.com

*Disney Specialist indicates a special knowledge of the
Disneyland Resort, Walt Disney World Resort, Disney
Institute, and Disney Cruise Line. Not an agent, affiliate,
or employee of Disney.

Index

ABC Commissary, 145
Adventurers Club, 174
Affection Section, The, 160
African Lounge, 158
All Star Gear, 172
All Star Resorts, 14–16
Aloha Isle, 71
AMC 24 Theatres Complex, 109–170
American Adventure, The, 112, 119, 121
American Gardens Theater, The, 112
AnaComical Players, 105
Anaheim Produce, 133
Anandapur Ice Cream, 163
Animal Cam, 160
Animal Encounters, 166–167
Animal Health and Care, 160
Animal Kingdom Lodge, 24
Animation Gallery, 138
Ariel's Grotto, 80–81
Artesanias Mexicanas, 123
Astro Orbiter, 87
Atlantic Dance Hall, 196, 197
Aunt Polly's, 75
Auntie Gravity's Galactic Goodies, 91
Avalunch, 188
Avigators Supply, 177

Backlot Express, 145
Backlot Theater, 140–141
Backstage Magic (tour), 57–58
Backstage Pass, 138–139
Bay Cove, 193
Beach Club Resort, 24
Beach Haus, 189
Bear in the Big House, 137
Beastly Bazaar, 153
Best Western Lake Buena Vista Resort Hotel, 38
BET SoundStage Club, 174, 177
Biergarten, 119
Big Al's, 76
Big River Grille & Brewing Works, The, 197
Big Thunder Mountain Railroad, 72–73
Blizzard Beach, 183, 185, 186
Boardwalk, The, 196
BoardWalk Baker, 197
BoardWalk Resort, 24
Body Wars, 105–106
Boneyard, The, 164
Bongos Cuban Café, 171
Boulangerie Patisserie, 120
Brass Bazaar, The, 124
Briar Patch, 76

Buzz Lightyear's Space Ranger Spin, 87
Bwana Bob's, 71

Cap'n Jack's Oyster Bar, 179
Caribbean Beach Resort, 20
Caribbean Coral Reef Ride, 102
Carousel of Progress, 87–88
Casablanca Carpets, 124
Casey's Corner, 63
Castaway Creek, 190
Catalina Eddie's, 133
Celebrity 5&10, 131
Celebrity Eyeworks Studio, 172
Chakranadi Chicken Shop, 163
Chapeau, The, 64–65
Character Greeting Pavillions, 155
Chair Lift, 186
Chester and Hester's Dinosaur Treasures, 166
Chip 'n' Dale's Cookie Cabin, 156
Cinderella's Golden Carrousel, 81
Cinderella's Royal Table, 83–84
Cinderella Castle, 81
Circle of Life, 101
Cirque de Soleil, 170
City Hall, 62
Columbia Harbour House, 77
Comedy Warehouse, The, 174
Contemporary Resort, 24–25
Coral Reef, 107–108

Cosmic Ray's Starlight Café, 90
Country Bear Jamboree, 73
County Bounty, 86
Courtyard by Marriott, 39
Cover Story, 129
Cranium Command, 106
Creature Comforts, 155
Cretaceous Trail, 164
Cross Country Creek, 187
Crossroads of the World, 131
Crow's Nest, The, 71
Crown and Crest, The, 124
Crystal Arts, 65
Crystal Palace, The, 63
Cypress Point Nature Trail, 193

D-Zertz, 177
Darkroom, The, 131
Delizie Italiane, 123
Der Bucherwurm, 122
Der Teddybär, 122
Diamond Horseshoe Saloon Revue, 73, 75, 93
Die Weihnachts Ecke, 122
Dino Diner, 166
DinoLand Snacks, 166
Dinosaur, 164–165
Dinosaur Gertie's Ice Cream of Extinction, 146
Dinosaur Jubilee, 165
Discovery Island Trails, 153
Disney & Co., 65, 131–32
Disney Clothiers, 65
Disney Cruise Line, 25
DisneyQuest, 170
Disney's Candy Cauldron, 172

Disney's Character Carnival, 198
Disney's Days of Christmas, 181
Disney's Doug Live!, 142–143
Disney Information Online, 7–8
Disney Traders, 125
Donald's Boat, 86
Doubletree Guest Suites, 39
Downhill Double Dipper, 187
Drinkwallah, 163
DTV, 177–178
Duka La Filimu, 159
Dumbo the Flying Elephant, 81

Echo Lake Café, 144
Echo Park Produce, 146
Eco Web, 160
Egg Roll Wagon, 70–71
8Trax, 175, 177
El Pirata Y el Perico, 71
El Rio del Tiempo, 123
Electric Umbrella, 108
Electrical Water Pageant, 93
Elephant Tales, 71
Ellen's Energy Adventure, 104–105
Emporium, The, 65
Enchanted Grove, 84
Enchanted Tiki Room, The, 67–68
EPCOT, 95–126
ESPN Club, 196, 197
EUROSPAIN, 182
ExtraTERRORestrial Alien Encounter, The, 88

Fantasia Gardens, 198–199
Fantasmic! 135, 146–148
Fantasy Faire, 84
Fantasy in the Sky Fireworks, 93
Festival of the Lion King, 155–156
50s Prime Time Café, 144–145
Fingas, 136
Firehouse Gift Station, 65
Fitness Fairgrounds, 106
Flame Tree Barbecue, 154
"Flights of Wonder" at Caravan Stage, 161–162
Flying Fish Café, 197
Food Rocks, 101–102
Forest Trail Funnel Cakes, 156
Fort Wilderness Resort and Campground, 13–14, 25–26
Forty Thirst Street, 172
Fossil Preparation Lab, 165
Fountain View Espresso & Bakery, 108–109
Frontierland Shootin' Arcade, 73
Frontier Trading Post, 76
Frontier Wood Carving, 76
Fruit and Vegetable Wagon, 79
Fulton's Crab House, 176
Fulton's Stone Crab Lounge, 177
Funny Photos, 86–87

Galaxy Palace Theater, 88
Galerie des Halles, 121

Garden Gate Gifts, 152
Garden Grill, The, 107
Gateway Gifts, 110
Geiger's Counter, 91
Ghirardelli Soda Fountain
    and Chocolate Shop, 180
Glas und Porzellan, 122
Golden Age Souvenirs, 146
Goofy About Health, 106
Goofy's Barnstormer, 86
Gourmet Pantry, 180, 182
Grand Floridian Beach
    Resort and Spa, 26
Great Movie Ride, The,
    129–130
Green Thumb Emporium,
    109
Grosvenor Resort, 39
Guitar Gallery by George's
    Music, 172

Habitat Habit!, 160
Hall of Presidents, The, 76–77
Harambe Fruit Market, 159
Harmony Barber Shop, 65
Harrington Bay Clothiers,
    182
Haunted Mansion, The,
    77–78
Heritage House, 79
Heritage Manor, 121
Hilton at Walt Disney World
    Village, 39
Hollywood and Vine, 145
Hollywood Brown Derby,
    The, 130
Honey, I Shrunk the
    Audience, 130

Honey, I Shrunk the Kids
    Movie Set Adventure, 141
Hook's Tavern, 84
House of Blues, 170, 171
House of Treasure, 71
Hoypoloi, 172
Hub Video Stage, 175
Humunga Kowabunga, 190

Ice Station Cool, 109
Ichabod's Landing, 80
Il Bel Cristallo, 123
IllumiNations, 125
Image Works, 100
Impressions de France, 144
Indiana Jones Adventure
    Outpost, 146
Indiana Jones Epic Stunt
    Spectacular, 143
Innoventions Pavilions, The,
    98–99
International Crossroads, 125
Island Depot, 178
Island Mercantile, 155
Island Supply, 71
It's a Small World, 82
It's a Wonderful Store, 142
It's Tough to Be a Bug!,
    153–154

Jellyrolls, 196
Jib Jammer, 191
Jim Henson's Muppet*Vision
    3-D 4D, 141
Journey Into Imagination,
    100, 109
Jungle Cruise, 68

Kali River Rapids, 162
Ketchakiddie Creek, 190–191
Keys to the Kingdom (tour), 57
Keystone Clothiers, 131
Kilimanjaro Safaris, 157–158
King's Gallery, The, 85
Kringla Bakeri og Kafe, 120
Kusafiri Coffee Shop, 159

La Boutique des Provinces, 121
La Cucina Italiana, 123
La Familia Fashions, 123
La Maison du Vin, 110, 120, 122
La Signature, 121
Laffitte's, 72
Land Pavilion, The, 101–102, 107, 108, 109
L.A. Prop and Storage, 131
Le Cellier Steakhouse, 116–117
Leaning Palms, 192
Leap Frog Fountains, 101
Legend of the Lion King, The, 82
LEGO Imagination Center, 182
Les Chefs de France, 117
Liberty Inn, 119
Liberty Square Portrait Gallery, 80
Liberty Square Riverboat, 78
Liberty Tree Tavern, 78–79
Liberty Tree, 78
Living Seas Pavilion, 102–103, 107–8, 109

Living with the Land, 101–103
L'Originale Alfredo di Roma Ristorante, 117
Lottawatta Lodge, 188
Lotus Blossom Café, 119
Low Tide Lou's, 192
Lumiere's Kitchen, 84
Lunching Pad at Rockettower, 90–91

Mad Tea Party, 82
Maelstrom, 115–116
Magic Carpets of Aladdin, 69
Magic of Disney Animation, The, 137–138
Magic of Wales, The, 125
Magnetron, 172
Maharajah Jungle Trek, 162
Main Street Cinema, 66
Making of Me, The, 106
Mama Melrose's Ristorante Italiano, 141
Mandala Gifts, 163
Mannequin's Dance Palace, 175
Many Adventures of Winnie the Pooh, The, 82–83
Maps, xx–xxi
March of the Animals Parade, 167
Marketplace in the Medina, 124
Matsu No Ma Lounge, 120
Medina Arts and Berber Oasis, 124
Melt Away Bay, 187
Merchants of Venus, 91

Mickey's of Hollywood, 131–132
Mickey's Star Traders, 91
Midway Games, 175
Mike Fink Keelboats, 78
Min and Bill's Dockside Diner, 146
Minnie's Country Home, 86
Missing Link, 177
Mitsukoshi Dept. Store, 123
Mme Leota's Cart, 80
Mogul Mania, 186
Mombasa Marketplace Ziwani Traders, 159
Mouse House, 178
Mr. Kamil's Burger Grill, 163
Mrs. Potts' Cupboard, 84
Mt. Gushmore, 187
Munch Wagon, 161
Music Legends, 178

New Year's Eve Street Party, 178
Nine Dragons, 117
Northwest Mercantile, 121

O Canada!, 113
Oasis, The, 71
Old Key West Resort, 26
Once Upon a Time, 133
Online Discount Travel, 6–7
Oscar's Classic Car Souvenirs, 132
Out of the Wild, 161
Outpost Shop, The, 152

Pangani Forest Exploration Trail, 157–158

Pasta Piazza Ristorante, 108
Patriot's Cart, 80
Pecos Bill Tall Tale Inn and Café, 75–76
Peter Pan's Flight, 83
Pinocchio Village Haus, The, 84
Pirates of the Caribbean, 69–70
Pizzafari, 154
Planet Hollywood, 133–134, 171
Plaza de los Amigos, 123
Plaza del Sol Caribe Bazaar, 72
Plaza Ice Cream Parlor, 64
Plaza Pavilion, The, 91
Plaza Restaurant, The, 63
Pleasure Island Jazz Company, 175, 177
Plume et Palette, 122
Pluto's Toy Palace, 131–132
Pocahontas and Forest Friend, 156
Polynesian Resort, 26–27
Pooh Corner, 182
Pop Century Resort, 16–17
Port of Entry, 125
Port Orleans Riverside, 18–20
Port Orleans French Quarter Resort, 19–20
Portobello Yacht Club, 176, 177
Prairie Outpost and Supply, 76
Pringle of Scotland, 125
Puffin's Roost, The, 124
Pure & Simple, 108

Queen's Table, The, 125
Quick Transportation, 5

Rafiki's Planet Watch, 159–161
Raft Rides, 191
Rainforest Café, 151–152, 179–180
Refreshment Outpost, 120
Refreshment Port, 120
Resortwear Unlimited, 182
Restaurant Akershus, 119
Restaurant Marrakesh, 118
Restaurantosaurus, 165–166
Rock 'n' Roller Coaster, 135
Rock N Roll Beach Club, 175, 177
Rose and Crown, 118–119, 120
Rosie's Red Hot Dogs, 133
Rudder Buster, 191
Runoff Rapids, 187

Safari Barbecue Hut, 154
Safari Pretzel, 154
Scary Apothecary, The, 134
Scary Rides, 239–240
Sci-Fi Dine-In Theater, 145
Screen Door General Store, 198
Scuttle's Landing, 84
Sea Base Alpha, 109
Seashore Sweets, 197
Seven Dwarfs Mining Co., 85
Shades of Green, 23
Shades of Motion's, 68–69
Shadow Box, The, 67

Shark Reef, 191
Showcase Gifts, 125
Shrunken Ned's Junior Jungle Boats, 70
Sid Cahuenga's One-of-a-Kind, 132
Silhouette Cart, 80
Singapore Sal's, 192
Sir Mickey's, 85
Ski Patrol Shelter, 186
Sleepy Hollow, 79
Slurp's Up, 192
Slush Gusher, 187
Snow Stormers, 187
Snow White's Adventures, 83
Sommerfest, 119
Song of the Rainforest, 160
Sosa Family Cigars, 172–173
Sounds Dangerous Starring Drew Carey, 143
Space Mountain, 88–89
Spaceship Earth, 103–104, 110
SpectroMagic Parade, 94
Splash Mountain, 73–74
Spoodles, 197–198
Stage One Company Store, 142
Star Tours, 143–144
Starabilias, 173
Starring Rolls Bakery, 130
Stern Burner, 191
Storm Slides, 191
Studio Catering Co., 140
Studio M, 182
Studios Backlot Tour, 139
Studio Store, The, 138
Suessigkeiten, 122
Summer Sands, 182

Summit Plummet, 188
Sunset Club Couture, 134
Sunset Cove, 180
Sunset Ranch Market, 133
Sunshine Season Food Fair, 108
Sunshine Tree Terrace, 71–72
Superstar Studios, 178
SuperStar Television, 144
Suspended Animation, 178
Sweet Spells, 134
Sweet Success, 132
Swiss Family Treehouse, The, 70
Switching Off, 241

Tamu Tamu Refreshments, 159
Tangier Traders, 124
Tarzan Rocks!, 165
Tea Caddy, The, 125
Team Mickey's Athletic Club, 182
Teamboat Springs, 188
Tempura Kiku, 117
Teppanyaki Dining Room, 118
Test Track Pavilion, 104–105
Theater of the Stars, 132–133
Thimbles and Threads, 198
Thin Ice Training Course, 186
Tike's Peak, 188
Tiki Tropics Shop, 72
Timekeeper, 89–90
Tinker Bell's Treasures, 85
Toboggan Racer, 188
Tom Sawyer Island, 74

Tony's Town Square Restaurant, 63
Toontown Farmer's Market, 86
Toontown Hall of Fame, 86
Tomorrowland Light and Power Company, 90
Tomorrowland Speedway, 90
Tomorrowland Transit Authority, 90
Toy Soldier, The, 125
Toy Story Pizza Planet, 141–142
Toys Fantastic, 183
Traders of Timbuktu, 72
Trail Creek Hat Shop, 76
Treasure Chest, 72
Tree of Life, The, 153
Tune In Lounge, 146
Turkey Leg Wagon, 75
Tusker House Restaurant, 158
TV Academy Hall of Fame Plaza, 144
Twilight Zone Tower of Terror, The, 135–136
2 R's Coffee Bar, 181
2 R's Reading and Riting, 183
Typhoon Lagoon, 191
Typhoon Tilly's Galley & Grog, 192

Under the Sea, 138
Universe of Energy, 104–105
Upstream Plunge Pool and Slippery Slides, 193
Uptown Jewelers, 67
Ursa Major Minor Mart, 91

Villains in Vogue, 134
Villas at Wilderness Lodge, The, 27
Virgin Cafe, 172
Virgin Megastore, 173
Volkskunst, 122
Voyage of the Little Mermaid, 138

Walt Disney Railroad, The, 62
Warming Hut, The, 189
Waterfront Stage, 175–176
Wildlife Express to Conservation Station Train, 158
Weinkeller, 120, 123
Well & Goods, 110
West End Stage, 176
Westward Ho, 75
White Water Rapids, 193–194
Who Wants to Be a Millionaire—Play It!, 139–140

Whoop-'N'-Holler Hollow, 194
Wilderness Lodge, 27
Wildhorse Saloon and Store, 173, 176–177
Winnie the Pooh's Gala Premiere, 134
Winter Summerland, 199
Wonders of China, 113
Wonders of Life Pavilion, 105–106, 108, 110
Wonders of the Wild, 155
World of Disney, The, 181
Writer's Stop, The, 142
Wyland Galleries, 198

Yacht Club Resort, 27–28
Yakitori House, 120
Yankee Trader, The, 80
Ye Old Christmas Shoppe, 80
Yong Feng Shangdian Shopping Gallery, 121

Zanzibar Shell Co., 72

The Cheapskate's Guide to
WALT DISNEY WORLD

The Cheapskate's Guide to
WALT DISNEY WORLD

THIRD EDITION

Time-Saving Techniques
and the Best Values in
Lodging, Food, and Shopping

MICHAEL LEWIS *and* DEBBI LACEY

CITADEL PRESS
Kensington Publishing Corp.
www.kensingtonbooks.com

CITADEL PRESS BOOKS are published by

Kensington Publishing Corp.
850 Third Avenue
New York, NY 10022

All Kensington titles, imprints, and distributed lines are available at special quantity discounts for bulk purchases for sales promotions, premiums, fund-raising, educational, or institutional use. Special book excerpts or customized printings can also be created to fit specific needs. For details, write or phone the office of the Kensington special sales manager: Kensington Publishing Corp., 850 Third Avenue, New York, NY 10022, attn: Special Sales Department, phone 1-800-221-2647.

First printing: February 2002

10 9 8 7 6 5 4 3 2 1

Printed in the United States of America

Library of Congress Control Number: 2001094192

ISBN 0-8065-2280-1

To my daughter, Samantha—Since your mommy and I welcomed you into the world during the Blizzard of '96, every day has been like a trip to Disney World for us. We love you this much!—ML

To my sister, Barbara Sanders, and friend Mary Wogisch—traveling companions extraordinaire! If it wasn't for Mary's insistence that my sister and I spend spring break from twelfth grade at Disney World, we probably wouldn't have become the vagabonds we are today. And instead of my next trip to the Magic Kingdom being my thirty-third, it might have been my first . . . and I, too, would be reading a travel guide, instead of writing one!—DL